Research and Development in Expert Systems XV

Springer
London
Berlin
Heidelberg
New York
Barcelona
Hong Kong
Milan
Paris
Santa Clara
Singapore
Tokyo

Roger Miles, Michael Moulton and Max Bramer (Eds)

Research and Development in Expert Systems XV

Proceedings of ES98, the Eighteenth Annual International Conference of the British Computer Society Specialist Group on Expert Systems, Cambridge, December 1998

 Springer

Roger Miles, BSc, PhD
XHP Consulting Ltd, Gloucester

Michael Moulton, BSc, MBA, CEng
Department of Accounting and Management Science, Portsmouth Business School, University of Portsmouth, Portsmouth

Max Bramer, BSc, PhD, CEng
Faculty of Technology, University of Portsmouth, Portsmouth

ISBN 1-85233-086-4 Springer-Verlag London Berlin Heidelberg

British Library Cataloguing in Publication Data
Reasearch and development in expert systems XV : proceedings
    of Expert Systems 98, the eighteenth SGES international
    conference on knowledge based systems and applied
    artificial intelligence, Cambridge, December 1998
    1.Expert systems (Computer science) - Congresses
    I.Miles, Roger II.Moulton, Michael III.Bramer, M.A. (Max A.), 1948-
    006.3'3
    ISBN 1852330864

Typesetting: Camera ready by contributors
Printed and bound at the Athenæum Press Ltd., Gateshead, Tyne and Wear
34/3830-543210 Printed on acid-free paper

TECHNICAL PROGRAMME CHAIRPERSON'S INTRODUCTION

R.G. MILES
XHP Consulting Ltd, Gloucester.

This book is one of two volumes containing papers for presentation at the British Computer Society Expert Systems 98 conference. This is the annual conference of the BCS Specialist Group on Expert Systems and is in its 18th year. During its lifetime it has established itself as the premier Expert Systems conference in the UK. The conference is attracting an increasing number of papers world-wide and this year in excess of 70% were from research groups outside the UK.

This volume includes all papers accepted for the Technical Stream of Expert Systems 98 and presented at the conference in December 1998. The papers within this stream present innovative, new research work. The companion volume, Applications and Innovations in Expert Systems VI, includes all papers accepted for the application stream of the conference. This stream has become the premier European conference on applications of Expert Systems.

The papers accepted for presentation within the Technical Stream cover a broad range of research within Expert Systems and fit into four broad categories: ontological frameworks, knowledge base development, classifiers and neuro-fuzzy systems.

The award for best Technical paper has been made to David McSherry, from the University of Ulster, for his paper entitled "Strategic Induction of Decision Trees". This paper describes an algorithm for decision-tree induction in which attribute selection can be explained in strategic terms providing support for incremental learning, problem solving and explanation. This paper is the clear award winner and the reviewers noted the breadth of application of the work.

The Keynote Technical paper by David Goldberg from the University of Illinois, entitled "3 Lessons of Genetic Algorithms for Computational Innovation", proposes that Genetic Algorithms are a first order model of certain processes in human innovation.

This volume once again shows the advanced techniques in general AI research which will in future be applied in several areas.

ACKNOWLEDGEMENTS

ES98 CONFERENCE COMMITTEE

Professor Max Bramer, University of Portsmouth	(Conference Chairperson)
Dr Ian Watson, University of Salford	(Deputy Conference Chairperson, Tutorial Co-ordinator)
Dr Roger Miles, XHP Consulting Ltd.	(Technical Programme Chairperson)
Michael Moulton, University of Portsmouth	(Deputy Technical Programme Chairperson)
Dr Rob Milne, Intelligent Applications Ltd.	(Application Programme Chairperson)
Ann Macintosh, AIAI, University of Edinburgh	(Deputy Application Programme Chairperson)

TECHNICAL PROGRAMME COMMITTEE

Roger Miles	(Chair)
Mike Moulton	(Deputy Chair)
Max Bramer	
Rick Magaldi	
Ian Watson	

TECHNICAL PROGRAMME REFEREES

Steve Battle, University of the West of England
Max Bramer, University of Portsmouth
Claudia Eckert, Open University
David Dodson, City University
John Hunt, University of Wales, Aberstwyth
Mark Keene, University of Dublin, Ireland
John Kingston, University of Edinburgh
Antonio Kreuger, Universitaet des Saarlandes, Germany
Brian Lees, University of Paisley
Rick Magaldi, British Airways plc
Roger Miles, XHP Consulting Ltd.
Rob Milne, Intelligent Applications Ltd.
Mike Mouton, University of Portsmouth
John Nealon, Oxford Brookes University
Barry O'Sullivan, University College Cork, Ireland
Duska Rosenberg, Brunel University
Jim Smith, University of the West of England
Rob Smith, University of Alabama, USA
Eva Stopp, Universitaet des Saarlandes, Germany
Humphrey Sorensen, University College Cork, Ireland
Peter Struss, Technical University of Munich, Germany
Ian Watson, University of Salford

CONTENTS

TECHNICAL KEYNOTE ADDRESS

3 Lessons of Genetic Algorithms for Computational Innovation
D.E. Goldberg 3

BEST TECHNICAL PAPER

Strategic Induction of Decision Trees
D. McSherry 15

SESSION 1: ONTOLOGICAL FRAMEWORKS

Exploiting Knowledge Ontology for Managing Parallel Workflow Systems
S. Aknine 29

A Generic Ontology for Spatial Reasoning
F. Coenen, P. Visser 44

Knowledge Modelling for a Generic Refinement Framework
R. Boswell, S. Craw 58

SESSION 2: KNOWLEDGE BASE DEVELOPMENT

CG-SQL: A Front-End Language for Conceptual Graph Knowledge Bases
S. Coulondre 77

Constraint-Based Knowledge Acquisition and Verification for Planning
R. Barruffi, E. Lamma, M. Milano, R. Montanari, P. Mello 96

Coping with Poorly Understood Domains: The Example of Internet Trust
A. Basden, J.B. Evans, D.W. Chadwick, A. Young 114

SESSION 3: Classifiers

Pruning Boosted Classifiers with a Real Valued Genetic Algorithm
S. Thompson 133

On Rule Interestingness Measures
A.A. Frietas 147

MVC - A Preprocessing Method to deal with Missing Values
A. Ragel , B. Crémilleux 159

SESSION 4: Neuro-Fuzzy Approaches

Alarm Analysis with Fuzzy Logic and Multilevel Flow Models
F. Dahlstrand 173

Learning Full Pitch Variation Patterns with Neural Nets
T. Zhu, W. Gao, C.X. Ling 189

A Neural Network Based Approach to Objective Voice Quality Assessment
R.T. Ritchings, G.V. Conroy, M.A. McGillion, C.J. Moore, N. Slevin,
S. Winstanley and H. Woods 198

REVIEW PAPER

Case-Based Reasoning is a Methodology not a Technology
I. Watson 213

Author Index 225

TECHNICAL KEYNOTE ADDRESS

3 Lessons of Genetic Algorithms for Computational Innovation[1]

David E. Goldberg

Department of General Engineering

University of Illinois at Urbana-Champaign

Urbana, Illinois 61801

deg@uiuc.edu

Reprinted from: Babovic, Vladan & Lars Christian Larsen, Hydroinformatics '98 - Proceedings of the Third International Conference on Hydroinformatics, Copenhagen, Denmark, 24-26 August 1998. 1998. C.1530 pp., Hfl.276/US$140.00/GBP92.00. A.A.Balkema, P.O. Box 1675, Rotterdam, Netherlands (e-mail: sales@balkema.nl).

Introduction

For some time, I have been struck by the connection between the mechanics of innovation and genetic algorithms (GAs)—search procedures based on the mechanics of natural selection and genetics. In this short paper, I explore those connections by invoking the *fundamental metaphor of innovation* as an *explanation* for GA power of effect. Thereafter, I reverse the argument, by setting out to construct *competent* GAs—GAs that solve hard problems quickly, reliably, and accurately—through a combination of effective (1) design methodology, (2) design theory, and (3) design. While, we won't have the opportunity to review the technical lessons in detail, the abstract does examine three crucial qualitative issues: (1) the key *race* between selection and the innovation operators, (2) the idea of a *control map* that helps us understand the genetic algorithm's

---

[1] A considerably extended version of this argument will appear in "The Race, the Hurdle, and the Sweet Spot: Lessons from Genetic Algorithms for the Automation of Design Innovation and Creativity," in P. Bentley (Ed.), *Evolutionary Design by Computers*, Academic Press.

sweet spot, and (3) the primary *hurdle* or impediment to competent GA design, a hurdle that has been overcome by three different algorithms that obey the same principle: the need to identify important substructures before deciding among them. The implications of these lessons in practical GA design and the construction of a computational theory of innovation are briefly explored.

The Nickel Tour of Genetic Algorithms

Elsewhere, I have written at length (Goldberg, 1989) about GA basics, and here we briefly review the elements of GA mechanics.

GAs search among *populations* of *chromosomes* that may be decoded to represent *solutions* to some *problem*. Basic to the operation of a GA is the ability to evaluate the *fitness to purpose* of one solution relative to another. With a population in place, *selection* and *genetic operators* can process the population iteratively to create a sequence of populations that hopefully will contain more and more good solutions to our problem as time goes on. There is much variety in the types of operators that are used in GAs, but quite often (1) *selection*, (2) *recombination*, and (3) *mutation* are used. Simply stated, selection allocates greater survival to better individuals, recombination combines bits and pieces of parental solutions to form, new, possibly better offspring, and mutation makes one or more changes to an individual's trait or traits.

The Fundamental Intuition

Our nickel tour doesn't do justice to GA mechanics, but even a longer explanation would leave us scratching our heads and asking how such simple operators might do anything useful, let alone promote an effective, robust search for good stuff. It is something of an intellectual mystery to explain why such individually uninteresting mechanisms acting in concert might together do something useful. Starting in 1983 (Goldberg, 1983), I have developed what I call the *fundamental intuition of genetic algorithms* or the *innovation intuition* to explain this apparent mystery. Specifically, I liken the processing of selection and mutation together and that of selection and recombination taken together to *different facets of human innovation*, what I will call the *improvement* and *cross-fertilizing* types of innovation. Here we will concentrate on the cross-fertilizing type of innovation exclusively.

Selection + Recombination = Innovation

To understand how selection and crossover might give us anything useful, we appeal to our own sense of human cross-fertilizing innovation. What is it that people do when they are being innovative in a cross-fertilizing sense? Usually they are grasping at a notion—a set of good solution features—in one context, and a notion in another context and juxtaposing them, thereby speculating that the combination might be better than either notion taken individually. My first thoughts on the subject were introspective ones, but others have written along similar veins, for example, the French poet-philosopher Valéry:

> It takes two to invent anything. The one makes up combinations; the other chooses, recognizes what he wishes and what is important to him in the mass of the things which the former has imparted to him.

Verbal descriptions are far from the exacting rigor of computer code, but it is interesting that the innovation intuition has been articulated by philosophers of earlier times.

The Race

The innovation intuition seems reasonable enough, but it would be nice to go beyond mere hand waving and understand some of the underlying issues of innovation. The first key to greater insight is to understand the critical *race* that goes on in a competitive innovating system. In an evolving system acted upon by selection alone, we expect to see an S-shaped time history of the market share of the best individuals in the population, and we may calculate the time it takes to go from a small market share to a large one as a characteristic *takeover time* or t^*. This seems reasonable enough, but real GAs have selection and recombination. What difference could it possibly make to understand the behavior of a competitive system under selection alone?

The answer to this question comes quickly and convincingly if we *imagine another characteristic time*, call it the *innovation time* t_i, which we shall define as the mean time for recombination or innovation operator to achieve a solution better than any achieved to this point. With such a characteristic time in mind there are two basic situations that we must be concerned with: the situation where the takeover time is greater than or equal to the innovation time, $t^* = t_i$, and that where the innovation time exceeds the takeover time $t^* < t_i$.

In thinking about these two situations, we immediately wonder which is the more advantageous for a selectorecombinative GA, and the answer is apparent with some straightforward reasoning as follows. The condition where innovation time leads (is less than or equal to) the takeover time is most advantageous for continuing innovation, because prior to the best individual dominating the population, recombination *creates a better individual.* Thereafter this better individual starts to dominate the population, and in essence, the innovation clock is reset. This cycle of partial takeover and continued innovation is repeated over and over again, resulting in the happy condition I have dubbed *steady-state innovation.*

A Schematic of a Control Map

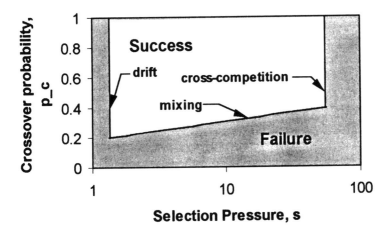

Figure 1. A control map shows the GA's sweet spot or zone of success for setting GA control parameters.

Contrast this virtuous setting with the condition where innovation time lags (is greater than) takeover time. In such a situation, the current best guy continually increases in market share without serious competition and ultimately takes the population to substantial convergence, and now it is too late because *diversity is a necessary condition of selectorecombinative success.* This situation was called *premature convergence* (De Jong, 1975) fairly early in the GA literature, but until the introduction of the above *time scales* argument (Goldberg, Deb, & Thierens, 1993), there was no means of analyzing the boundary between innovative success and failure. With the understanding of the crucial role of time scales and the race, rational analysis and design of competitive innovating GAs has advanced quite rapidly.

The Sweet Spot

One of the tools critical to these rapid advances is the so-called *control map*, which helps us delimit a genetic algorithm's *sweet spot*. Technical details of these developments are in the original papers (Goldberg, Deb, & Thierens, 1993; Thierens, 1995; Thierens & Goldberg, 1993), but here we strive for qualitative understanding of the key points. These can best be obtained by focusing on the schematic of the sweet spot of a genetic algorithm operating on an easy problem as shown in figure 1. In this map, we plot the feasible settings of the GA's control parameters, s, the selection pressure, and p_c, the probability of crossover. The selection pressure is simply the number of copies that are given to the best individual in the population under selection alone. The crossover probability is the frequency with which mated chromosomes actually undergo the exchange of crossover.

In the previous section, we discussed the race between innovation and selection. If we take this argument seriously and develop an equation from the condition when the takeover time is of the same order as the innovation time, we obtain the mixing or innovation boundary shown on the graph, where the crossover probability must increase as the logarithm of the selection pressure. Any value of crossover probability above this line is expected to succeed and any value below this boundary is expected to fail.

There are two other boundaries shown on the control map. To the left we see the region of success bounded by the so-called *drift boundary*, where convergence is controlled by the vagaries of random fluctuation when the selection pressure is small. To the right, we see the region of failure dominated by what we call *cross-competition*, when semantically independent traits end up competing with one another when the selection pressure is close to the population size.

The Hurdle

GA control maps and the sweet spot can be used with some precision to predict the success (or failure) of a given GA on some specified problem. It has been demonstrated both theoretically ·and empirically elsewhere (Goldberg, Deb, & Thierens, 1993) that easy problems—problems that may be solved through bitwise exchanges—have large sweet spots, and almost any selectorecombinative GA with any reasonable choice of crossover operator can be expected to do well in such cases. On the other hand, as a problem becomes more difficult—that is as a problem has building blocks larger than single bits—the size of the sweet spot shrinks even as the population size is increased nominally to account for the increased noise of the more difficult problem instance. This is a big problem, and ultimately the sweet spot vanishes. Another way to view the same problem is to ask the question what size population is required to solve problems of increasing difficulty and length. Both theoretically and empirically it has been shown (Thierens & Goldberg, 1993; Thierens, 1995) that population sizes must grow exponentially to accommodate harder problems.

This leaves us with a split decision regarding the efficacy of simple GAs. If a problem is bitwise solvable, modest population sizes may be used and accurate, reliable solutions may be expected in small numbers of function evaluations, and we should expect those numbers to scale well, growing no more quickly than a subquadratic function of the number of decision variables or bits. On the other hand, with a more difficult problem instance, simple recombination operators scale badly, requiring a superexponential number of function evaluations to get reliable answers to even boundedly difficult problems, and therein lies the rub, the hurdle to the design of competent GAs. Is there some way to design crossover mechanisms that allow solutions to hard problems to scale more like those of easy problems?

Competent GA Design

Remarkably, the answer to this question is a resounding "yes," and the trick is to both *identify* and *exchange* clusters of genes appropriate to solving a problem without the need for human intervention or advice.

A line of work dating back to 1989 (Goldberg, Korb, & Deb, 1989) has set this as its goal, and succeeded in achieving this goal for the first time in 1993 (Goldberg, Deb, Kargupta, & Harik, 1993) with the creation of the *fast messy genetic algorithm* (fmGA). Two other mechanisms have also achieved competence in the sense of solving boundedly hard problems quickly, reliably, and accurately, and these are Kargupta's (1996) *gene expression messy genetic algorithm* (gemGA) and Harik's linkage learning GA (LLGA) (Harik & Goldberg, 1997; Harik, 1997). Detailed descriptions are beyond the scope of this treatment, and the mechanisms are surprisingly different from one another in their details of operation. Despite these differences, the need to tame the race between selection and crossover pushes the GA designer to do one thing above all else: *identify building blocks before deciding among them.* This is easy to say, but hard to do, and all the efforts thus far have had to overcome this hurdle to achieve effective operation.

Title:

Creator:
gnuplot
Preview:
This EPS picture was not saved
with a preview included in it.
Comment:
This EPS picture will print to a
PostScript printer, but not to
other types of printers.

Figure 2. The fast messy GA results reported in Goldberg et al. (1993) demonstrate subquadratic growth in the computation time compared to the original messy GA and simple mutation-based hillclimbers, which grow as the fifth power of the number of variables and are much slower across the board than the fmGA.

Figure 2 shows the results from the first competent GA, the fast messy GA (Goldberg, Deb, Kargupta & Harik, 1993). In a problem with order-5 difficult building blocks, the fast messy GA is able to find global solutions in times that grow as a subquadratic function of the number of decision variables as expected. By contrast, the original messy GA and mutation-oriented hillclimbing (Mühlenbein, 1992), have numbers of function evaluations that grow as a quintic function of the number of decision variables, and the exponent on this polynomial gets worse as problems get harder. On the other hand, a competent GA appears to require only subquadratic growth on all problems of fixed difficulty, and this kind of performance characteristic is the kind of robust solution genetic algorithmists have been seeking for so long.

Conclusions

Many practitioners approach genetic algorithms as yet another tool to toss in the tool kit, but this paper has suggested that they might be much more. Specifically, the paper has suggested that as we try to improve genetic algorithms to live up to their search potential, we are actually constructing computational models of the processes of innovation. This is an exciting prospect, both from the standpoint of the practical problem-solving capability that such competent GAs might add to our tool kit and for the understanding and insight that such models might give us regarding the processes of innovation within our minds, our organizations, and our human institutions and society itself. Effective application of these tools across the spectrum of human endeavor has begun in earnest, while the role of genetic algorithms in the understanding of innovation processes has just begun, but the combination bodes well for an exciting era whose signature will be the increased scientific and technological reliance on computational engines of innovation and creation.

Acknowledgments

This paper was written while I was on sabbatical at the Section on Medical Informatics at Stanford University. I am grateful to Mark Musen, Russ Altman, and John Koza for inviting me to Palo Alto.

My contribution to this study was sponsored by the Air Force Office of Scientific Research, Air Force Materiel Command, USAF, under grants F49620-94-1-0103, F49620-95-1-0338, and F49620-97-1-0050. The US Government is authorized to reproduce and distribute reprints for Government purposes notwithstanding any copyright notation thereon.

The views and conclusions contained herein are my own and should not be interpreted as necessarily representing the official policies or endorsements, either expressed or implied, of the Air Force Office of Scientific Research or the U. S. Government.

References

De Jong, K. A. (1975). *An analysis of the behavior of a class of genetic adaptive systems*. Doctoral dissertation, University of Michigan, Ann Arbor.

Goldberg, D. E. (1983). *Computer-aided pipeline operation using genetic algorithms and rule learning*. Doctoral dissertation, University of Michigan, Ann Arbor.

Goldberg, D. E. (1989). *Genetic algorithms in search, optimization, and machine learning.* Reading, MA: Addison-Wesley.

Goldberg, D. E., Deb, K., & Clark, J. (1992). Genetic algorithms, noise, and the sizing of populations. *Complex Systems, 6,* 333–362.

Goldberg, D. E., Deb, K., Kargupta, H., & Harik, G. (1993). Rapid, accurate optimization of difficult problems using fast messy genetic algorithms. *Proceedings of the Fifth International Conference on Genetic Algorithms,* 56–64.

Goldberg, D. E., Deb, K., & Thierens, D. (1993). Toward a better understanding of mixing in genetic algorithms. *Journal of the Society of Instrument and Control Engineers, 32*(1), 10–16.

Goldberg, D. E., Korb, B., & Deb, K. (1989). Messy genetic algorithms: Motivation, analysis, and first results. *Complex Systems, 3*(5). 493–530.

Harik, G. (1997). *Learning gene linkage to efficiently solve problems of bounded difficulty using genetic algorithms.* Doctoral dissertation, University of Michigan, Ann Arbor.

Harik, G., & Goldberg, D. E. (1997) Learning linkage. *Foundations of Genetic Algorithms, 4,* 247–262.

Kargupta, H. (1996). *SEARCH, evolution, and the gene expression messy genetic algorithm* (Unclassified Report LA-UR 96-60). Los Alamos, NM: Los Alamos National Laboratory.

Mühlenbein, H. (1992). How genetic algorithms really work: I. Mutation and hillclimbing. *Parallel Problem Solving from Nature,* 15–25.

Thierens, D. (1995) *Analysis and design of genetic algorithms.* Doctoral dissertation, Katholieke Universiteit Leuven, Leuven, Belgium.

Thierens, D., & Goldberg, D. E. (1993). Mixing in genetic algorithms. *Proceedings of the Fifth International Conference on Genetic Algorithms,* 38–45.

BEST TECHNICAL PAPER

Strategic Induction of Decision Trees

David McSherry

School of Information and Software Engineering, University of Ulster, Coleraine BT52 1SA, Northern Ireland

Abstract

An algorithm for decision-tree induction is presented in which attribute selection is based on the evidence-gathering strategies used by doctors in sequential diagnosis. Since the attribute selected by the algorithm at a given node is often the best attribute according to Quinlan's information gain criterion, the decision tree it induces is often identical to the ID3 tree when the number of attributes is small. In problem-solving applications of the induced decision tree, an advantage of the approach is that the relevance of a selected attribute or test can be explained in strategic terms. An implementation of the algorithm in an environment providing integrated support for incremental learning, problem solving and explanation is presented.

1 Introduction

In top-down induction of decision trees (TDIDT), selection of the best attribute at each node of the tree is analogous to the selection of the most useful test in sequential diagnosis. Interestingly, the use of information-theoretic measures to guide test selection in programs for sequential diagnosis, as in the method of minimum entropy [1], predates their use for attribute selection in supervised learning [2] although the latter use was first suggested by Hunt et al. [3]. In diagnostic reasoning, a limitation of the minimum entropy approach is that the absence of a specific goal can lead to the selection of tests which appear irrelevant to doctors [4]. Similarly, problem-solving behaviour based on a decision tree induced by an algorithm in which attribute selection is based on information-theoretic measures may be difficult to explain in terms that would be meaningful to a domain expert. It is argued in this paper that for problem-solving behaviour based on an induced decision tree to emulate the problem-solving behaviour of a domain expert, the attribute-selection criteria used in the induction process must reflect the problem-solving strategies of the expert.

In medical diagnosis, doctors rely on hypothetico-deductive reasoning, selecting tests which may be useful for confirming a target hypothesis, eliminating an alternative hypothesis, or discriminating between competing hypotheses [5,6]. Hypothesist is an intelligent system for sequential diagnosis whose evidence-gathering strategies are based on the strategies used by doctors [7]. Developed within the independence Bayesian framework, it is essentially a sequential Bayesian classifier with the ability to explain its reasoning in terms of the diagnostic strategy it is currently pursuing.

This paper describes an adaptation of the model of hypothetico-deductive reasoning [7,8,9] on which Hypothesist is based to the machine-learning task of decision-tree induction. An algorithm for TDIDT called Strategist is presented in which attribute selection is based on the test-selection strategies used by doctors in diagnosis. There is no assumption of the conditional independence of attributes as in Hypothesist. Like any TDIDT algorithm, Strategist partitions the data set into subsets corresponding to the values of a selected attribute, and recursively applies the same procedure to each subset, whereas there is no partitioning of the data set in Hypothesist.

Interestingly, the attribute selected by Strategist is often the best attribute according to the information gain criterion from ID3 [10]. The decision tree it induces is therefore often identical to the ID3 tree when the number of attributes is small. However, an advantage of Strategist is that in applications of the induced decision tree in sequential classification or diagnosis, the reasoning process can be explained in strategic terms. Strategist's attribute-selection strategies are described in the following section. Two well-known data sets are used to illustrate the induction process. An implementation of the algorithm in an environment providing integrated support for incremental learning, problem solving and explanation is presented in Section 3.

2 Attribute Selection in Strategist

Strategist differs from most TDIDT algorithms in that the induction process is goal driven. In the current subset S of the data set, the *target* outcome class is the one which is most likely in S. That is, the outcome class C for which $p(C|\xi)$ is maximum, where ξ is the combination of attribute values, if any, on the path from the root node to S. Instead of a single splitting criterion like information gain in ID3 (or gain ratio in later versions) attribute selection is based on a multi-strategy approach.

2.1 Attribute Selection Strategies

In each subset of the data set generated by the induction process, Strategist attempts to apply one of the attribute-selection strategies listed below in order of priority:

1. CONFIRM   : confirm the target outcome class
2. ELIMINATE   : eliminate the likeliest alternative outcome class
3. VALIDATE   : increase the probability of the target outcome class
4. OPPOSE   : decrease the probability of the likeliest alternative outcome class
5. DISCRIMINATE   : increase the probability of the target outcome class relative to the likeliest alternative outcome class

First priority is given to attributes with values which occur only in the target outcome class (CONFIRM), reflecting the importance in diagnostic reasoning of test results which confirm outright a diagnostic hypothesis. Second priority is given to attributes with values which occur in the target outcome class but not in the likeliest alternative outcome class (ELIMINATE), reflecting the importance in diagnostic reasoning of a test result that eliminates a likely alternative hypothesis. In the absence of tests which can confirm outright or eliminate a hypothesis, doctors must often look instead for findings that will increase the probability of a target hypothesis (VALIDATE), decrease the probability of an alternative hypothesis (OPPOSE), or discriminate between two competing hypotheses (DISCRIMINATE).

As shown by the following theorem, adapted from [7], attributes which support a given attribute-selection strategy can be identified from the conditional probabilities, in the current subset of the data set, of their values in each outcome class. For example, an attribute will support the CONFIRM strategy in Strategist if, in the current subset, one of its values occurs only in the target outcome class. An attribute will support the VALIDATE strategy if, in the current subset, one of its values is more likely in the target outcome class than in any other surviving outcome class.

Theorem 1 Let S be the current subset of the data set, and let ξ be the combination of attribute values, if any, on the path from the root node of the induced decision tree to S. Among the outcome classes $C_1, C_2, ..., C_n$ surviving in S, let C_t be the target outcome class and let C_a be the likeliest alternative outcome class in S. An attribute value E will:

(a) confirm C_t if, among the examples in S, it occurs only in C_t

(b) eliminate C_a if, among the examples in S, it occurs in C_t but not in C_a

(c) increase the probability of C_t if, for $1 \leq i \leq n$, $p(E|C_t, \xi) \geq p(E|C_i, \xi)$

(d) decrease the probability of C_a if, for $1 \leq i \leq n$, $p(E|C_a, \xi) \leq p(E|C_i, \xi)$

(e) increase the probability of C_t relative to C_a if $p(E|C_t, \xi) > p(E|C_a, \xi)$

In (c) and (d), the inequalities must be strict for at least one $i \leq n$.

Although five attribute-selection strategies are available in Strategist, fewer are needed in most induction tasks. As the following theorem shows, only two distinct strategies are required in a two-class induction task.

Theorem 2 If there are only two outcome classes in the data set (or in the current subset of the data set) then the CONFIRM and ELIMINATE strategies are equivalent. The VALIDATE, OPPOSE and DISCRIMINATE strategies are also equivalent in such a data set.

When two or more attributes will support the same attribute-selection strategy, some measure of attribute usefulness is required to identify the most useful attribute. Different measures are used depending on the strategy supported and are adapted from those used in Hypothesist to select the most useful test in sequential diagnosis [7]. Similar measures are used in Xcavator, an algorithm for hypothetico-deductive data mining [11,12].

Definition 1 In a given subset S of the data set, the expected weight of evidence in S of an attribute A in favour of a given outcome class C_1, relative to an alternative outcome class C_2, is:

$$\psi(A, C_1, C_2, \xi) = \sum_{i=1}^{m} \frac{p(A=V_i|C_1,\xi)\, p(A=V_i|C_1,\xi)}{p(A=V_i|C_2,\xi)},$$

where $V_1, V_2, ..., V_m$ are the values of A, and ξ is the combination of attribute values, if any, on the path from the root node to S.

If the strategy of highest priority which can be supported in the current subset is VALIDATE, OPPOSE or DISCRIMINATE, and two or more attributes will support this strategy, the attribute selected is the one for which $\psi(A, C_t, C_a, \xi)$ is greatest, where C_t is the target outcome class and C_a is the likeliest alternative outcome class. Where the current subset of the data set and combination of attribute values ξ used to generate it are specified in the text we will simply write $\psi(A, C_t, C_a)$ instead of $\psi(A, C_t, C_a, \xi)$.

In a given subset S of the data set, the expected weight of evidence in S of an attribute A is infinite if, among the examples in S, there is a value of A which occurs in C_1 but not in C_2. Expected weights of evidence cannot therefore discriminate between attributes that support the CONFIRM or ELIMINATE strategies in Strategist. Interestingly, Hunt et al. [3] considered a *ratio* rule based on weights of evidence but rejected it for similar reasons. In Strategist, as in Hypothesist [7], the solution to this problem is to use a different quantitative measure for these attributes.

Definition 2 In a given subset S of the data set, the eliminating power in S of an attribute value E, denoted el(E, ξ), is the sum of the probabilities $p(C|\xi)$ of all the outcome classes C in S which are eliminated by E, where ξ is the combination of attribute values, if any, on the path from the root node to S. If none of the outcome classes in S is eliminated by E, the eliminating power of E in S is zero.

Definition 3 In a given subset S of the data set, the expected eliminating power in S of an attribute A with values $V_1, V_2, ..., V_m$, in favour of an outcome class C in S, is :

$$\gamma(A, C, \xi) = \sum_{i=1}^{m} p(A=V_i \mid C,\xi)\, el(A=V_i,\xi),$$

where ξ is the combination of attribute values, if any, on the path from the root node to S.

If the attribute-selection strategy of highest priority which can be supported in the current subset of the data set is CONFIRM or ELIMINATE, and two or more attributes will support this strategy, the attribute selected is the one for which $\gamma(A, C_t, \xi)$ is greatest, where C_t is the target outcome class. Where the current subset of the data set and combination of attribute values ξ used to generate it are

Table 1. Conditional probabilities of attribute values in the contact lens data and in the subsets generated by successive selection of the attribute values: tear production rate = normal, astigmatism = absent, and age = presbyopic.

	Contact lens type									
	N	S	H	N	S	H	N	S	N	S
	0.63	0.21	0.17	0.25	0.42	0.33	0.17	0.83	0.50	0.50
Spectacle prescription										
myope	0.47	0.40	0.75	0.33	0.40	0.75	1.00	0.40	1.00	0.00
hypermetrope	0.53	0.60	0.25	0.67	0.60	0.25	0.00	0.60	0.00	1.00
Age of patient										
young	0.27	0.40	0.50	0.00	0.40	0.50	0.00	0.40		
pre-presbyopic	0.33	0.40	0.25	0.33	0.40	0.25	0.00	0.40		
presbyopic	0.40	0.20	0.25	0.67	0.20	0.25	1.00	0.20		
Astigmatism										
present	0.53	0.00	1.00	0.67	0.00	1.00				
absent	0.47	1.00	0.00	0.33	1.00	0.00				
Tear production rate										
normal	0.20	1.00	1.00							
reduced	0.80	0.00	0.00							

specified in the text, we will simply write $\gamma(A, C_t)$ instead of $\gamma(A, C_t, \xi)$.

2.2 The Contact Lens Data

The contact lens data set is based on a simplified version of the optician's real-world problem of selecting a suitable type of contact lenses, if any, for an adult spectacle wearer [13]. Outcome classes in the data set are no contact lenses (N), soft contact lenses (S) and hard contact lenses (H). Table 1 shows, from left to right, the conditional probabilities of the attribute values in the contact lens data and in the subsets generated by successive selection of the attribute values: tear production rate = normal, astigmatism = absent, and age = presbyopic. The probabilities of the surviving outcome classes in each subset are also shown.

Initially in Strategist, the target outcome class is no contact lenses, and the likeliest alternative outcome class is soft contact lenses. Only one attribute, tear production rate, has a value which occurs only in the target outcome class and will therefore support the CONFIRM strategy. Though not required on this occasion, its expected eliminating power in favour of the target outcome class is:

γ(tear production rate, no contact lenses) = 0.20 x 0 + 0.80 x (0.21 + 0.17) = 0.30

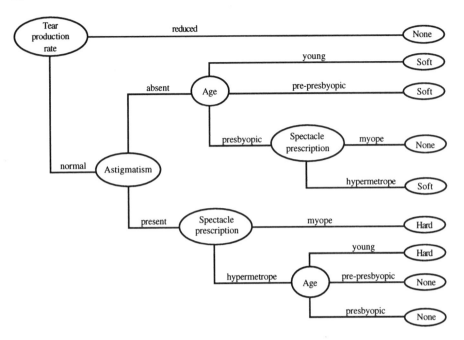

Figure 1. Decision tree induced by ID3, and by Strategist, from the contact lens data

Astigmatism has a value which occurs in no contact lenses but not in soft contact lenses and would therefore, if required, support the ELIMINATE strategy. Age has a value (presbyopic) which is more likely in no contact lenses than in any other outcome class and would therefore support the VALIDATE strategy. Its expected weight of evidence in favour of the target outcome class is:

$$\psi(\text{age, no contact lenses, soft contact lenses}) =$$
$$0.27^2/\ 0.40 +\ 0.33^2/\ 0.40 + 0.40^2/\ 0.20 = 1.25$$

Finally, spectacle prescription has a value (myope) which is less likely in soft contact lenses, the likeliest alternative outcome class, than in any other outcome class and would therefore support the OPPOSE strategy.

Since the CONFIRM strategy is given priority, and tear production rate is the only attribute which can support this strategy, tear production rate is selected to appear at the root node of the induced decision tree. The next three columns in Table 1 show the probabilities of the three outcome classes, and conditional probabilities for the remaining attributes, in the subset of the contact lens data in which tear production rate = normal.

The target outcome class now changes to soft contact lenses, the likeliest outcome class in the current subset of the data set, and hard contact lenses becomes the likeliest alternative outcome class. None of the three remaining attributes has a value which occurs only in the new target outcome class, so the CONFIRM strategy cannot be supported in this subset of the data set. However, astigmatism has a value which occurs in soft contact lenses but not in hard contact lenses and will therefore support the ELIMINATE strategy. As the only such attribute, it is selected by Strategist as the attribute to partition this subset of the data set.

The next two columns in Table 1 show the probabilities for the two surviving outcome classes and conditional probabilities for the remaining attributes in the subset of the contact lens data in which tear production rate = normal and astigmatism = absent. Soft contact lenses is again the target outcome class in this subset. Both age and spectacle prescription now have values which occur only in the target outcome class and will therefore support the CONFIRM strategy.

Since γ(age, soft contact lenses) = 0.14, while γ(spectacle prescription, soft contact lenses) = 0.10, age is selected as the best attribute for partitioning the current subset. Two of its values confirm the target outcome class, so only the presbyopic subset can be further partitioned. As shown in the next two columns of Table 1, the surviving outcome classes in the presbyopic subset are equally likely. If soft contact lenses is arbitrarily selected as the target outcome class, spectacle prescription has a value which occurs only in the target outcome class and will therefore support the CONFIRM strategy. Since its other value occurs only in no contact lenses, the subsets that result from partitioning the current subset correspond to leaf nodes of the induced decision tree.

The complete decision tree induced by Strategist is shown in Figure 1 and is identical to the tree induced by ID3 with the information gain criterion. Only two of Strategist's attribute-selection strategies, CONFIRM and ELIMINATE, were required to induce the tree. A quantitative measure of attribute usefulness was required at only two of the nodes.

2.3 The Voting Records Data

The congressional voting records data [14] collected by Jeff Schlimmer from a 1984 session of the United States Congress, records the party affiliations of congressmen and their votes on 16 budget issues such as education spending, freezing of physician fees, and synthetic fuel funding.

Initially in Strategist, the target outcome class in this two-class induction task is Democrat. None of the 16 attributes will support the CONFIRM strategy, but all will support the VALIDATE strategy. The attribute for which the expected weight of evidence in favour of the target outcome class is greatest, and therefore the most useful attribute according to Strategist, is the vote on the freezing of physician fees. This is also the most useful attribute according to the information gain criterion in ID3.

In the decision trees induced by Strategist and ID3, the sub-trees corresponding to physician fee freeze = n are identical. The sub-trees corresponding to physician fee freeze = u involve different attributes but are identical in structure and size. The Strategist sub-tree for physician fee freeze = y is slightly larger than the ID3 sub-tree. Both algorithms were applied without a stopping criterion in the experiment to facilitate comparison of the results.

3 Lazy Problem Solving in Strategist

Potential benefits of lazy problem solving, in which computation is performed on a demand-driven basis, include incremental learning and reduced effort in knowledge acquisition [15]. In this section, a lazy version of Strategist and its implementation in an environment providing integrated support for incremental learning, problem-solving and explanation are presented. As in instance-based algorithms like IB3 [16], an explicit decision tree is not constructed in the lazy version of Strategist. Instead, the entire data set is stored and used as necessary to classify problem cases presented by the user.

Attribute selection is based on the strategies described in Section 2. However, instead of partitioning the data set into subsets corresponding to all values of a selected attribute, Strategist now asks the user for the value of the selected attribute for the problem case and forms a single subset of the data set consisting of those examples for which the attribute's value matches the reported value. If the subset contains instances with different outcome classes, the same procedure is recursively applied to the subset, thus generating a nested sequence of subsets. The process continues until an empty subset is generated, or one that contains only examples with the same outcome class, or until no further attributes remain.

In effect, Strategist generates a single path in a conceptual decision tree for the problem case. Integration of the induction and problem-solving processes in the lazy version of Strategist has a number of advantages. One is a form of incremental learning, in that new examples can be added to the data set at any time without modification of a stored decision tree. Another is a natural method of tolerating missing data in problem cases. As in an expert system, the user may answer *unknown* when the value of an attribute is requested. Strategist simply ignores the attribute and uses the attribute-selection strategy of highest priority which can now be supported to select another attribute. The example consultation below, based on the contact lens data, shows its ability to uniquely classify a problem case when the value of a relevant attribute is unknown.

Strategist:	The target hypothesis is no contact lenses. What is the tear production rate?
User:	unknown
Strategist:	Is astigmatism present?
User:	yes
Strategist:	What is the spectacle prescription?
User:	hypermetrope
Strategist:	What is the age of the patient?
User:	presbyopic
Strategist:	No contact lenses has been confirmed

A practical limitation of the algorithm's ability to tolerate missing data is that when unknown attributes are eliminated, the remaining attributes may not provide enough information to uniquely classify the problem case. For example, a unique classification is not possible if both the tear production rate and astigmatism are unknown.

A third advantage of integration, and perhaps the most significant, is Strategist's ability to explain the problem-solving process in strategic terms. Before answering a question, the user may ask *why* the question is relevant. A similar facility is often provided in rule-based expert systems. Strategist's explanation depends on the strategy it is currently pursuing. If currently pursuing its VALIDATE strategy, it tells the user which value (or values) of the selected attribute will increase the probability of the target outcome class. Examples of the explanations generated in the CONFIRM and ELIMINATE strategies can be seen in the following consultation extract.

Strategist: The target outcome class is no contact lenses. What is the tear production rate?
User: why
Strategist: Because if the tear production rate is reduced this will confirm no contact lenses. What is the tear production rate?
User: normal
Strategist: The target outcome class is soft contact lenses. Is astigmatism present?
User: why
Strategist: Because the absence of astigmatism will eliminate hard contact lenses

The following consultation extract illustrates the explanations provided by Strategist in the VALIDATE and OPPOSE strategies, which are required in the contact lens task only when the values of certain attributes are unknown for the problem case.

Strategist: The target outcome class is no contact lenses. What is the tear production rate?
User: unknown
Strategist: Is astigmatism present?
User: unknown
Strategist: What is the age of the patient?
User: why
Strategist: Because if the age of the patient is presbyopic, this will increase the probability of no contact lenses. What is the age of the patient?
User: unknown
Strategist: What is the spectacle prescription?
User: why
Strategist: Because if the spectacle prescription is myope, this will decrease the probability of soft contact lenses

Strategist's explanation of the reasoning process in strategic terms may resemble more closely the explanations a domain expert would provide than those of a rule-based expert system. Its explanations are certainly more concise. When asked to explain the relevance of astigmatism in the second example consultation, Strategist's explanation is simply that the absence of astigmatism will eliminate hard contact lenses. An expert system would instead generate an explanation based on its current goal and the conditions of the rule it is trying to fire. The following example of the type of explanation a rule-based system is likely to provide is based on one of the rules for no contact lenses induced from the contact lens data by PRISM [13].

Expert System: Is astigmatism present?
User: why
Expert System: Because if astigmatism is present and the spectacle prescription is hypermetrope and the age of the patient is presbyopic, then the conclusion is no contact lenses

Strategist's continual revision of the target outcome class as new evidence is obtained, a feature it shares with Hypothesist [7], is another way in which it differs from a rule-based expert system, which may stubbornly pursue a goal, regardless of how unlikely it has become, until the supply of matching rules is exhausted.

When expert knowledge is captured in the form of rules, strategic knowledge often remains implicit in the ordering of the rules and their conditions [17]. Strategic knowledge may also be implicit in the ordering of goals in the knowledge base and therefore unavailable to the expert system for explanation. While some of the strategic aspects of human problem solving are explicitly modelled in Strategist, its assessment of the usefulness of attributes (or tests) is solely based on the evidence they provide and not, for example, their relative costs.

In PRISM, the induction of a set of modular rules associated with each outcome class was intended to overcome a limitation of decision trees which arises from their requirement for information which may be relevant only in the classification of certain cases. For example, the tear production rate requires a lengthy and expensive examination which can be avoided in practice if other tests show that the patient is unsuitable for contact lenses [13]. Provided the rules (and goals) are strategically ordered in the knowledge base, an expert system based on the PRISM rules can reach a conclusion of no contact lenses without asking the user for the tear production rate. An alternative solution to this limitation of decision trees is to constrain the selection of attributes in the induction process [18]. For example, Strategist's attribute-selection strategies could be modified to give priority to attributes other than the tear production rate.

4 Conclusions

An algorithm for TDIDT has been presented in which attribute selection is based on the test-selection strategies used by doctors. Its main advantage is that in problem-solving applications of the induced decision tree, the problem-solving process can be explained in strategic terms.

Strategist's method of handling missing data in problem cases is simpler than the approaches used in CART and C4.5 [19,20]. Its simple strategy of ignoring the unknown attribute and selecting the next best attribute often enables a unique classification to be made without complicated arithmetic. A similar strategy is not possible in an explicit decision tree induced, for example, by ID3 as there is no record of the attribute which was second best at a given node. However, any TDIDT algorithm can be modified to produce a decision tree which can tolerate missing data in problem cases [18].

Algorithms in which decision-tree induction and classification are integrated as in Strategist, and which handle missing values in problem cases in a similar way, include IBID [18] and LAZYDT [21]. Incremental learning in Strategist is gained at the expense of improvements in accuracy which might be possible by the use of post-pruning techniques [22]. In any approach to lazy problem solving, another trade-off is the additional computational effort required to answer information queries [15]. In tasks where explanation of the problem solving process is considered a priority, but not at the expense of accuracy or speed of response to queries, a non-incremental version of Strategist with explanations stored at the nodes of an on-line, post-pruned, explicit decision tree may provide a practical solution.

Experiments show that the decision trees induced by Strategist and ID3 are often identical when the number of attributes is small. When they differ, the Strategist tree tends to be larger. Issues to be addressed by further research include the conditions under which Strategist differs from ID3 in its choice of attribute and the effects of such differences on classification accuracy.

References

1. Gorry GA, Kassirer JP, Essig A, Schwartz WB. Decision analysis as the basis for computer-aided management of acute renal failure. American Journal of Medicine 1973; 55:473-484

2. Quinlan JR. Discovering rules by induction from large collections of examples. In: Michie D (ed) Expert systems in the micro-electronic age. Edinburgh University Press, UK, 1979, pp 168-201

3. Hunt EB, Martin J, Stone PJ. Experiments in induction. Academic Press, New York, 1966

4. Spiegelhalter DJ, Knill-Jones RP. Statistical and knowledge-based approaches to clinical decision-support systems with an application in gastroenterology. Journal of the Royal Statistical Society Series A 1984; 147:35-77

5. Elstein AS, Schulman LA, Sprafka SA. Medical problem solving: an analysis of clinical reasoning. Harvard University Press, Cambridge, 1978

6. Shortliffe EH, Barnett GO. Medical data: their acquisition, storage and use. In: Shortliffe EH, Perreault LE (eds) Medical informatics: computer applications in health care. Addison-Wesley, 1990, pp 37-69

7. McSherry D. Hypothesist : a development environment for intelligent diagnostic systems. In: Keravnou E, Garbay C, Baud R, Wyatt J (eds) Artificial intelligence in medicine. Springer-Verlag, Heidelberg, 1997, pp 223-234 (Lecture notes in artificial intelligence no. 1211)

8. McSherry D. A domain independent theory for testing fault hypotheses. In: Colloquium on intelligent fault diagnosis - part 1: classification techniques. Institution of Electrical Engineers, London, 1992, pp 3/1-3/4 (Digest no. 1992/045)

9. McSherry D. Intelligent dialogue based on statistical models of clinical decision making. Statistics in Medicine 1986; 5:497-502

10. Quinlan JR. Induction of decision trees. Machine Learning 1986; 1:81-106

11. McSherry D. Qualitative assessment of rule interest in data mining. In: Nealon JL, Hunt J (eds) Research and development in expert systems, vol 13, Proceedings of Expert Systems 96. SGES Publications, UK, 1996, pp 204-215

12. McSherry D. Hypothetico-deductive data mining. Applied Stochastic Models and Data Analysis 1998; 13:415-422

13. Cendrowska J. PRISM: an algorithm for inducing modular rules. International Journal of Man-Machine Studies 1987; 27:349-370

14. Merz CJ, Murphy PM. UCI repository of machine learning databases [http://www.ics.uci.edu/~mlearn/MLRepository.html]. University of California, Irvine, 1998

15. Aha DW. The omnipresence of case-based reasoning in science and application. Expert Update 1998; 1:29-45

16. Aha DW, Kibler D, Albert MK. Instance-based learning algorithms. Machine Learning 1991; 6:37-66

17. Clancey WJ. The epistemology of a rule-based expert system - a framework for explanation. Artificial Intelligence 1983; 20:215-251

18. McSherry D. Integrating machine learning, problem solving and explanation. In: Bramer MA, Nealon JL, Milne R (eds) Research and development in expert systems, vol 12, Proceedings of Expert Systems 95. SGES Publications, UK, 1995, pp 145-157

19. Breiman L, Friedman JH, Olshen RA, Stone CJ. Classification and regression trees. Wadsworth, Pacific Grove, 1984

20. Quinlan JR. C4.5: Programs for machine learning. Morgan Kaufmann, San Mateo, 1993

21. Friedman JH, Kohavi R, Yun Y. Lazy decision trees. In: Proceedings of the thirteenth national conference on artificial intelligence. AAAI Press/The MIT Press, 1996, pp 717-724

22. Langley P. Elements of machine learning. Morgan Kaufmann, San Francisco, 1996

SESSION 1: ONTOLOGICAL FRAMEWORKS

Exploiting Knowledge Ontology for Managing Parallel WorkFlow Systems

Samir Aknine

Lamsade (laboratoire d'analyse et modélisation
de systèmes pour l'aide à la décision)
Université Paris Dauphine
Place du Maréchal De Lattre de Tassigny
75775 Paris cedex 16
Samir.Aknine@lamsade.dauphine.fr

Abstract

In this article, we propose a framework for cooperation among human actors of a cooperative work system supported by software agents based on a common knowledge representation ontology. Ontology gives a background of knowledge to share among autonomous agents of a cooperative system and solves indirect conflicts between actors' activities. We realised and tested our mediating system by an experimentation on cooperative writing process in the domain of telecommunications.

1 Introduction

With the increase of the possibilities offered by the World-Wide-Web, the necessity to build tools for cooperative work has been more and more obvious. Also, we think that Workflow systems must evolve to parallel Workflow systems (PWS). As we have already claimed in [4], PWS are capable of managing complex and dynamic activity processes, this can significantly increase these systems' productivity and the quality of their results. The main difficulty induced by the paralleling introduced in the execution of activities in these systems is the solving of indirect conflicts between partially independent activities. Therefore, we suggest that a multidisciplinary approach may be an essential element for the construction of these systems.

Workflow systems have been largely used for automating activity processes in several domains. However, most of these systems are very limited in the aid and the support for human actor's coordination [8]. Often these systems declare actor's assistance; anyhow the most tasks are delegated for actors [9]. In our research, we particularly orient ourselves towards the aspects, which have not been largely studied in these systems [6] [10] [13]. So, we propose the paralleling of activity processes with managing the coherence of these systems. The purpose of this article is to introduce the ontology used for knowledge representation which plays the most important role in the management of workflow processes.

To move forward in this project, we also define multi-agent architecture models [4], which use process conceptual models to achieve the desired fonctionnalities. So, our research will lead us to represent two cooperation strategies: the human actors' strategy, the activity processes of which are described in our ontology, and the software agents' strategy in the system we are confronted to.

The agent architecture, we propose for this type of systems is doted with several control agents, an execution agent, a supervisor agent, an interface module to communicate with the actor and a working memory. The first flexibility of our architecture resides in the forced separation between the agent control (totally independent from the application domain) and the behaviours executing the domain tasks. This constraint facilitates the reuse of the mediating system for other applications only by redefining the tasks that an agent must execute.

The second flexibility of this architecture is the agent capacity to accomplish several tasks at the same time, in particular, the execution of active tasks and the planning of future tasks. The third flexibility is the result of its recursive structure, which allows the incorporation of other agents to its structure without loosing its flexibility. Finally, the forth flexibility is related to the requirements of the recent mobile applications, the interest of which have largely been argued in [21] [22].

Barry Crabtree [19] outlined: "imagine having to download many images just to pick up one. Is it not more natural to get your agent to 'go' to that location, do a local search and only transfer the chosen compressed image back across the network?"

The question we will also try attempt to answer in this article deals with the partial migration of the agent's code, i.e., only the part which is capable of executing the requested task in the destination site and maintaining the modules which are not directly involved in the achievement of this task in the initial site. The partial migration of code is particularly interesting in the sense that it can reduce the submersion risk of the network by an unusable code.

This article is divided in eight sections. In the 2nd section, we study the conceptual choices oriented agents we have proposed for the implementation of the cooperative work aided systems. In the 3rd section, we illustrate the parallel Workflows reactive coordination paradigm with a technique specification cooperative writing process in the telecommunications domain. In the 4th section, we present our ontology of knowledge representation. In the 5th section, we introduce our software agent architecture in details. In the 6th section, we introduce the control architecture of the global cooperative work aided system. In the 7th section, we discuss the implementation of our software prototype. In the 8th section, we wind up our discussion.

2 Why do we talk about a distributed approach for cooperative work aided systems?

The interest of making research on multi-agent systems has particularly grown in several domains. In our research on cooperative work aided systems, we have chosen a Multi-Agent orientation because of the potential power an agent community offers for solving a complex problem, by incorporating it into a cooperative system. The most attractive aspects, which led us to the distributed implementation of these systems, are the following ones:

- The centralisation of the tasks of a cooperative process is almost unexploitable. A fundamentally distributed cooperative system it is easier to think about it as a software agents group in permanent interactions with a community of actors.
- The large dynamicity of the system in the execution phase of the cooperative tasks processes, more recent researches on planning are widely related to this class of problems [14][7].
- The existence of several forms of cooperation and interactions in this domain, i.e., a horizontal cooperation form (between agents) and a vertical one (between agents and actors) especially adapted to the research on Distributed Artificial Intelligence (DAI), on the decomposition and the allocation of tasks [7] [14] and on the negotiation between agents [11].

3 A reactive coordination mechanism for cooperative activity processes

Before describing the proposed ontology and agent model, we will briefly come back to the main characteristics of the cooperative application we studied to make this model valid. The application consists of organising activities of actors and in controlling them during the cooperative writing process of technique specifications. We are faced to several problems particularly due to the parallel execution form of the tasks we have.

We suppose that an activity A_i is possibly or semi-independent from an activity A_j if the outputs of A_j "can be" the inputs or the supports for the activity A_i. A relation "can exist" between the outputs of A_j and the inputs and the supports of A_i shows the existence of some situations in which the execution of the activity A_i is independent from the execution of the activity A_j. To reach these cases of independence, we have introduced the possibilist relation "possible independence or semi-independence" to model parallel Workflow activities. In order to not make the parallel workflow processes fail, if the outputs of the activity A_j are necessarily the inputs or the supports of A_i, A_i functionally depends on A_j. Of course, if the outputs of A_j are neither inputs, nor supports for the activity A_i, A_i is thus considered as independent from A_j.

In the cooperative writing process, the achievement of a technique specification requires four operations (writing, reading, reviewing and verification) on the three sub-specifications (the functional specification, the detailed specification and the referential specification). After the writing of the functional specification has been over, the reviewing and the reading of the functional specification and the writing of the detailed specification activities are immediately activated. The fact of disposing of a representation ontology of the possible independence relation between activities and of a reactive control mechanism which immediately warns the reviewer of the (FS), its reader and the writer of the detailed specification for each modification done on the (FS), enables us to take the risk of paralleling the execution of independent activities and the possibly independent ones.

This form of possibilist paralleling notes a reduction of the global execution time of the activities of the system. The two cases described in figure 1 illustrate the favourable and the unfavourable cases regarding the parallel execution of possibly independent activities. In the first case, the nongeneration of a new version of the functional specification during the reviewing of this specification confirms the possible independence relation between the reviewing and the reading of the (FS) and its independence from the writing of the detailed specification. In the second case, the generation of a new version of the functional specification by the reviewing activity turns the possible independence relation into a functional dependence relation between the paralleled activities.

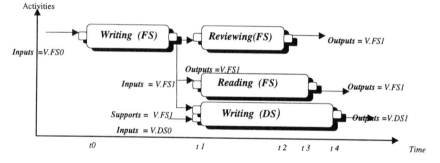

(a) A favourable paralleling: the reviewing task did not change the document.

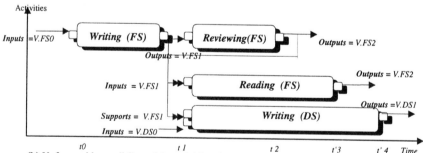

(b) Unfavourable paralleling of the activities: the system reactivates writing and reading.

Legend

FS: Functional specification; DS: Detailed specification; V. ξ_j: Version 'j' of the document ξ.

Figure 1 Illustration of the paralleling of the possible independent activities on a fragment of a cooperative writing process.

4 Ontology for actors cooperation

Our aim is to define an ontology for knowledge representation suited for parallel workflow systems at knowledge level [18]. At a conceptual level, a task is a description of actions allowing the achieving of a goal [12]. We propose a script of a task combining a declarative description, a behavioural description and a control structure extended of the task description proposed in [23] [8] (cf. figure 2).

- **The declarative description** is composed of the following elements:
  - ➢ The sufficient inputs which represent in our application the documents allowing the achievement of a task. For example, the sufficient document for the reading task of the functional specification is V. FS1.
  - ➢ The necessary inputs are the necessary documents to validate the results of a task execution. For example, the document in output of the reviewing task is the necessary document to validate the results of the reading task. When the necessary inputs are the same as the sufficient inputs, the paralleled activity process is favourable.
  - ➢ The sufficient supports represent the documents that a task consults during its execution.
  - ➢ The necessary supports validate the final results of tasks (cf. definition 2).
  - ➢ The task preconditions are the sufficient conditions for the execution of a task. These conditions control the existence of the sufficient inputs and the sufficient supports of the task.
  - ➢ The failure conditions are constraints made on the necessary inputs and the necessary supports which invalidate the task execution according to definition 2.
  - ➢ The success states and the failure states define the states of the necessary inputs and the necessary supports with which a task has been considered as valid or invalid and which are in our case the different document versions.
  - ➢ The priority is a numerical value attributed for each task. It allows the resolution of conflicts between semi-independent tasks. The priority permits the separation between correct paralleled tasks and incorrect tasks.
  - ➢ The status defines the state of a task : active (i.e., the preconditions are satisfied), inactive (i.e., the preconditions are unsatisfied), executed or inhibited which corresponds to a temporary state for a task during the occurrence of an incoherence in the system.

- **The behavioural description** indicates the necessary operational elements for a task execution. As in our application of cooperative writing, the tasks are performed by an actor in cooperation with its software agent, the part of task reserved for an agent is limited to actions of answering to queries submitted by the actor. This description contains inference rules and procedures.

- **The control structure** allows software agents to be totally independent of domain problems. It contains five types of methods: methods of preconditions control for the task execution; activation methods which activate the execution of a task once the preconditions are verified; execution methods of the behavioural part of a task; task execution control methods; task inhibition methods activated when a conflict appears between semi-independent tasks and methods of task resumption.

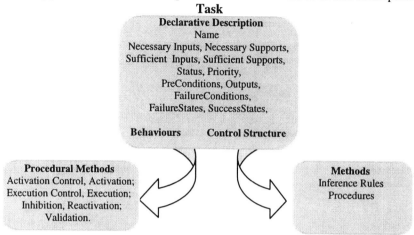

Figure 2 Task description

In the following part, we present the definitions which subtend our ontology for knowledge managing.

Definition 1: Active Task
We consider that a task is active at instant t_i, if its activation conditions are satisfied at t_i or if these same conditions were satisfied at a previous t_k instant, but its failure conditions have not been satisfied in the interval $[t_k, t_i]$.

The formal definition of an active task is given as follows.
Let T be a set of tasks in the system, T_i be a task of T. Let p be a PreCondition of T_i, Satisfied(p, t_i) a formula which gives a true value if p is satisfied at instant t_i. T_i is considered as an active task at instant t_i if one of these following conditions is satisfied :

. $\forall\ p_m \in$ PreCondition(T_i), Satisfied (p_m, t_i).
. $\forall\ p_m \in$ PreCondition(T_i), Satisfied (p_m, t_k) $k < i$ and
    $\rceil \exists\ e_n \in$ FailCondition(T_i), as Satisfied(e_n, t_j), $k < j \le i$.

Definition 2: A valid task execution
We consider that the execution of a task T_i done from its sufficient inputs and sufficient supports is valid, if no task T_j executed in parallel with T_i and which has an equal or a greater priority in comparison with the priority of T_i has created a new output which can be a necessary input or a necessary support of the task T_i.

Formally, this definition is translated as follows.

Let T be a set of domain tasks and T_i be a task of T. Let $I_{suf}(T_i)$, $I_{nec}(T_i)$ and $S_{suf}(T_i)$, $S_{nec}(T_i)$ be the sufficient and the necessary inputs and supports for the execution of a task T_i respectively and Outputs(T_i) the outputs of T_i. Let $t_{init}(T_i)$ and $t_{final}(T_i)$ be the beginning and the ending instants of the execution of T_i. Let Valid a predicate which returns true if the execution of the task T_i is valid, Priority (T_i) the priority of the T_i task in the system and state(x, t_i) an operator[2] which returns the state of the sufficient and the necessary, input or support x at instant t_i.

Valid (T_i) = true if $\forall$ $T_j \in$ T such that Priority $(T_i) \leq$ Priority (T_j)
$$\forall x \in [I_{suf}(T_i) \cap Output(T_j)] \cup [S_{suf}(T_i) \cap Output(T_j)]$$
$$state\ (x, t_{init}(T_i)) = state\ (x, t_{final}(T_j))$$

In order to allow the agents to automatically verify the coherence of the paralleled tasks in the system and to solve conflicts (cf. figure 1.b), we need to define the task execution coherence.

Definition 3: Task execution coherence
We consider that an execution of a task T_j is coherent in comparison with the execution of a task T_i if T_i does not share the inputs of T_j. In the opposite case, the execution of the task T_j must not modify the sufficient inputs and the sufficient supports of the task T_i (cf. figure 1.a).

Formally, this definition is translated as follows.
Let T be a set of tasks in a system, T_i and T_j two tasks of T, state(x, δ_i) an operator which returns the state of the input or support x at δ_i instant. Let $I_{suf}(T_i)$, $I_{nec}(T_i)$ and $S_{suf}(T_i)$, $S_{nec}(T_i)$ be the sufficient and necessary inputs and supports for the execution of T_i respectively. Let Outputs(T_i) the outputs of the task T_i. Let Coherence (T_j, T_i) be a predicate which gives a true value if the execution of the task T_j is coherent compared with the execution of T_i, $\delta_{init.}(T_i)$ and $\delta_{final}(T_i)$, the beginning and the ending instants of the task T_i.

Coherence (T_j, T_i) = True   if
$$\rceil \exists x \in [inputs(T_i) \cap inputs(T_j)] \cup [supports(T_i) \cap inputs(T_j)]$$
such as inputs $(T_i) = I_{suf}(T_i) \cup I_{nec}(T_i)$ and supports $(T_i) = S_{suf}(T_i) \cup S_{nec}(T_i)$
Or
$$\forall x \in [I_{suf}(T_i) \cap Output(T_j)] \cup [S_{suf}(T_i) \cap Output(T_j)],$$
$$state\ (x, t_{init}(T_i)) = state\ (x, t_{final}(T_j))$$

In our application, this definition indicates that the version of a document which corresponds to the state of a sufficient input or a sufficient support of a task Ti must not be modified by a task T_j executed in parallel with a task T_i.
With this predicate, we define the tasks whose execution is valid at the instant t_i and the set of tasks authorised at instant $t_{k\ (k\ >\ i)}$. For this reason, we introduce the notion of a coherent process.

---

[2] In the example of figure 1, we represent the version of the document FS at the instant t_1 with state(FS, t_1)= V.FS$_1$.

Definition 4: A coherent activity process
Let T_a be the set of active tasks at the instant δ_i in the cooperative system, t a task
of T_a and ω a set of tasks, $\omega \subset T_a$. ω is a coherent process if, for each $t \in \omega$:
1. $\forall$ t' $\in$ ω, we have Coherence (t , t').
2. $\forall$ t'' $\in$ T_a / ω // T_a / ω is a set of tasks for which the execution has been considered as invalid
           and then will be reactivated in the next cycles of the system.
We have:

    a. if $\rceil$ Coherence (t , t'') then t. priority $\geq$ t''. priority or

        $\exists$ t* $\in$ ω such as t* . priority $>$ t''. priority.

    b. if Coherence (t , t'') then $\exists$ t* $\in$ ω such as $\rceil$ Coherence (t* , t'')
        and t*. priority $>$ t''. priority.

To affect the priority attributed for the tasks in the cooperative activity process, the
agent refers to its task dependence and independence models. The strategy we have
retained to do this affectation is to allot the highest weight for the tasks having a
maximal semi-independence value (more a task has many relations of semi-
dependence with other tasks, the task generates more conflicts).
As we have outlined, the paralleling of semi-independent tasks causes some
situations of conflicts. For these conflicts, the agents in the system react by the
validation of the execution of some tasks and the invalidation of others when the
priority attributed for each task allows for the agents this decisional process. For
example, a new version of the functional specification generated by the reading
task cannot affect the task of reviewing the functional specification executed in
parallel, since the modifications done during the reading of the document deal only
with the linguistic quality of the document without any effects on its semantic and
so no conflict appears. In other cases, i.e., when tasks have same priorities, the
agents delegate the problem of conflict solving for the actors that they assist.

5 The software agent model

In most of the works dealing with Multi-Agent systems, researchers agreed on the
main components of a software agent (i.e., a knowledge base, an internal control
system and a processing system) and a communication system by which the agent
revels his state and affects his environment. An agent has one or several
behaviours. He uses them after he had received explicit message, to answer for
questions or for the monitoring [12].
From the description of cooperative activity process, we have drawn attention to
the five following needs: (1) the agents have to recognise the events which took
place in their environment; (2) they have to answer to these events and to react at
the right time; (3) selecting dynamically the tasks to be executed, which enables to
build up dynamically the activities plans of the actors they assist; (4) they have to
check whether all the conditions regarding tasks are satisfied before, during and
after their execution; (5) coordinate their tasks with those of the actors during the

execution of the cooperative writing process. Therefore, these aspects have been necessarily taken into account in the proposed architecture.

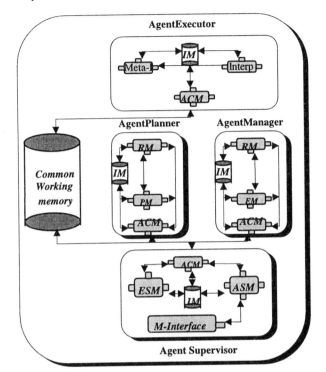

Figure 3 The control architecture of a software agent

So, we have defined a new recursive agent model endowed with several agents of control (i.e., an AgentPlanner and an AgentManager), an execution agent AgentExecutor, a supervisor agent. The first control agent (the AgentManager) integrates the behaviours which manage the execution of the domain tasks. The second control agent (the AgentPlanner) plans dynamically the sequence of the tasks which implies a dynamic generation of the actors' activity plans. Both the AgentExecutor and his actor participate to the execution of the selected tasks.

As we have introduced it, the proposed software agent architecture has been conceived to support the idea of a partial migration of the agent's code. Indeed, the separation between the four agents making up our architecture enables the AgentExecutor to migrate from his site to another in order to execute the desired task by interpreting the existing code in the other sites. As for the other agents of the architecture, they can stay in the same site and exchange messages with the AgentExecutor through their communication module.

• The central unit

It contains the two most important agents (the AgentPlanner and the AgentManager) on which the architecture is built. It acts as a controller, which activates, inhibits, validates and invalidates the executed tasks in the cooperative system. The central unit authorizes the inhibition of some tasks if the perceived events by the supervisor agent require an immediate reaction. After perceiving an event created by the AgentSupervisor, the AgentManager's recognition module (RM) constructs a description of the actions concerning this event, transmitted to the AgentPlanner. This one analyses the actions claimed by the AgentManager. He responds on by another description of actions retransmitted to the AgentManager. The AgentManager sends it to the supervision modules (ASM and ESM) or to the AgentExecutor. Whatever the case, the action will be executed either by the actor, or interpreted by the Interpreter of the AgentExecutor, or by both of them. The operating of each agent (AgentPlanner or AgentManager) described in figure 3 is interweaving in the operating of the other. At each control cycle of the super agent, the AgentSupervisor updates his knowledge. The recent knowledge is inserted in the common working memory of the four agents. This knowledge is then analysed and send by the AgentManager to the AgentPlanner, which leads to the appropriate decisions.

At each control cycle, the AgentManager checks the activation conditions of tasks which correspond to the "PreConditions" and the execution conditions of the tasks to be executed. For each recent activated or inactivated task, the agent manager sends an information message to the AgentPlanner. At the reception of the messages sent by the AgentManager, the AgentPlanner reacts with an application of a validation algorithm for the activated and inactivated tasks. The algorithm calculates the set of parallel tasks, the execution of which is coherent within the system.

Task Execution Validation Algorithm (EVA)

The algorithm receives as inputs the set T of task T_i inactivated and activated at δ_i instant.

Method ValidationOfTasks (T)

Begin

    T' = Order(T);   // Order is a method which orders the tasks of T by a diminished priority.

    Pile = ()

    While (T' ≠ ())

    Begin

        Unstuck (S, T');

        If $\forall\ x_j \in$ Pile, Coherence (S , x_j)

                Stuck (Pile, S) ;

    End

    Return Pile;

End

- **The supervision agent (AgentSupervisor)**

The descriptors of the events, which come in the Environmental Supervision Module (ESM), are the results of the actions executed by the agent himself or by the other agents. The descriptors of the actions are the commands created by the AgentPlanner for contracts which will be signed [24][3] and those transmitted by the AgentManager for the events related to the execution of tasks. The descriptors of events, which come in the Actor Supervision Module (ASM), are the results of actions executed by the actor and the descriptors of actions are the commands received by the central unit of the agent transmissible to the actor. In these commands, we can find those indicating the beginning and the ending of the execution, the interruption and the reactivation of tasks. These messages are sent to the agents from the same environment and to the actor with which they cooperate.

6 The architecture of the mediating system of cooperative work

In our prototype, a cooperative work process is defined as a set of tasks specified by the designer of the process. He determines the knowledge and the dependencies between tasks, which reinforce the control during the execution of a work process. Since our tool is decentralized, there is no central control unit. The control mechanism is totally decomposed between all the agents of the system.

Each agent executes several tasks: the activation of the tasks within the work process; the control and the management of the mistakes made during the execution of the tasks; the management of the declarative part of the tasks and the management of the functional dependencies and possible independence between these tasks. They communicate between themselves by a common memory workspace. They contribute to the control of the coherence and the validation of the obtained results in the cooperative system.

Finally, to reach the coherence of the system, we have imposed that each agent creator of an agent's group executing a set of paralleled tasks, must be responsible of each incoherent situation occurring during the execution of these tasks by the agents of the same group [24][3]. Therefore, he validates some tasks and invalidates others when such a situation is to be faced by using the task validation algorithm (cf. section 5).

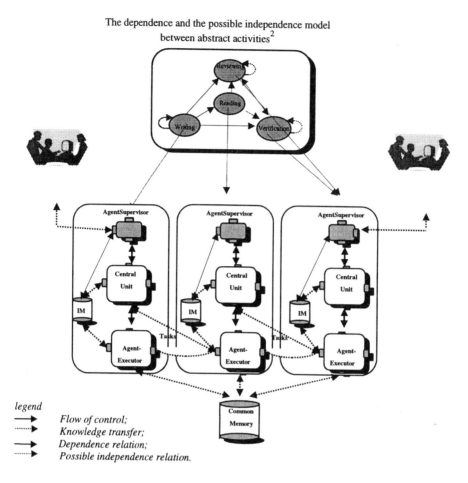

Figure 4 The control architecture of the cooperative work aided system.

7 Experiments and first results

It is important for the interface of the agent to adapt itself to the users' needs and to enable an interactivity with the actor during the execution of the work process. To take these needs into account, we have decided to implement the interface of the actors with the Java applets. As the user interest is limited to the achievement of a task and to the coherence of his results in comparison with the results of concurrent tasks executed by other actors in the cooperative system, we have decided to make totally transparent the representation and the validation of the results of these tasks

---

[2] The process of constructing the dependence and possible independence models between the abstract tasks is explained in [1].

for the actors. Figure 5 shows the actor's interface in the mediating system. The interface is made of the following parts:

- A window meant for the agent's notifications, which enables the agent to post the internal events, which took place in the system.
- A window meant for the actors' requests, which enables to show external events as the beginning, the ending and the interruption of the execution of a task.
- A window meant for the posting of the internal tasks in a list of the actor's planned tasks and the task to be executed.
- A window meant for the sticking of concurrent tasks to the current actor's task, which can alter its execution. On the right, down, a part is reserved for the execution of the current tasks, i.e., the writing of the document.

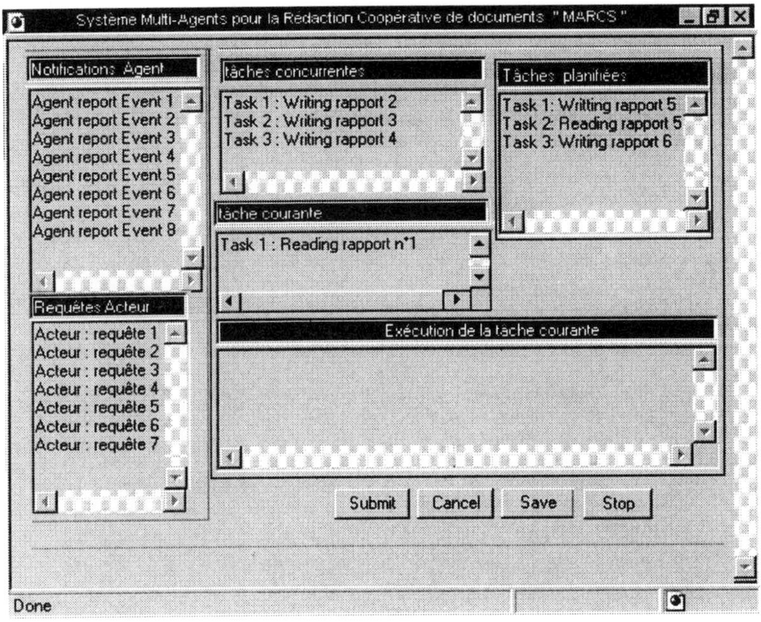

Figure 5 Graphical interface meant for the execution of the task within a cooperative writing process

8 Conclusion

In a cooperative system an intelligent agent has to coordinate his activities with the actor's and with other agents. He has to identify and execute logically correct tasks in response to the external events. We aimed at constructing autonomous agents capable of reasoning about their representation (of their environment, of the other agents, of the actor with which they cooperate and their own knowledge).

In this article, we have introduced an innovative ontology for the representation and the management of parallel workflow systems. We have also presented an architecture for these agents centred on the three main aspects of the recent applications: the mobility, the reusability and the parallel processing. This architecture is perfectly reusable for other cooperative systems, in the sense that the description and the implementation of the software agents are totally independent from the domain of application, i.e., the cooperative writing of documents. The agents' control is totally independent from the domain tasks that they execute [23] [8]. Domain tasks are described in activity representation formalism inspired from the KADS methodology and interpreted by the agents during their execution.

Our ontology dealing with the representation of the activity processes enables us to create new applications by only specifying the domain tasks the agents have to execute without redefining their control. We have also shown how we used our architecture to solve technical specification writing problems in the telecommunication domain. The prototype has been implemented with VisualJ++. It was specially created to meet the requirements of the recent applications by proposing an interesting solution of a partial migration of the agent's code.

In the current work, we are building a new conceptual model for designing parallel workflow systems [5]. Our conceptual model is principally based on the knowledge representation ontology proposed in this article.

References

[1] Aknine, S. Task Languages and Cooperation, Master Thesis, Paris Dauphine University, 1997.

[2] Aknine, S. A Reflexive Agent Architecture applied to Parallel WorkFlow Systems, CE'98, 5th ISPE International Conference on Concurrent Engineering Research and Applications, Tokyo, Japan, July 15-17, 1998a.

[3] Aknine, S., Issues in Cooperative Systems. Extending the Contract Net Protocol, IEEE ISIC/CIRA/ISAS'98, A Joint Conference on the Science and Technology of Intelligent Systems, Maryland U.S.A., September 14-17, 1998b.

[4] Aknine, S., Using Multi-Agent Systems to support Workflow Telecommunications Applications, IEEE ISIC/CIRA/ISAS'98, A Joint Conference on the Science and Technology of Intelligent Systems, Maryland U.S.A., September 14-17, 1998c.

[5] Aknine, S. & Pinson, S. Ontologie et Modèles Conceptuels pour la Modélisation des Systèmes de Workflow Parallèle dans une Perspective Multi-agent, Internal report (submitted), 1998.

[6] Borghoff, M., Bottoni, P., Mussio, P. & Pareschi, R. Reflective agents for adaptive Workflows, 2nd International Conference on the Practical Application of Intelligent Agents and Multi-Agent Technology (PAAM'97), 1997.

[7] Decker, K. & Lesser, V. Designing a family of co-ordination Algorithms, 13th International Workshop on Distributed Artificial Intelligence, 1994.

[8] De Hoog, R., Martil, R. & Wielinga, B.J. The CommonKads Model Set, Research Report, Esprit Project, KADS-II Consortium, 1993.

[9] Divitini, M., Simon, C. & Schmidt, K. ABACO : Coordination Mechanisms in a Multi-agent Perspectives, Second International Conference on the Design of Cooperative Systems, 1996.

[10] Ellis, C.A. Information Control Nets: A Mathematical Model of Office Information Flow, Conference on Simulation, Measurement and Modeling of Computer Systems, 1979.

[11] Ephrati, E. & Rosenschein, J. Multi-Agents planning as a dynamic search for social consensus, International Joint Conference on Artificial Intelligence, IJCAI'93, San Mateo, Calif. : Morgan Kaufmann, 1993.

[12] Ferber, J. Les systèmes Multi-agent. Vers une Intelligence collective, InterEditions, 1995.

[13] Glance, N.S., Pagani, D.S., & Pareschi, R. Generalised Process Structure Grammars (GPSG) for Flexible Representations of Work, ACM Conference on Computer Supported Cooperative Work, November 16-20, Boston, Mass, 1996.

[14] Haddawy, P. & Hanks, S. Issues in decision theoretic planning : symbolic goals and numeric utilities, DARPA, Workshop on Innovation Approaches to Planning, Scheduling and Control. San Mateo, Calif. : Morgan Kaufmann, 1990.

[15] Lesser, V. (edt). ICMAS-95, First International Conference on Multi-Agents Systems, MIT Press, 1995.

[16] Malone, T. What is Coordination Theory, National Science Foundation Coordination Theory Workshop, MIT, 1988.

[17] McCarthy, D.R., & Sarin, S.K., Workflow and Transaction in InConcert, Bulletin of the Technical Committee on Data Engineering, Vol. 16 N°2 - IEEE, June. Special Issue on Workflow Extended Transaction Systems, 1993.

[18] Newell, A. The knowledge level, Artificial Intelligence,18, 1982.

[19] Nwana, H.S. & Azarmi, N. Software Agents and Soft Computing : Toward Enhancing Machine Intelligence : Concepts and Applications, Springer, 1997.

[20] O'Hare, G.M.P. & Jennings, N.R. (ed.), Foundations of Distributed Artificial Intelligence, John Wiley, 1996.

[21] Parc, A.S. & Leuker, S. A Multi-agent Architecture Supporting Service Access, Rothermel, K. & Popescu-Zeletin, R.S. (ed.), First International Workshop on Mobile Agents, MA'97, Berlin, Germany, 1997.

[22] Rothermel, K. & Popescu-Zeletin, R.S. (ed.), First International Workshop on Mobile Agents, MA'97, Berlin, Germany, 1997.

[23] Schreiber, G., Breuker, J., Biedeweg, B. et Wiellinga, B.J. (1993). KADS A Principled Approach to Knowledge Based Systems Development Academic Press.

[24] Smith, R.G. The Contract Net Protocol: High-Level Communication and Control in a Distributed Problem-Solver, IEEE Transactions on Computers,1980.

A Generic Ontology for Spatial Reasoning

Frans Coenen and Pepijn Visser

CORAL*Research Group

Department of Computer Science, The University of Liverpool

Liverpool, UK

Abstract

In this paper we describe a generic ontology to support N-dimensional spatial reasoning applications. The ontology is intended to support both quantitative and qualitative approaches and is expressed using set notation. Using the ontology; spatial domains of discourse, spatial objects and their attributes, and the relationships that can link spatial objects can be expressed in terms of sets, and sets of sets. The ontology has been developed through a series of application studies. For each study a directed application ontology was first developed which was then merged into the generic ontology. Application areas that have been investigated include: Geographic Information Systems (GIS), noise pollution monitoring, environmental impact assessment, shape fitting, timetabling and scheduling, and AI problems such as the N-queens problem.

1   Introduction

In this paper we describe an generic ontology for spatial reasoning applications. The aim is to produce a mechanism which will facilitate the high level conceptualization of such applications in a manner which is both simple and as widely applicable as possible using ontologies. As a consequence researchers and manufacturers of spatial reasoning systems will benefit from the advantages that ontologies offer as demonstrated in other fields, for example Knowledge Based System (KBS) development [9].

The ontology is expressed using well established set theoretic notation. This approach was adopted because spatio-temporal objects naturally lend themselves to definition in terms of sets of addresses (coordinates). The ontology thus provides a mechanism whereby a spatial domain of discourse, spatial objects and their attributes, and the relationships that can link spatial objects can be expressed in terms of sets, and sets of sets. Application directed task ontologies can then be expressed using a subset of the available generic conceptualization.

A spatial reasoning system, the SPARTA (SPAtial Reasoning using Tesseral Addressing) system, which operates using a constraint logic programming paradigm, has also been developed. This system is designed to read directed problem

---

*Conceptualization and Ontology Research at Liverpool

statement expressed using the generic ontology described here, and then to "run" the conceptualization so as to produce appropriate results. Although this system is referred to within this paper its precise nature is not described (interested readers are directed to Coenen et al. [5, 6] for further information).

We commence by presenting an introduction to ontologies (section 2) and the application area of spatio-temporal reasoning (section 3). Specific application ontologies, using the general ontology, are expressed using set notation. The advantages offered by this representation and some details with respect to syntax are thus presented in section 4. In section 5 some assumptions regarding the nature of multi-dimensional space and its definition with respect to the ontology are established. This is followed in section 6 and section 7 with discussion concerning the expression of spatial entities and the attributes that may be associated with such entities using the ontology. Finally in section 8 we present some conclusions and consider directions for further research into the field of spatial ontologies.

2   Ontologies

Building knowledge systems involves the creation of a model of a particular domain (e.g., electronic circuits, legislation, plants). Such a model is necessarily an abstraction of the domain under consideration. This is what makes a model useful, it abstracts from irrelevant details and thereby allow us to focus on the aspects of the domain we are interested in. Building a model of a domain involves deciding upon what entities in the domain are to be distinguished, and what relations will be recognized between these entities. Moreover, it involves deciding upon what types of entities, and what types of relation exist. Often, the latter kind of decisions are straightforward and not always explicitly documented. For instance, in building a model of the blocks world we use predicates like block(A), holds(A) and on(A,B) thereby implicitly assuming the domain to consist of blocks, tables, and hands, and that blocks, tables and hands have spatial relations. Making these assumptions requires the domain to be carved up in concepts. Alternatively stated, they reflect a conceptualization of the domain under consideration. The conceptualization tells us the types of entities and how they relate. In the blocks world the conceptualization tells us that there are blocks, tables, hands and that blocks and tables have spatial relations. It does not, however, tell us what blocks, tables and hands there are, nor how they are spatially related. To be able to compare conceptualizations of a domain, it is necessary to make them explicit. Thus, we need to have an explicit conceptualization. This is what the word ontology is used for in AI research: an ontology is defined as an explicit specification of a conceptualization ([8]).

Recently the result of gathering vocabularies and structuring domains has been recognized as a valuable effort in its own right, deserving of attention (Wiederhold p.7 [18]). In general, we can say that ontologies may contribute to the following five areas:

1. **Knowledge acquisition**. Ontologies describe and structure the entities

and relations that need to be acquired for the domain under consideration. Examples of this kind of ontology use are CUE [10], and MOBAL [14].

2. **Knowledge exchange**. Ontologies can be used to define assumptions that enable knowledge exchange between different systems. Examples of this kind of ontology use can be found in SHADE [11], and also in the work of Wiederhold [18]

3. **Knowledge-system design**. Ontologies are reusable constructs in the design of knowledge systems because they can be used to represent the invariant assumptions underlying different knowledge bases in the same domain. As such, they can be considered as initial building blocks of the knowledge base under construction. An example of this kind of ontology use can be found in the GAMES methodology [9].

4. **Domain-theory development**. Because an ontology explicitly states the building blocks of particular domains, it can be used for the analysis, comparison, and development of domain theories. Examples of this kind of ontology use can be found in Sim and Rennels [15], and Visser and Bench-Capon [17].

5. **System documentation**. Ontologies provide a meta-level view (vocabulary, structure) on their application domain which facilitates adequate system documentation for end-users. An example of this kind of ontology use is found in the Cyc project [13].

Although the ontologies concept is now well established in the Knowledge Based Systems (KBS) community ([9]) very little work has been undertaken in the field of spatial ontologies. Some work has been done on the language of spatial reasoning, i.e. "what is meant by the term nearby?" Etc. In addition mereology has been taken up as a theory of part-whole relations in formal philosophical ontology ([16]), although this has not been generally extended to spatial reasoning contexts. The ontology described here seeks to lay the foundation for a generic abstract ontology to support spatio-temporal reasoning applications so that the researchers and builders of such systems can gain similar advantages to does gained by the KBS community through the use of ontologies.

3 SPATIAL-TEMPORAL REASONING

Spatial reasoning can be defined, very broadly, as the automated manipulation of data objects belonging to spatial domains so as to arrive at application dependent conclusions. A spatial domain, in this context, is then considered to imply any N-dimensional space (real or imaginary, including 1-D temporal spaces) in which objects of interest may be contained. Automated manipulation then implies the computer simulation of some higher mental processes (not just the simple response to some stimulus or the mechanical performance of an algorithm). We are therefore not concerned with (say) the automated retrieval of spatially referenced data contained in some database format. Thus, at its simplest, spatial reasoning can be considered to revolve round the identification of (previously unknown) relationships that exists between spatial objects according to the relationships that are known or desired to exists between such data objects. In more complex systems the identified relations are then used as the foundation whereby further reasoning can take place, and consequently additional conclusions drawn.

4 Syntax

A number of languages/tools are available in which ontological conceptualizations may be expressed. The most well known example is Ontolingua [8] which is directed at ontologies for the conceptualization of expert systems and developed as part of the KSE project. Another example is KRSL (Knowledge Representation Specification Language) which is directed at a similar domain (Leher [12]).

The core ontology described here is presented using set notation. The principal reason for this is that space is conceptualized as a comprising groups of "cells" — the Cartesian coordinate system is the most widely used mechanism for referencing such cells. It is thus a natural step to consider such groups of cells in terms of sets. Further reasons for using set notation are that the theory is long established and is consequently well understood, and secondly that there is a recognized notation for expressing sets and the operations that can be performed on it.

Using the proposed spatio-temporal ontology a task dependent application ontology is described in terms of a "singleton" set, $TaskOntology$, which comprises a 3-tuple each element of which, in turn, is a set:

$$TaskOntology = \{\langle Space, Objects, Relations \rangle\}$$

The set $Space$ describes the nature of the domain of discourse. The set $Objects$ defines the set of spatial entities of interest, and the attributes that may be associated with those entities. The set $Relations$ then defines the relationships that can exist between pairs of spatial entities. The more precise nature of each of these sets is described in the following sections.

5 Space

The ontology assumes that:

- N-dimensional space comprises a set of N-dimensional isohedral cells each of which is identified by a unique *address* (the SPARTA system uses a tesseral addressing system — see Diaz and Bell [7] for an overview of this technique).

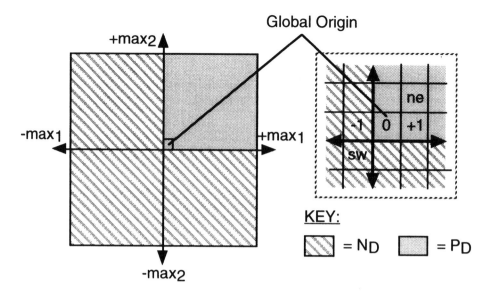

Figure 1: Example 2D space

- The addressing systems has the effect of linearising space so that an ordering can be imposed on sets of addresses (regardless of the number of dimensions under consideration).

- The addressing system has an origin to which all other addresses can be referenced

- The system has an arithmetic superimposed that facilitates translation through the space

Given this representation we can identify a domain of discourse U which may be defined as follows:

$$U = P \amalg N$$

(the disjoint union of the sets P and N) where:

$$P = \{p \mid p : (the \ set \ of \ all \ references representing \ positive \ space)\}$$
$$N = \{n \mid n : (the \ set \ of \ all \ references representing \ negative \ space)\}$$

The reasons for this distinction will become apparent when we go on to consider the attributes that can be associated with spatial objects in section 6.

An example 2-D space is given in Figure 1. Note that the maximum dimensions are denoted by the labels max_1 and max_2. The nature of these dimensions will be domain dependent. Note also that the *globalOrigin* of the space, the cell 0, is located at the intersection of the two axis. For the purposes of this document it is necessary to identify a number of further addresses with respect to the *globalOrigin*. These are shown in the inset in Figure 1 which assumes a linearisation the flows from the bottom-left cell up to the top-right cell. The addresses -1 and $+1$ indicate the addresses immediately before and after the *globalOrigin* as defined by the linearisation. The addresses *sw* and *ne* indicate the addresses which are "corner adjacent" to the *globalOrigin* but furthest away (in the negative and positive directions) with respect to the linearisation. The values that may be associated with the variables *sw* and *ne* will be implementation dependent.

The domain of discourse of any task is then either equivalent to U or is some subset of U (but such that the origin is included). In this paper we will indicate task domain sets using the notation U_D which is then comprised of the disjoint intersection of the positive and negative component spaces (P_D and N_D respectively).

Given a particular application the set *Space* will be defined as follows:

$$Space = \{max_1, max_2, ...max_N\}$$

where N is an integer representing the number of dimensions under consideration. Thus, in the context of a particular task ontology, a 1-D space would be defined as $\{max_1\}$, a 2-D space as $\{max_1, max_2\}$, and so on. This in turn will define the nature of the sets U_D, P_D and N_D. Once the domain of discourse has been defined we can define sub-spaces within this domain in terms of subsets of U_D, as dictated by the nature of the application.

5.1 Local Origins

We have seen that any set U_D has a *globalOrigin*. Similarly any subset of U_D will have a *localOrigin* which is defined as the reference nearest to the *globalOrigin* as dictated by the nature of the linearisation. Thus, given a subset X of the set U_D we define a function $f_{localOrigin}$ that returns the reference for the local origin of the set X. This function is defined as follows:

$$Dom(f_{localOrigin}) = Pow(U_D)$$
$$Cod(f_{localOrigin}) = U_D$$
$$Gr(f_{localOrigin}) = \{\langle X, a\rangle \mid a : X \land a \ nearest \ the \ (global) \ origin$$

where *Dom*, *Cod* and *Gr* are the domain, codomain and graph of the indicated function, and *Pow* is a function that returns the power set its argument (which must be a set).

5.2 Linearisation and sequences of addresses

The linear representation assumed offers many computational advantages. In particular it allows for the unambiguous identification of local origins and the definition of sequences of addresses. With respect to the latter we use the infix operator .. to define such sequences. The prefix operand for this operator then represents the start of the sequence (the address closest to the origin) and the postfix operand the end of the sequence (the address furthest away from the origin).

6   Objects

Any spatial application will comprise a number of spatial entities. These may describe points, intervals, events, areas, volumes and so on. Using the general ontology spatial entities of interest are described in terms of a set of sets, *Objects*, which is defined as follows:

$$Objects = \{Obj_1, Obj_2, ..., Obj_N\}$$

where the elements Obj_1 through to Obj_N are themselves set of sets whose elements describe attributes that may be associated with spatial entities. Spatial entities may have many attributes. The following are currently addressed by the general ontology:

- Identifier
- Location
- Shape
- Rotation
- Size (actual, maximum, minimum)
- Connectivity (a spatial entity does not have to be comprised of a continuous set of cells)
- Class (type)

This list of possible attributes is not complete, although it does cover those attributes most commonly encountered. Work is currently in progress to identify a more complete list. Each of the above attributes is discussed further in the following subsections.

6.1   Identifier

To do anything with a spatial entity we need to be able to identify it in some manner. The simplest approach is to give the entity in question a unique *name* selected from a set *Names*:

$$Names = n \mid the\ set\ of\ all\ possible\ names$$

Thus one (and only one) element of any set *Obj* is always a member of the set *Names*.

6.2 Location

Other than an identifier the second most important attribute that may be associated with a spatial entity is its location. There are two possibilities, either an entity's location is precisely known (i.e. it is fixed) or we know of some *location space* in which the entity can be said to exist (this may extend to the entire domain). What ever the case the location or location space is described in terms of some subset (*Location* or *LocationSpace*) of P_D, i.e. in terms of a positive set of cells contained within the domain. In the absence of any other information these sets are assumed to be equivalent to P_D. Thus:

$$\begin{aligned} Location &= \{L \mid L \subseteq P_D\} \\ LocationSpace &= \{L \mid L \subseteq P_D\} \end{aligned}$$

the definitions are the same, the interpretations are different. Note also that, given a spatial entity whose location is known (i.e. there exists a set *Location* as opposed to a set *LocationSpace*), further attributes such as shape, size, connectivity etc., are defined by default. We will refer to such an object as a *fixed object*.

6.3 Shape

Shape is probably the third most significant attribute that a spatial entity has. We have already seen that in the case of a fixed object shape is defined by default. However, in the absence of a fixed location, shape is often significant. Shape is defined (in a similar manner to the *Location* and *LocationSpace* sets) as follow:

$$Shape = \{S \mid S \subseteq U_D \wedge globalOrigin \in S\}$$

Note that any shape definition must include the origin address of U_D. This is required because if we wish to do anything useful with the shape it must have some reference (a local origin) with respect to which it can be manipulated.

We will refer to spatial entities that have a known shape, but no definite location other than some location space within which they are considered to exist, as *free objects* (in the sense that they are not fixed). Given a free object, the shape definition also defines further attributes such as size and connectivity. Note also that a free object must have some location space associated with it — somewhere within which it is known to exist. This may be either the entire space P_D or some subset of P_D as defined in the previous sub-section.

6.4 Rotation

A further important attribute associated with free objects is orientation — this may be either fixed or we may be free to rotate the object. Whether a shape/object can be rotated or not is defined in terms of a singleton set *Rotation*:

$$Rotation = \{r \mid r \in Bool\}$$

where *Bool* is the Boolean set comprised of the elements $\{true, false\}$.

6.5 Size

In the absence of location and shape information we may have knowledge of size. The size of a spatial object is expressed in terms of the number of members of a set describing its shape, i.e. the *cardinality* of this set. In the case of a fixed object this will be the set *Location*, in the case of a free object this will be the set *Shape*. Where the nature of this set is not known we can still express the required number of elements for this set. The minimum size of any object (that can be physically realized) is 1 indicating that it is represented by a single cell. The maximum size of an object is equivalent to $f_{cardinality}(P_D)$ (where $f_{cardinality}$ is a function that returns the "size" of its argument which must be a set), other wise the object exceeds the application domain. In addition the nature of the size of an object can be expressed in terms of (i) a minimum size, (ii) a maximum size, or (iii) an actual size — the set of operators $\{<, =, >\}$. Thus we can define a set *Size*, comprising a single 2-tuple, as follows:

$$Size \; = \; \{\langle q, z\rangle \mid q \in \{<, =, >\} \cdot z \in \{1 \; .. \; cardinality(P_D)\}\}$$

6.6 Connectivity

Finally we may know something about whether an object's location/shape is represented by a contiguous set of addresses or not. In this context continuity is defined as the situation where each element of a *Location* or *shape* set of addresses associated with any object is adjacent to at least one other element of this set (by adjacent we mean either edge or corner adjacency). We define the nature of the connectivity attribute in terms of a singleton set *Contiguity* as follows:

$$Contiguity = \{c \mid c \in Bool\}$$

6.7 Class

From the above we can conclude that (so far) the attributes of any object are taken from the set of all possible attributes (*Attributes*) defined as follows:

$$Attributes = \{identifiers, locations, locationspaces,$$
$$shapes, rotation, size, connectivity\}$$

Given any spatial object only a sub-set of this possible set of attributes will be associated with it. The nature of this subset is, in turn, described by the *classes* of an object. This is defined by a singleton set *Class*:

$$Class = \{c \mid c \in \{fixed, free, shapeless\}\}$$

Thus the complete *Attribute* set should more properly be expressed as follows:

$$Attributes = \{identifiers, classes, locations, locationspaces,$$
$$shapes, rotation, size, connectivity\}$$

The nature of the attributes that can be associated with each class has been discussed in the foregoing, however, a summary is presented below.

- **Fixed objects**: Objects whose locations are "fixed". Consequently they have only three attributes: an identifier, a class and a *Location* set (all other attributes are defined by default). Thus given a particular fixed object this will be defined as follows:

$$FixedObject = \{name, class, Location\}$$

- **Free objects**: Objects whose location is not known, but who have a fixed shape. Objects belonging to this class have five attributes: an identifier, a class, *LocationSpace* and *Shape* sets, and whether rotation is permitted or not (the size and connectivity attributes are implied by the shape attribute and therefore do not need to be explicitly included). Thus given a specific free object this would be defined thus:

$$FreeObject = \{name, class, LocationSpace, Shape, rotation\}$$

- **Shapeless objects**: Objects whose location and shape are both not known. These may be objects for which we know nothing (other than they exist), or we may know details about size and/or connectivity. Their definition will also require a description of the location space in which they are known to be contained. Thus:

$$ShapelessObject = \{name, class, LocationSpace\} \vee$$
$$\{name, class, LocationSpace, Size\} \vee$$
$$\{name, class, LocationSpace, Contiguity\} \vee$$
$$\{Name, Class, LocationSpace, Size, Contiguity\}$$

7 Relations

In addition to the above attributes, applicable to individual objects, there are a further set of attributes that serve to link pairs of objects or objects and locations. We will refer to such attributes as relationships. For example, given two objects we might say that one is contained within the other. The relation "contained" as used here is a predicate in the sense that the relation is either true or false. More precisely we are saying that the location (or locationSpace) of one of the objects is such that it is contained wholly within the location (or location space) of the other. We have seen that in the generic ontology, as outlined so far, all locations and location spaces are expressed as sets. Therefore the most natural way of describing relations in the context of the ontology described here is in terms of the standard set relations expressed as a Boolean functions:

$$f_{filterEquals}(A, B) \Rightarrow true \ if \ A = B$$
$$f_{filterIntersects}(A, B) \Rightarrow true \ if \ A \cap B$$
$$f_{filterSubset}(A, B) \Rightarrow true \ if \ A \subset B$$
$$f_{filterSubsetOrEquals}(A, B) \Rightarrow true \ if \ A \subseteq B$$
$$f_{filterSuperset}(A, B) \Rightarrow true \ if \ A \supset B$$
$$f_{filterSupersetOrEquals}(A, B) \Rightarrow true \ if \ A \supseteq B$$

where A and B are sets of addresses. We use the term filter here to indicate that these relations are, in practice, used to express constraints that are desired to hold between objects. If we add the negation of these predicates we have 12 possible relations.

Alternatively we can also conceive of relations as non-Boolean functions which can be used to refine the location space associated with shapeless objects, i.e. given such an object we can get some idea of its nature through a set of relations. We can identify two such relations:

$$f_{mapIntersects}(A, B) \Rightarrow A_n = A \cap B$$
$$f_{mapComplement}(A, B) \Rightarrow A_n = B \setminus A$$

We refer to these relations as mappings in the sense that we "map" some set operation (intersection, union, complement) on to the first argument (A) with respect to the second argument (B) so as the produce a revised set (A_n). Given a set of such relations we can continuously revise the location space for a shapeless object with respect to fixed or free objects until we have a desired location for the shapeless object.

The total possible set of relations is then as follows:

$$Relations \ = \ \{equals, intersects, subset, subsetEqual, superset,$$

$$superset Equal, not Equals, not Intersects, not Subset,$$
$$not Subset Equal, not Superset, not Superset Equal,$$
$$intersection, complement\}$$

In the ontology a relation, at its simplest, is expressed as a set of three elements

$$Relation \quad = \{\{a, r, b\} \mid a, b \in Names \cdot r \in Relations\}$$

Note that locations/location spaces are referenced using object names.

7.1 Offsets

To increase the expressiveness of these relations we can apply an *offset* to the location of an object. An offset is a set of addresses, defined as some subset of U_D, which is applied either to (a) all the elements describing a location (or location space) or (b) the local origin for this set. The effect in the first case is to translate or expand (or both) the space. In the second case this allows us to define other "locations" with respect to the given location or location space.

Although the offset principle allows us to expand objects the only way in which objects can be "shrunk" is to define a space with respect to the local origin of the object in question so that it appears that the object has been shrunk. This is often a cumbersome process, thus a facility is also provided to "shrink" by a given number of addresses.

What ever the case offsets are defined by a 2-tuple as follows:

$$Offset \quad = \quad \{\langle t, F \rangle \mid t \in \{ref, all, shrink\} \cdot F \subseteq U_D\}$$

Thus a relation can, more broadly, be defined as follows:

$$Relation = \{a, r, b\} \vee \{a, \langle t_a, F_a \rangle, r, b\} \vee$$
$$\{a, r, b, \langle t_b, F_b \rangle\} \vee \{a, \langle t_a, F_a \rangle, r, b, \langle t_b, F_b \rangle\}$$

7.2 Quantifying the intersection relations

The expressiveness of the *intersects* and *intersection* relations (either in addition to or as an an alternative to the use of offsets) may be further expanded by quantifying the size of the intersection. In the ontology we achieve this by allowing two optional arguments for the intersection predicate — an operator and a desired cardinality. The set of possible operators is as follows:

$$<, <=, =, =>, >$$

The cardinality is expressed as a positive integer in the range of 1 to $f_size(P_D)$. Thus we can (say) insist that an intersection is equal to a cardinality of 4 as follows:

$$\{a, intersection(=, 4), b\}$$

8 Conclusions

In this paper we have describe the foundation for an "all purpose" general purpose ontology to support the development of spatio-temporal reasoning applications. Although the technique has been applied to a great many applications — Geographic Information Systems (GIS) [4], noise pollution monitoring [2], environmental impact assessment [1], shape fitting [6], scheduling and timetabling [3], and AI problems such as the N-queens problem — the ontology is not yet complete. There are still many application areas, such as map and chart interaction, spatial simulation, environmental planning; which may require further mechanisms to increase the expressiveness of the relations. With respect to the attributes that can be associated with spatial entities there are still a number of variations on the given list that require further investigation. For example we can conceive of partially shaped objects in that we may know a minimum shape for the object. There is thus still much work to do. However, work to date, indicates that the ontology described in this paper provides a sound foundation for this further work.

References

[1] Beattie, B., Coenen, F.P., Hough, A., Bench-Capon, T.J.M., Diaz, B.M. and Shave, M.J.R. (1996). Spatial Reasoning for Environmental Impact Assessment. Third International Conference on GIS and Environmental Modeling, Santa Barbara: National Center for Geographic Information and Analysis, WWW and CD.

[2] Brown, A.G.P., Coenen, F.P., Shave, M.J. and Knight, M.W. (1998). An AI Approach to Noise Prediction. To appear in Building Acoustics.

[3] Coenen, F.P., Beattie, B., Bench-Capon, T.J.M., Shave, M.J.R and Diaz, B.M. (1995). Spatial Reasoning for Timetabling: The TIMETABLER system. Proceedings of the 1st International Conference on the Practice and Theory of Automated Timetabling (ICPTAT'95), Napier University, Edinburgh, pp57-68.

[4] Coenen, F.P., Beattie, B., Bench-Capon, T.J.M, Diaz, B.M. and Shave. M.J.R. (1996). Spatial Reasoning for Geographic Information Systems. Proceedings 1st International Conference on GeoComputation, School of Geography, University of Leeds, Vol 1, pp121-131.

[5] Coenen, F.P., Beattie, B., Bench-Capon, T.J.M, Diaz, B.M. and Shave. M.J.R. (1997). A tesseral Approach to N-Dimensional Spatial Reasoning.

In Hameurlain, A. and Tjoa, A.M. (Eds), Database and Expert Systems Applications, (Proceedings DEXA'97), Lecture Notes in Computer Science 1308, Springer Verlag, pp633-642.

[6] Coenen, F.P., Beattie, B., Bench-Capon, T.J.M., Diaz, B.M. and Shave. M.J.R. (1998). Spatio-Temporal Reasoning Using A Multi-Dimensional Tesseral Representation. Proceedings ECAI'98, pp140-144.

[7] Diaz, B.M. and Bell, S.B.M. (1987). Spatial Data Processing using Tesseral Methods. Natural Environment Research Council publication, Swindon, England.

[8] Gruber, T. (1992). Ontolingua: A Mechanism to Support Portable Ontologies. Knowledge Systems Laboratory, Standford University, Stanford, USA.

[9] Heijst, G. van (1995). The Role of Ontologies in Knowledge Engineering, Doctoral Thesis, University of Amsterdam, Amsterdam, The Netherlands.

[10] Heijst, G. Van, and G. Schreiber (1994). CUE: Ontology-based knowledge acquisition, L. Steels, A. Th. Schreiber, and W. Van de Velde (eds.), A Future for Knowledge Acquisition, Proceedings of the 8th European Knowledge Acquisition Workshop EKAW'94, Vol. 867 of Lecture Notes in Artificial Intelligence, pp.178-199, Springer-Verlag, Berlin/Heidelberg, Germany.

[11] Kuokka, D.R., J. McGuire, J.C. Weber, J.M. Tenenbaum, T.R. Gruber, and G.R. Olsen (1993). SHADE: Knowledge-Based Technology for the Re-Engineering Problem, Annual Report 1993.

[12] Leher, N. (1990). Knowledge Representations Specification Language. Technical Report, DARPA/Rome Laboratory Planning and Scheduling Initiative, Reference manual.

[13] Lenat, D.B. and R.V. Guha (1990). Building Large Knowledge-Based Systems; Representation and Reasoning in the Cyc Project, Addison-Wesley, Reading, Massachusetts, United States.

[14] Morik, K., S. Wrobel, J-U. Kietz, and W. Emde (1993). Knowledge Acquisition and Machine Learning; Theory, Methods and Applications, Knowledge-Based Systems, Academic Press Limited, London, United Kingdom.

[15] Sim, I., and G. Rennels (1995). Developing A Clinical Trial Ontology: Comments on Domain Modeling and Ontological Reuse, Knowledge Systems Laboratory Medical Computer Science, KSL-95-60, June 1995.

[16] Simons, P. (1987). Parts — A study in Ontology. Clarendon Press, Oxford.

[17] Visser, P.R.S. and T.J.M. Bench-Capon (1998). A Comparison of Four Ontologies for the Design of Legal Knowledge Systems, Artificial Intelligence and Law, Vol 6,N0 1, pp3-26.

[18] Wiederhold, G. (1994). Interoperation, Mediation, and Ontologies, Proceedings International Symposium on Fifth Generation Computer Systems (FGCS94), Workshop on Heterogeneous Cooperative Knowledge-Bases, Vol. W3, pp.33-48, ICOT, Tokyo, Japan.

Knowledge Modelling for a Generic Refinement Framework

Robin Boswell and Susan Craw

School of Computer and Mathematical Sciences

The Robert Gordon University

Aberdeen, UK

Abstract

Refinement tools assist with debugging a KBS's knowledge, thus easing the well-known knowledge acquisition bottleneck, and the more recently recognised maintenance overhead. Existing refinement tools are developed for specific rule-based KBS environments, and have usually been applied to artificial or academic applications. Hence there is a need for tools which are applicable to industrial applications. However, it would be wasteful to develop separate refinement tools for individual shells; instead, the KRUSTWorks project is developing re-usable components applicable to a variety of KBS environments.

This paper develops a knowledge representation that embodies a KBS's rulebase and its reasoning, and permits the implementation of core refinement procedures, which are generally applicable and can ignore KBS-specific details. Such a representation is an essential stage in the construction of a generic automated knowledge refinement framework, such as KRUSTWorks. Experience from applying this approach to CLIPS, POWERMODEL and PFES KBSs indicates its feasibility for a wider variety of industrial KBSs.

1   Introduction

The well-known knowledge acquisition bottleneck encompasses both the original knowledge elicitation, and the debugging of the knowledge while the knowledge based system (KBS) develops. As KBSs become more routinely used in industry, their maintenance becomes a further knowledge management issue. The evolution of methodologies such as KADS (Schreiber, Wielinga & Breuker 1993) organises the knowledge development process, but there is a demand for knowledge refinement tools that assist with the acquisition, debugging and maintenance of the knowledge itself. A knowledge refinement tool assists a knowledge engineer by identifying places where the knowledge may need to be changed. For knowledge acquisition, it identifies potential gaps in the knowledge and incorporates missing knowledge into the KBS. For debugging, it identifies potential faults in the knowledge and suggests possible repairs. In contrast to debugging, knowledge maintenance refines the knowledge because the problem-solving environment has changed in some way; in this case, the knowledge must be updated to match the new environment.

Knowledge refinement tools each perform the same general steps. The tool is presented with a faulty KBS and some evidence of faulty behaviour; often this consists of examples that the KBS fails to solve correctly, together with the correct solutions. The refinement tool reacts to a piece of evidence by undertaking the following three tasks: *blame allocation* determines which rules or parts of rules might be responsible for the faulty behaviour; *refinement generation* suggests rule modifications that may correct the faulty behaviour; and *refinement selection* picks the best of the possible refinements. The goal of refinement is that the refined KBS correctly solves as many of the examples as possible, with the expectation that novel examples will also have an improved success rate.

Most knowledge refinement systems are designed to work with KBSs developed in a single language (Ourston & Mooney 1994, Richards & Mooney 1995, Murphy & Pazzani 1994), or a particular shell (Ginsberg 1988). However, it is wasteful to develop refinement tools for individual languages and shells. We prefer to investigate re-usable refinement components that can be applied to a variety of KBS environments. This paper concentrates on the knowledge representation issues, and the rest of this section investigates the knowledge demands of the core refinement processes. Section 2 considers how they can be satisfied by generic structures that organise the key roles adopted by components of rules. In Sections 3 and 4 we describe our experience of applying these generic knowledge structures to various KBSs. Section 5 investigates the approaches used by other refinement tools. In Section 6 we draw some conclusions about the usefulness of these structures and their utility in our long term goal of providing a framework of refinement components in the KRUSTWorks project.

1.1   The Refinement Process of a KRUSTTool

We base this paper on experience with our KRUST refinement system (Craw 1996). Figure 1 shows a KRUSTTool[1] performing the operations highlighted above. The KBS's problem-solving for one training example is analysed, and blame is allocated to the knowledge that has taken part in the faulty solution, or which failed to contribute to the solution as intended. The experiment toolset generates repairs that correct this faulty behaviour. A rule is prevented from firing by making its conditions harder to satisfy, or by preventing rules that conclude the knowledge required by the original rule's conditions. Conversely, a rule is encouraged to fire by making its failed conditions easier to satisfy, or by encouraging rules that conclude the knowledge required by the original rule's failed conditions. Knowledge specific refinement operators implement these repairs on the rules. KRUSTTools are unusual in proposing many faults and generating many repairs initially, and so a KRUSTTool applies filters to remove unlikely refinements before any refined KBSs are implemented. It then evaluates the performance of these refined KBSs on the training example itself

---

[1]We now refer to refinement tools that apply the basic mechanism of the original KRUST system as KRUSTTools. We are developing a KRUSTWorks framework (Section 6) from which an individual KRUSTTool for a particular KBS will be assembled; i.e. there is not one unique KRUSTTool.

and other examples that are available. A detailed description of the execution of an early KRUST appears in (Craw & Sleeman 1990).

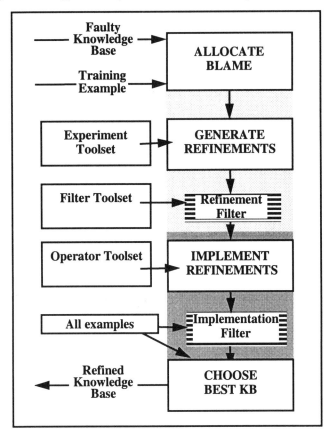

Figure 1: The Operation of a KRUSTTool

1.2   The Knowledge Demands of a KRUSTTool

The refinement process relies on determining what knowledge was applied to solve the given training example and what knowledge might have been applied instead (Blame Allocation), and how to alter the knowledge (Refinement Generation). A refinement tool therefore reasons about actual and potential interactions within the KB, and in particular rule chaining behaviour. An important result of our work on knowledge refinement is the conclusion that the necessary information for the refinement of any KBS may be represented in two structures.

The *Knowledge Skeleton* is an internal representation of the rules in a KBS. The knowledge skeleton allows the refinement tool to determine what knowledge is applied and how rules can chain. The creation of a knowledge skeleton requires the existence of a common knowledge representation language, which can represent any feature in any shell to which KRUSTWorks is to be applied. The skeleton itself is built by a shell-specific translator. The remaining sections of this paper concentrate on the representation language for the knowledge skeleton and the use of the knowledge skeleton in KRUSTTools.

The *Problem Graph* represents the KBS's problem-solving for an incorrectly solved example. Details of the problem graph and its use in KRUSTTools will appear in a later paper. Figure 2 shows a problem graph when the KBS solution is '−' but the correct answer is '+'. The initial facts are shown as circular leaf nodes, provable knowledge is also shown as circles, and square nodes represent knowledge that is currently not provable but would help to correct the error. Each rule is labelled by a diamond, linked to its conditions beneath it and its conclusion above. A circular arc indicates that a rule has two or more conditions forming a conjunction. For example, rule $R7$ has conditions G ∧ H and conclusion B. Rule $R8$ has condition H and conclusion C.

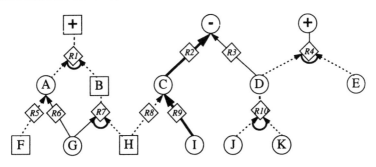

Figure 2: A Sample Problem Graph

The *positive* part of the problem graph is shown as solid lines and represents the knowledge that was applied during the problem-solving. The *negative* part of the problem graph is shown with dotted lines and highlights those parts of rules which may be changed to deduce the correct answer '+'. The negative part of the graph is constructed with reference to the desired goal and the knowledge skeleton, since it can not be derived from the observed behaviour of the KBS. We represent the control strategy by organising the sub-graphs in a left-to-right order, where the leftmost rules are those chosen earliest for execution. The chain of reasoning that leads to the KBS's conclusion is therefore the leftmost sub-graph containing circled nodes only; nodes are circled because these rules' conditions were satisfied, and they appear as the leftmost of the satisfied rules because they were selected in preference to other satisfied rules. This chain has been highlighted using bolder lines in Figure 2. Blame allocation identifies square nodes leading to '+' that should be altered to allow them to fire (leftmost sub-graph), circular nodes leading to '−' that should be prevented from firing (middle sub-graph), and circular nodes leading to '+' that should be altered to make them more competitive in the control strategy (rightmost sub-graph).

It is important to note that the positive half of the problem graph is derived from the actual observed behaviour of the KB, not from an internal simulation, so is guaranteed correct. On the other hand, the negative half of the graph does require a simulation of potential KB behaviour, and hence may introduce inaccuracies. However, any consequent incorrect repairs will be detected during testing; and if the ideal repair is missed, then the best of the many other refinements that the KRUSTTool generates will be applied instead.

1.3 Using the Knowledge Structures

The core refinement procedures adopted by all KRUSTTools were shown in figure 1. Figure 3 places the refinement procedures in context, and shows how a KRUSTTool interacts with a KBS to create the knowledge skeleton and the problem graph. These provide the information needed to carry out refinement. The KRUSTTool performs the following steps.

1. The tool translates the KBS's rules into the knowledge skeleton, representing the static knowledge in the KBS.

2. The tool is given a training example, for which the KBS gives an incorrect solution, together with information about how the KBS reaches its conclusions. This information may be provided either in the form of an execution trace, or via queries submitted to the KBS. The tool uses the information to build a problem graph: an internal structure representing the reasoning of the KBS for the particular training example.

3. The refinement algorithm analyses the problem graph and the knowledge skeleton to determine where changes may be made to correct the errors made by the KBS. In general, the correct fix can not be uniquely determined, so the tool generates a number of alternative refinements, which are then filtered, implemented and tested. Testing consists of translating the modified knowledge skeletons back into the language of the KBS, and then executing them on the training example and others.

One distinguishing feature of KRUSTTools is that the refinement algorithm and the KBS run as separate processes. In contrast, EITHER (Ourston & Mooney 1994) is written in PROLOG and refines only PROLOG KBSs, using a single process for both tool and KBS. The KRUSTTools approach is necessary for a generic refinement tool, since a separate refinement tool and KBS is necessary to allow the refinement of a KBS written in any language.

2 The Knowledge Skeleton Representation Language

The purpose of this language is to represent the rules in any KBS to which a KRUSTTool is to be applied. This seemingly over-ambitious task is made feasible because, despite the variety of different syntax and functionality apparently

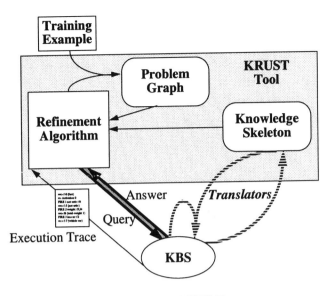

Figure 3: KRUST and KBS Processes

available in current KBS shells, there are in fact only a limited number of roles that a rule element can play (Palmer & Craw 1996a, Johnson & Carlis 1997). Furthermore, we are interested only in the ability to reason about which rules fire and the capability of the KRUSTTool to repair faults. Therefore, the knowledge representation language needs to represent faithfully only those parts of the knowledge that should be reasoned about and can be repaired. In contrast, for example, knowledge that contains external function calls does not need to be transformed into any special internal format since it will remain unchanged and so can be copied into any refined KBSs.

2.1   Basic Rule Elements

Each rule condition and conclusion is said to be a *rule element*. Three basic classes of rule element have been identified, corresponding to the fundamental roles they play in rules.

Tests can succeed or fail; e.g., retrievals from working memory, or comparisons such as ?amp-price $\leq$?amp-budget where ?var is a variable name.

Expressions are rule elements that return a value, and always succeed; e.g., arithmetical calculations or function calls.

Assignments assign a value to a variable, and again always succeed.

These three basic classes form the first level of the hierarchy of rule elements shown in Figure 4.

It is clear that by defining an internal representation for each rule element type, we can create an internal data structure representing the static rules in the KBS. However, in addition to simply representing the rules, the knowledge skeleton must also allow a KRUSTTool to reason about the knowledge in order to refine it. The most direct way of changing the behaviour of any rule element is to change the rule element itself by applying an appropriate refinement operator. We therefore wish to establish a rule element hierarchy so that each leaf node is associated with a set of refinement operators that apply to rule elements of this type.

2.2 A Usable Knowledge Hierarchy

The initial partition above is too coarse for defining refinement operators. Therefore, we continue to partition these roles until each partition contains a class of rule element with a well-defined set of associated refinement operators. Each of the new nodes in the extended hierarchy of Figure 4 is now described.

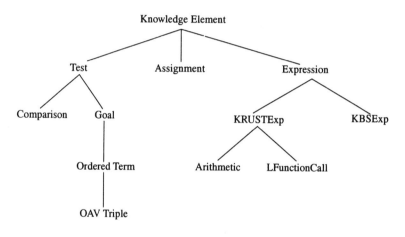

Figure 4: Hierarchy of Knowledge Elements

2.2.1 Tests

There are two sub-classes of test depending on whether the truth of the test comes from information local to the rule or knowledge deduced by other rules.

Comparisons are equations or inequalities. Their truth depends only on local information: the relational operator and the values being compared. Suitable refinement operators change the operator (`adjust-operator`) or the values (`adjust-value`).

Goals are rule elements that use the KBS's working memory; a conclusion that adds a fact to working memory, and a condition that uses that fact, are both classified as Goals[2]. We now identify two common sub-classes, but further sub-classes are added in Section 4.

Ordered Terms consist of a keyword followed by arguments; e.g., the PROLOG literal `colour(sky, blue, light)`.

OAV Triples are a sub-class of Ordered Term where the keyword is the attribute and the object and value form the remaining two arguments; e.g., `colour(sky, blue)`.

Goals offer another way to modify the behaviour of a rule's condition: by changing rules whose conclusions unify with the condition. Therefore, the knowledge skeleton must allow the KRUSTTool to determine when two Goals chain; i.e. a condition in one rule matches a conclusion of another rule. The `goals-match` function determines that two Ordered Terms (or OAV Triples) chain if and only if they have the same keyword and arity, and the corresponding arguments unify. As we propose further sub-classes of Goal we shall describe relevant refinement operators and modify the `goals-match` function.

2.2.2 Expressions

An expression is a piece of procedural knowledge which calculates and returns a value. There are two sub-classes, reflecting whether the calculation can be performed within the KRUSTTool or must be passed to the KBS for external execution.

KRUSTExps are evaluated within the KRUSTTool and are further divided.

Arithmetic expressions use the four standard arithmetical operators $+, -, \times, /$.

LFunctionCall expressions are Lisp functions and are executable in the KRUSTTool since it is implemented in Lisp. They represent KBS rule elements which are either written in Lisp or can be translated into Lisp. Alternatively, it would be possible to pass all non-arithmetical expressions to the KBS for evaluation, with the consequence however, that these expressions could not be refined.

KBSExps include all those expressions which cannot be evaluated within the KRUSTTool and so are passed to the original KBS for evaluation. KBSExps deal with situations where a KBS shell allows calls to procedural code, such as C functions, in rule elements. KBSExps cannot be refined.

---

[2]Describing Goals in terms of working memory applies particularly to forward-chaining rules. However, the distinguishing property of Goals is their ability to chain, so that we can identify and reason about Goals equally well for either backward or forward-chaining rules.

2.2.3 Assignments

Many rule elements, including those described so far, consist of a single element from the hierarchy, but a rule element can consist of an arbitrarily deep recursive structure. This is particularly relevant for Assignments and Arithmetic Expressions; e.g.,

`?amp-budget = (?budget - ?cd-price) / 0.6`

is an Assignment, whose right-hand side is the Arithmetic Expression

`(?budget - ?cd-price) / 0.6`

These recursive style rule elements have also proved useful for more complex knowledge formats found in some KBS languages. Further examples appear in the following two sections.

We therefore now introduce the term *knowledge element* for the classes identified in the knowledge hierarchy, and reserve the term *rule element* for complete conditions or conclusions. Thus, rule elements are made up of one or more knowledge elements. We are therefore building a representation language for knowledge elements which can then be used to construct rule elements and hence rules.

3 Applying the Knowledge Skeleton

The hierarchy we have described (Figure 4) is fairly basic and was based on our experience with PROLOG KBSs and some simple KBSs written in CLIPS (Giarratano 1998). Figure 5 shows a rule broken down into the knowledge elements we have met in the previous section. We now investigate the hierarchy's expressiveness when applied to more advanced KBS shells. For this investigation we consider the knowledge structures available in three commercial KBS shells: CLIPS[3], POWERMODEL[4] and PFES[5] (Alvey 1987). Both PFES and CLIPS use exclusively forward-chaining rules; POWERMODEL permits the use of both forward and backward-chaining rules. Many features of these shells corresponded to knowledge element types already present in the hierarchy, and this section explores the features to which the existing hierarchy was applicable.

3.1 CLIPS Patterns

CLIPS patterns correspond to Ordered Terms and provide rule chaining; e.g.,

```
(preferences amplifier denon-amp-40 cd marantz-cd-75)
(preferences amplifier ?amplifier cd marantz-cd-75)
```

Rules containing these elements as conclusion and condition respectively will chain. However, CLIPS has a more general wildcard than ?var; $? matches 0 or more arguments. Such wild-cards require an appropriate extension to the goals-match function.

---

[3] CLIPS is an expert system shell widely used in both academia and industry.

[4] POWERMODEL is developed by IntelliCorp Ltd and is the successor to KAPPA.

[5] PFES (Product Formulation Expert System) is a development environment for KBSs that solve design and formulation problems.

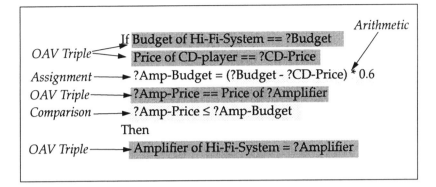

Figure 5: Sample Knowledge Elements in a Rule

3.2 PFES Agendas

There is a group of rule elements that appear at first unique to PFES, and therefore potentially difficult to represent within a common knowledge hierarchy. These *agendas* are untyped lists, where items can be read/written at the top or bottom, or directly below another given item. Agendas pass data between routines that generate values and those that subsequently test or filter them.

PFES agendas can also be viewed as a mechanism for storing attribute-value data; this better indicates how they may be represented within the existing hierarchy. Not all agendas have the same semantics, but the number of different possibilities actually employed within PFES applications is fairly limited. Two examples from the HI-FI program, whose purpose is to select the components of a hi-fi system, appear in Figure 6 where

speaker-agenda is a list of speakers; they are on it if they have the correct impedance

cd-price-agenda is a list of CD players, but now each item is associated with its price.

Each example shows the contents of an agenda at some point during the running of HI-FI, together with the PFES rule elements that write to and read from the agenda, and the KRUSTTool representation of these elements as Ordered Terms. Note that a conclusion that writes to the agenda, and the corresponding condition that reads from it, have the same KRUSTTool representation, though the two appear different in PFES.

Another feature of this representation is the fact that, while ?price's role as an attribute of ?cd-player is implicit in the PFES statements, it is made explicit in the KRUSTTool representation, where both the CD player and its price are arguments. One consequence is that PFES commands of the type add ?item to-bottom-of ?agenda have different KRUSTTool representations, depending on whether ?item represents an attribute. Fortunately it is possible to determine the correct translation from the context, both in the situations described here, and in other more complex situations also arising in HI-FI.

Snapshot of speaker-agenda

ar-18bx dean-alto-11 castle-pembroke

PFES Read/Write Operations on speaker-agenda

Conclusion:	add ?speaker to-bottom-of speaker-agenda
Condition:	?speaker is-on speaker-agenda

KRUSTTool representation of each operation

on-agenda(speaker-agenda, ?speaker)

Snapshot of cd-price-agenda

philips-cd650 429 sony-cdp103 399 marantz-cd 429

PFES Read/Write Operations on cd-price-agenda

Conclusions:	1) add ?cd-player to-bottom-of cd-price-agenda
	2) add ?price to-bottom-of cd-price-agenda
Conditions:	1) ?cd-player is-on cd-price-agenda
	2) ?price is-the-item-after ?cd-player on cd-price-agenda

KRUSTTool representation of each operation

1) on-agenda(cd-price-agenda, ?cd-player)
2) agenda-unlabelled-attribute(cd-price-agenda, ?cd-player, ?price)

Figure 6: Agendas and their PFES Operations

3.3 Compound Rule Elements

A powerful way to increase the expressiveness of the existing knowledge elements is to build compound rule elements from several knowledge elements. We met this idea already in Section 2.2.3 where we embedded an Arithmetic Expression as the body of an Assignment.

CLIPS, POWERMODEL, and many expert system shells allow conditions whose effect is to access a value and then test it; e.g., selecting CD players whose price is less than £200:

CLIPS **version**	(cd-player ?name ?price &: (< ?price 200))
POWERMODEL **version**	?cd-player.price < 200;

We have chosen to represent these as compound rule elements; here, a Comparison embedded in an Ordered Term: (cd-player ?name (?price < 200)).

This has consequences for `goals-match` and the refinement operators, which need to decompose the rule elements to which they are applied. In this example, the refinement operators for Ordered Terms are applicable to the term, but will not affect the Comparison element, while the refinement operators for Comparison are applicable to the Comparison nested within the term.

4 Extensions to the Hierarchy

We encountered several rule element types which could not be represented by the elements of the existing hierarchy shown in Figure 4. However, these new knowledge elements were found to be more specialised versions of existing knowledge elements and so could be added to the hierarchy without any revision to the basic structure. Figure 7 shows how the hierarchy has been expanded by the addition of the new Goal sub-class AV Tuple, described below.

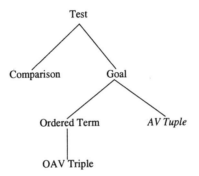

Figure 7: Adding a New Term to the Knowledge Element Hierarchy

4.1 Attribute Value Tuples

Many shells have a frame-based knowledge representation. Frames are similar to Ordered Terms, but the significance of each argument is determined by a preceding keyword rather than by the argument's position in a list; e.g., a CLIPS `amplifier` frame can be defined as:

```
(deftemplate amplifier
  (slot name)
  (slot price)
  (slot power)
  (slot impedance)
```

and a rule condition which tests the properties of `amplifier` looks like

```
(amplifier (name ?name) (power ?power) (price ?price))
```

The inherently unordered nature of this condition precludes its representation as an Ordered Term, so a new sub-class of Goal called an AV (Attribute-Value) Tuple was introduced. The AV Tuple consists of a keyword followed by a series of attribute-value pairs, so that the condition above is represented by the AV Tuple

```
(amplifier name ?name power ?power price ?price)
```

and matches conclusions such as

```
(amplifier name marantz-pm26 price 125 power 30 impedance 8)
```

The goals-match function is defined to use keywords rather than order for matching, and refinement operators are adapted so that they do not alter keywords.

4.2 Future Knowledge Elements

POWERMODEL permits the use of a variety of iterative operators within its rule conditions. A typical example is the loop:

```
for find ?x = instanceof Tuner;
    do ?x.presets = 7;
```

which retrieves each instance of Tuner, and sets its presets slot to 7. Currently, knowledge like this is simply copied verbatim in the knowledge skeleton, ignored during refinement generation, and re-created in its original form in the refined KBSs. However, this approach may be unnecessarily restrictive, given that within the procedural "wrapping" there are statements which *can* be refined. This is an area requiring further work, but the find loop above suggests the following. The statement contains an Assignment which can have an Assignment refinement operator applied. For example, suppose for the training example ?x is bound to quad-fm4 and its presets should be 9, then the refined knowledge might look as follows:

```
for find ?x = instanceof Tuner;
    do if ?x = quad-fm4
        then ?x.presets = 9
        else ?x.presets = 7;
```

5 Comparison with Other Work

Johnson & Carlis (1997) have also classified the rule elements in expert systems shells, but have taken a more syntax based approach. Their work confirms our view that it is possible to build a common representation for expert system shells while avoiding the need to introduce particular shell-specific items, and hence the feasibility of our generic approach to refinement. We now consider the restrictions imposed on KBSs by other refinement tools.

EITHER (Ourston & Mooney 1994) and FORTE (Richards & Mooney 1995) rely on PROLOG's Horn Clauses for their reasoning and ignore the control imposed by PROLOG's depth first search when multiple solutions are available. Each condition in a PROLOG rule is a PROLOG literal, and corresponds to an Ordered Term in the KRUSTTool hierarchy; the literal's predicate name is the Ordered Term's keyword. PROLOG's depth first search of clauses easily provides information for our problem graph. Therefore PROLOG KBSs have KRUSTTool representations.

NEITHER (Baffes & Mooney 1993) extends EITHER's refinement process by having specialised refinement operators for m-of-n rules. An *m-of-n* condition contains a set of n conditions, and is defined to be true if and only if at least m of the n conditions are true. Similarly, SEEK (Ginsberg 1988) refines rules in a specialised form where normal conditions are supplemented with m-of-n type conditions, but now the n conditions are symptoms associated with a diagnosis rather than explicitly listed in the condition. An m-of-n condition is a new Goal sub-class requiring a specialised `goals-match` function and specific refinement operators.

CLIPS-R (Murphy & Pazzani 1994) is similarly restrictive, since it refines only CLIPS KBSs. It uses example traces to build a data structure which groups together those examples that share an initial sequence of rule firings. This data structure guides CLIPS-R towards the most common errors. Since the CLIPS-R data structure represents the execution on training examples, it is similar in purpose to our problem graph.

ODYSSEUS (Wilkins 1990) illustrates a different approach to the use of control information from that of the other programs surveyed. Meta-rules contain the control knowledge, and failure to solve problems is attributed to missing domain knowledge which should have been available to be used by the control knowledge. By representing the control knowledge explicitly, ODYSSEUS is able to guide the refinement process.

6 Conclusions

The knowledge element hierarchy we have developed has been shown to provide a powerful representation mechanism for rule-based KBSs. It has evolved in a disciplined way from experience with several basic KBSs. Many of the new constructions found in more sophisticated KBSs have been directly equivalent to existing knowledge elements; e.g. PFES agendas. However, the hierarchy is also extensible in a natural way, by incorporating novel rule elements in two ways: new knowledge elements have extended the hierarchy without destroying its basic structure; or a recursive structure of existing knowledge elements represents the new rule element. It has thus been shown to be able to accommodate novel rule elements from a variety of shells.

In this paper we have concentrated on the feasibility of a knowledge element hierarchy as the basis of a representation language for knowledge skeletons. Knowledge skeletons contain the essential knowledge content of a KBS, and the hierarchy additionally identifies suitable refinement operators for the knowledge elements. Therefore, it is possible to have a common core of routines for blame allocation, refinement generation and filtering that explore the problem graph and manipulate the knowledge skeleton. We have not been concerned here with the efficacy of refinement, but other papers have shown KRUSTTools being successfully applied to a range of KBSs. The PROLOG-based student loan rules (Pazzani 1993) have been translated into CLIPS and POWERMODEL, and KRUSTTools have been applied to fix artificially introduced faults in all 3 versions (Palmer 1995, Palmer & Craw 1996b). A KRUSTTool has successfully been applied to the debugging and maintenance of the PFES-based tablet formulation system TFS developed by Zeneca Pharmaceuticals (Craw, Boswell & Rowe 1997, Boswell 1998).

The KRUSTWorks project is applying these ideas to provide a framework of re-usable refinement components from which to assemble a KRUSTTool for a particular KBS. Figure 8 illustrates the process. The knowledge engineer

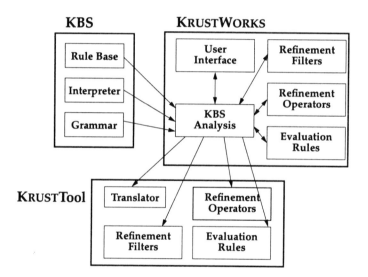

Figure 8: Creating a KRUSTTOOL from the KRUSTWorks Framework

provides the rulebase and interpreter for a KBS, together with a grammar for parsing the rules. KRUSTWorks performs an analysis of the KBS, determining properties such as the kinds of rule elements present, and the direction of rule chaining. Guided by the knowledge engineer, KRUSTWorks generates and customises modules to perform translation and the standard refinement tasks. The resulting specific KRUSTTool, shown at the bottom of the diagram, is customised to the needs of the particular application and does not contain unnecessary functionality.

References

Alvey (1987). The PFES report, volume three: The formulations kernel, Logica UK Ltd.

Baffes, P. T. & Mooney, R. J. (1993). Symbolic revision of theories with M-of-N rules, *in* R. Bajcsy (ed.), *Proceedings of the Thirteenth IJCAI Conference*, Chambery, FRANCE, pp. 1135–1140.

Boswell, R. (1998). *Knowledge Refinement for a Formulation System*, PhD thesis, School of Computer and Mathematical Sciences, The Robert Gordon University.

Craw, S. (1996). Refinement complements verification and validation, *International Journal of Human-Computer Studies* **44**(2): 245–256.

Craw, S., Boswell, R. & Rowe, R. (1997). Knowledge refinement to debug and maintain a tablet formulation system, *Proceedings of the 9TH IEEE International Conference on Tools with Artificial Intelligence (TAI'97)*, IEEE Press, Newport Beach, CA, pp. 446–453.

Craw, S. & Sleeman, D. (1990). Automating the refinement of knowledge-based systems, *in* L. C. Aiello (ed.), *Proceedings of the ECAI90 Conference*, Pitman, Stockholm, Sweden, pp. 167–172.

Giarratano, J. C. (1998). *Expert Systems : Principles and Programming*, 3rd edn, International Thomson.

Ginsberg, A. (1988). *Automatic Refinement of Expert System Knowledge Bases*, Research Notes in Artificial Intelligence, Pitman, London.

Johnson, V. M. & Carlis, J. V. (1997). Building a composite syntax for expert system shells, *IEEE Expert* **12**(6): 60–66.

Merz, C. J. & Murphy, P. M. (1996). UCI Repository of machine learning databases (http://www.ics.uci.edu/~mlearn/MLRepository.html), Irvine, CA: University of California, Department of Information and Computer Science.

Murphy, P. M. & Pazzani, M. J. (1994). Revision of production system rule-bases, *in* W. W. Cohen & H. Hirsh (eds), *Proceedings of the Eleventh International Conference on Machine Learning*, Morgan Kaufmann, New Brunswick, NJ, pp. 199–207.

Ourston, D. & Mooney, R. (1994). Theory refinement combining analytical and empirical methods, *Artificial Intelligence* **66**: 273–309.

Palmer, G. (1995). Applying KRUST to a new KBS tool: experience with Kappa, *Technical Report 95/9*, SCMS, Robert Gordon University.

Palmer, G. & Craw, S. (1996a). An extensible knowledge refinement tool, *Technical Report 96/2*, SCMS, Robert Gordon University.

Palmer, G. J. & Craw, S. (1996b). The role of test cases in automated knowledge refinement, *Proceedings of the 16th Annual Technical Conference of the British Computer Society Specialist Group on Expert Systems*, SGES Publications, Cambridge, UK, pp. 75–90.

Pazzani, M. J. (1993). Student loan relational domain, In UCI Repository of Machine Learning Databases (Merz & Murphy 1996).

Richards, B. L. & Mooney, R. J. (1995). Refinement of first-order horn-clause domain theories, *Machine Learning* **19**(2): 95–131.

Schreiber, G., Wielinga, B. & Breuker, J. (eds) (1993). *KADS: A Principled Approach to Knowledge Based Systems Development*, Academic Press.

Wilkins, D. C. (1990). Knowledge base refinement as improving an incorrect and incomplete domain theory, *in* Y. Kodratoff & R. S. Michalski (eds), *Machine Learning Volume III*, Morgan Kaufmann, San Mateo, CA, pp. 493–513.

SESSION 2: KNOWLEDGE BASE DEVELOPMENT

CG-SQL: A Front-end Language for Conceptual Graph Knowledge Bases

Stéphane Coulondre

L.I.R.M.M. (U.M.R. 9928 Université Montpellier II / C.N.R.S)
161 rue Ada, 34392 Montpellier Cedex 5 - France
e-mail: coulondr@lirmm.fr

Abstract

The conceptual graphs (CG) model is a knowledge representation model capable of clearly and formally representing a wide range of knowledge forms, from predicate logic to natural language. CG knowledge bases contain facts and rules. The model includes inference mechanisms that allow automated reasoning, by deciding whether a CG goal is implied by the knowledge base, and by giving a set of solutions. In this paper, we show that it is impossible to express some queries only by a CG goal: in particular, conventional operators like projection, selection, union and cartesian product, can not be expressed unless a set of rules is added to the knowledge base prior to the inference. We claim that expressing a query should not require modification of the knowledge base. Therefore, we propose in this paper an algebra and a SQL-like language for the CG model called CG-SQL, which permits the expression of complex queries with the above four operators, leaving the knowledge base unchanged. CG-SQL is an easy-to-use language, providing both the intuitive query capabilities of the CG model, and a declarative front-end query interface that follows the SQL style. We also prove that CG-SQL is complete with respect to safe sets of rules and that queries are decidable if no unsafe rules are present in the knowledge base.

1 Introduction

The conceptual graphs (CG) model is a knowledge representation model, which is part of the semantic networks family. CG were introduced by Sowa [11]. The base model consists of simple CG that aims at modeling static knowledge (facts) by way of the graph theory. The core operation, called *projection*, is a graph morphism between labelled graphs. This operation is behind several inference mechanisms that gives the model the ability to reason [8, 10]. CG have an associated semantic in first-order logic (FOL), but some of these mechanisms, which will be outlined in this paper, are not based on FOL and use exclusively graph operations. They are sound and complete with respect to the CG logical semantic. One of the most interesting mechanisms has been presented in [10], introducing CG rules and their treatment with sound and complete forward and backward chaining inference procedures. CG rules also have a logical semantic [10]. Forward chaining consists of inferring all the deducible knowledge by applying rules on facts, thus generating new facts. Testing for a particular piece of knowledge (goal) is then simply made by checking its presence within the enriched base. However, the procedure is not goal-directed, thus generating information that may not be useful. The philosophy of backward chaining is close to the classical SLD-resolution, although it is much more complex. The goal G and a rule R are analyzed in order to detect if R may have produced G. This analysis is called the *piece unification*. If it is successful, the procedure constructs a new goal G' which, when applying R on it, gives G. If the new goal is deductible from the same base, then G is deductible too. The inference ends when obtaining the empty goal. This inference procedure is goal-directed.

All these mechanisms decide whether a CG goal is implied by the knowledge base, and give a set of solutions. In this paper, we show that it is impossible to express some queries only by a CG goal: in particular, conventional operators like projection, selection, union and cartesian product, can not be expressed unless a set of rules is added to the knowledge base prior to the inference. We claim that expressing a query should not require modification of the knowledge base.

Therefore, we propose an algebra for the CG model which permits the expression of complex queries with the above four operators, leaving the knowledge base unchanged. The algebra redefines the classical monotone relational operators, and the only non-monotone operator (set difference) needs to be removed because of the absence of negation in the CG model. CG-SQL is an easy-to-use language providing both the intuitive query capabilities of the CG model, and a declarative front-end query interface that follows the SQL style. We cannot express all sets of rules of a CG knowledge base by CG-SQL. However, we can express all *safe* sets of rules. Knowledge bases that are composed of only safe rules lead to the decidability of queries. Therefore, we show that CG-SQL is complete with respect to the decidable part of the CG calculus. Nevertheless, this does not prevent the presence of non safe rules within the knowledge base.

There has already been an attempt to link the relational model with the CG model [9, 2, 3]. But these papers aimed at embedding the relational model in the CG model, by translating a relational database with a CG knowledge base. Therefore, the queries are asked on the knowledge base that is equivalent to the relations of the database. Answering these queries requires specific algorithms. In this paper, we address a different problem: we do not try to embed the relational model into the CG model, but we define algebraic operators that can deal with the whole CG knowledge base and all its expressive power, which is more expressive than a relational database. Moreover, the inference procedures are part of the CG model and need no further implementation.

Section 2 is devoted to the conceptual graphs model. In section 3, we present CG rules as well as their treatment in forward and backward chaining. In section 4, we present an algebra for the CG model and propose CG-SQL. Finally, we show that CG-SQL is complete with respect to the decidable part of the CG calculus.

2   The model of conceptual graphs

This section describes the CG model. Firstly, we present the *support* and the conceptual graphs, and then define the projection operator which aims at finding specializations of a graph. By describing the logical semantic of a CG, we point out the soundness and completeness of projection with respect to first-order logic.

2.1   Preliminaries

This section presents the basic conceptual graphs model, and the adding of rules as well as their treatment in backward chaining. This introduction is based on [4] for the model and on [10] for the rules.

Conceptual graphs are made of relations and concepts. They are defined on a support, which describes syntactic constraints, and provides background information on a specific application domain.

Definition 1 *[Support [4]] A support is a 5-tuple* $S = (T_C, T_R, \sigma, I, \tau)$ *where:*

- T_C, the set of concept types, is partially ordered by the relation $is - a$ (denoted $\leq$), and has a greatest element ($\top$ universal type) and a lowest element ($\bot$ absurd type).

- T_R, the set of relation types, is divided in several set of relation types with the same arity. $T_R = T_{Ri_1} \cup ... \cup T_{Ri_p}$, where T_{Ri_j} is the set of relation types of arity i_j, $i_j \neq 0$. Each T_{Ri_j} has a greatest and a lowest element.

- σ associates with every relation type the maximum type of its arguments. More precisely, it is an application which associates $\sigma(t_r) \in (T_C)^{ij}$ to each $t_r \in T_{Ri_j}$, and obeys the following : for every t_{r1}, t_{r2} of T_{Ri_j}, if $t_{r1} < t_{r2}$ then $\sigma(t_{r1}) \leq_{i_j} \sigma(t_{r2})$. We denote $\sigma_i(t_r)$ the ith argument of $\sigma(t_r)$.

- I, the set of individual markers. An individual marker is an entity of the knowledge base. There is also a generic marker is $*$. The set of markers $M \cup \{*\}$ has the following order : $*$ is greater than every individual marker, which are incomparable between them.

- τ is an application from I to $T_C\backslash\{\bot\}$, which associates a concept type t to every individual marker m.

Definition 2 *[Conceptual graph [4]] A conceptual graph (CG) G related to a support S, is a non oriented bipartite graph $G = (R, C, U, label)$, not necessarily connected where:*

- R and C are two different classes of vertices, called relation and concept vertices. $C \neq \emptyset$.

- U is the set of edges; for every relation vertex r, the set of edges is totally ordered, and we number these edges from 1 to $degree(r)$. We denote $G_i(r)$ the ith neighbour of r in G.

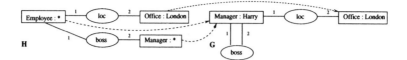

Figure 1: An example of projection

- *label* is an application which associates a label with every vertex, and obeys the following :

    - If $r \in R$, $label(r) \in T_R$, it is the type of the relation vertex, denoted $type(r)$.

    - If $c \in C$, $label(r) \in (T_C \backslash \{\perp\}) \times (I \cup \{*\})$. The label of a concept vertex is a couple $(type(c), marker(c))$. If c has a generic marker, c is called generic concept vertex. Otherwise c is a individual concept vertex. *label* obeys the constraints imposed by the applications σ and τ. For every $r \in R$, $type(G_i(r)) \leq \sigma_i(type(r))$ and every $c \in C$, if $marker(c) \in I$, then $type(c) = \tau(marker(c))$.

2.2 Projection

The core operation over CGs is the *projection*, which is a graph morphism. This operation allows the determination of the specialization relation on CGs: let G and H be two CGs, there is a projection from H to G if and only if G is a specialization of H (noted $G \leq H$) [11].

Definition 3 *[Projection [4]]. A projection from a CG $H = (R_H, C_H, U_H, label_H)$ to a CG $G = (R_G, C_G, U_G, label_G)$ is an ordered pair $\pi = (f, g)$ of mappings, f from R_H to R_G, and g from C_H to C_G, such that:*

- edges and their numbering are preserved: for each edge rc in U_H, $f(r)g(c)$ is an edge of U_G. If the ith edge of r is linked to c then the ith edge of $f(r)$ is linked to $g(c)$

- vertex labels may be restricted: for each r in R_H, $label_G(f(r)) \leq label_H(r)$ and for each c in C_H, $label_G(g(c)) \leq label_H(c)$.

Figure 1 shows an example of two conceptual graphs. We assume that in the support, *manager* $\in T_C$ and *employee* $\in T_C$ and we have *manager* $\leq$ *employee* (every manager is an employee). Thus there is a projection from the first graph H, which can be interpreted by "In the London office, there is an employee who is under a manager's command", to the second one G, which can be interpreted by "In the London office, the manager Harry is under his own command". Therefore the second graph implies the first one: $G \leq H$.

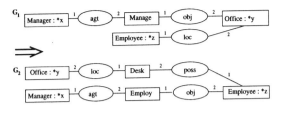

Figure 2: A CG rule

2.3 Logical semantic

Conceptual graphs, as well as the support, have an associated semantic in first-order logic. The operator Φ constructs the associated formula, which is an existential conjonctive and positive formula of the form $\exists x_1 \ldots x_s (A_1 \wedge \ldots \wedge A_p)$. There are no functional symbols. Details of this construction can be found in [4]. The projection is shown sound and complete with respect to the FOL semantic of graphs. In order to prove the completeness, we need the notion of normal form: a graph is in normal form if all individual vertices have different markers. A graph can be put in normal form by merging all its concept vertices with the same individual marker. Therefore we have:

Theorem 1 *Let $\Phi(S)$ be the set of formulae associated with the support. Let G and H be two conceptual graphs in normal form. Then $G \leq H$ if and only if $\Phi(S), \Phi(G) \models \Phi(H)$. (Soundness: [11] , Completeness: [4])*

3 Inference procedures in the CG model

The CG basic model has been extended with inference rules [10]. This section describes the rules and their forward and backward treatment by way of graph operations.

3.1 The rules

Rules are of the type "If G_1 then G_2 ", where G_1 and G_2 are conceptual graphs with possible co-reference links between some concept vertices of G_1 and G_2. A co-reference link indicates that two vertices denote the same individual. A rule is denoted $R : G_1 \to G_2$, where G_1 and G_2 are called the *hypothesis* and the *conclusion* of R. We use the notation of lambda-abstraction $\lambda x_1 \ldots x_n G$, with $n \geq 0$, which is composed of a graph G and n special generic vertices of G. A *fact* is a rule with an empty hypothesis.

Definition 4 *[Conceptual graph rule [10]] A conceptual graph rule $R : G_1 \to G_2$ is a couple of lambda-abstractions $(\lambda x_1 \ldots x_n G_1, \lambda x_1 \ldots x_n G_2)$. $x_1 \ldots x_n$ are called connection points. In the following, we will denote by x_i^1 (resp. x_i^2) the vertex x_i of G_1(resp. G_2). For each $i \in [1..n]$, x_i^1 and x_i^2 are co-referent.*

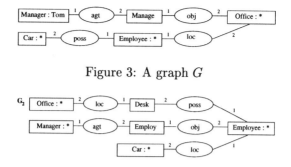

Figure 3: A graph G

Figure 4: A new graph G' obtain by application of R on G

The rule in figure 2 informally means the following: "If an employee z is in an office y managed by a manager x, then z has got a desk which is inside the office y, and x employs z".

Φ is extended to the graph rules. A knowledge base is composed of a support S and a set of rules, in which there is a subset (possibly empty) of facts. Let us now consider a goal Q to be proven. The following two procedures allow us to determine, given a knowledge base KB, whether $\Phi(KB) \models \Phi(Q)$; that is whether the knowledge base logically implies a goal. If the implication is proven, then a set of solutions, which are specializations of the goal Q, are built. These procedures use only graph operations and do not refer to the underlying FOL semantic.

3.2 Forward chaining

Forward chaining consists of inferring all the deductible knowledge by applying rules on facts, thus generating new facts. Each time a new graph is obtained, we add it to the knowledge base. To prove a goal Q, we apply each rule as many times as possible on each graph of the base. Testing for a particular knowledge (goal) is then simply made by checking its presence within the enriched base, that is if there is a projection of Q in a graph of the base. The latter is a specialization of Q, and thus is a solution to the goal Q.

The procedure is not goal-directed, thus generating information that may not be useful. For a extended presentation of forward chaining, we refer the reader to [10].

In order to prove the completeness, we need to extend the notion of normal form. A knowledge base is in normal form if for each rule $R : G_1 \rightarrow G_2$, G_2 is in normal form, and if the set of facts considered as one global graph is in normal form (each individual marker occurs once within the facts).

Theorem 2 *[Soundness and completeness of forward chaining [10]] Let KB be a knowledge base and Q be a request. Then:*

- *If Q is obtained by a sequence of rule applications, then $\Phi(KB) \models \Phi(Q)$.*

Figure 5: A request Q

Figure 6: A new request Q' built by unification of the Q and R

- *If $\Phi(KB) \models \Phi(Q)$, and KB and Q are in normal form then there is a graph Q' that can be obtained from KB by a sequence of rule applications, such that there is a projection from Q in Q'.*

3.3 Backward chaining : The piece resolution procedure

The philosophy of backward chaining is close to the classical SLD-resolution, though it is much more complex. The goal G and a rule R are analyzed in order to detect if R may have produced G, i.e. one searches an unification between G and the conclusion of R. If a unification is found, the procedure constructs a new goal G', which when applying R on it, gives a specialization of G. If the new goal is deductible from the same base, then G is deductible too. This basic operation is called the piece unification. This procedure is therefore goal-directed. The inference ends when obtaining the empty goal.

Piece resolution uses the structure of the graph as much as possible. To do this, it looks for the smallest information that can be considered as a whole. This unit of information is called *piece*. It is a subgraph of the conclusion of a rule, composed of a set of concept vertices linked by a set of relation vertices. Other backward chaining procedures split the goal into units of information which are smaller that a *piece* [7, 8], as also for Prolog [5] for first-order logic. In [6], we showed that piece resolution can considerably improve the number of backtracks needed for a SLD-resolution; this lets us hope to get some improvement of time too with a more efficient algorithm.

We do not describe in details here the way pieces are defined and how the new goal is built. For a extended presentation of piece resolution, we refer the reader to [10].

In figure 2, G_2 has two pieces. The first one includes all vertices from y to z and the second one includes all vertices from z to x . Indeed, x, y and z are cut points, and G_2 is split at z vertex.

For example, the request Q of figure 5 can unify with the rule of figure 2. Indeed, we can unify the subgraph of Q containing the vertices from Manager to Employee with the piece of G_2 from the concept vertex with the marker x to the concept vertex with the marker z. We obtain the new request Q' of figure 6.

A piece resolution is a sequence of piece unifications. It ends successfully if the last produced goal is the empty graph. It needs the definition of a tree exploration strategy (breadth-first or depth-first search like in Prolog for example). By keeping trace of the unifications, a specialization of the initial request Q can be built, that is a solution to the goal Q.

Theorem 3 *[Soundness and completeness of piece resolution [10]] Let KB be a knowledge base and Q be a request. Then:*

- *If a piece resolution of Q on KB ends successfully, then $\Phi(KB) \models \Phi(Q)$.*

- *If $\Phi(KB) \models \Phi(Q)$, then there is a piece resolution of Q on KB that ends successfully.*

4 A CG algebra and the CG-SQL query language

Let G be a goal conceptual graph with only one relation vertex r. Here we assume that goals have only one relation vertex. This assumption can be lifted by adding at run time a CG rule in the knowledge base whose hypothesis is a goal with more than one relation vertex and conclusion is to have one new relation vertex. Therefore, a new goal can be asked with only one relation vertex. We denote the *extension* of G by G_e, which is the set of solutions to G, built by forward or backward chaining. In the first subsection, we show the limitations of the goal-based query language. In the second subsection, we present an algebra for conceptual graphs that we prove complete with respect to a restricted set of CG rules, which we explain in the fourth subsection. In the third subsection, we present the CG-SQL language based on the algebra.

4.1 Preliminaries

Consider the simple query: give all the cars of the employees. This query can be expressed by mean of the following goal G:

Therefore, the extension G_e of G contains all the specializations of G that are implied by the knowledge base, thus giving a set of couples $(employee, car)$. But we only want the second term, that is, the car. If the goal was only a concept vertex of type Car (i.e. the left vertex of G only), we would have obtained all the cars of the knowledge base, even those not belonging to an employee. To obtain the desired query, we must add to the knowledge base the following rule, that "isolates", by mean of a new relation vertice *poss_emp*, the cars that belong to the employees:

and ask for the goal:

Thus, we could not obtain the desired query only by mean of a goal. We can of course get the answer by adding the rule in the knowledge base, but we claim that this *must not* be part of a query. Indeed, a query *must not* require some modifications of the knowledge base.

We propose an algebra that allows expressing more complex queries in an algebraic expression form that can use several goals, without adding any rule. This algebra relies on four operators that extend those of relational algebra in order to work on conceptual graphs. In addition, we show at the end of the section that *any* safe set of rules, a notion we will explain, can be expressed by mean of an algebraic expression. As already stated, we assume that goals which appear in algebraic expressions have only one relation vertex. In the case of a goal with more than one relation vertex, we can add a CG rule in the knowledge base at the run time whose hypothesis is that goal, and the conclusion has one new relation vertex and the same concept vertices. Therefore, a new goal, corresponding to the conclusion, can be asked,which has only one relation vertex. Note that this construction is not unique. We can easily prove that there is a bijective transformation between the extension of the new goal and the extension of the old one.

4.2   The algebra

It is important to notice the absence of negation within the CG model. Therefore, the set difference operator which consists of keeping CGs that belong to a set and that do *not* belong to another set is impossible, because it requires the use of negation. Our algebra contains four basic operators: projection, selection, cartesian product and union. We can of course define more operators which are derivable from these four, like equijoin, natural join, and semijoin.

4.2.1   Projection

Let G be a conceptual graph with only one relation vertex r.

Definition 5 *The (algebraic) projection of G_e is denoted by $\pi_{i_1,...,i_n}(G_e)$, where i_j , $j \in [1..n]$ is the position of a concept vertex within r and n is the arity of r. The projection returns the set of CGs with one relation vertex r' of arity n such that there is at least one CG $Q \in G_e$ with one relation vertex r such that the i_jth position of r' , $j \in [1..n]$ is linked to a concept vertex identical (i.e. same type and same maker) to the jth concept vertex of r. These links are sequentially numbered.*

Example 1 *Let G be the following goal, which means: "Give all the employees who are in a desk whose number is 2, their office and their manager":*

Let G_e be the set containing the following CGs, which are the solutions to the goal G:

Suppose we want to get all CGs that associates an employee with its office only. This can be obtained by the projection $\pi_{1,2}(G_e)$, giving the following set of CGs:

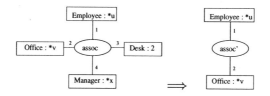

Remark 1 *The algebraic projection can be expressed by a CG rule and a goal. The projection in the previous example is equivalent to the following rule, in which we construct a new CG with a new relation vertex assoc', such that its extension is $\pi_{1,2}(G_e)$. The goal to be asked is the conclusion of the rule.*

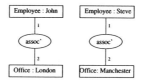

4.2.2 Selection

Definition 6 *Let S be a formula of the form $\$i_1 = j_1 \wedge \ldots \wedge \$i_n = j_n$, where i_k, $k \in [1..n]$ is a position number, and j_k, $k \in [1..n]$ is either an individual marker or a position number denoted by $\$j_k$. Then $\sigma_F(G_e)$ returns the set of CGs of G_e such that the marker of the i_kth concept vertex of r is identical to j_k if it is a marker, or to the marker of the j_kth concept vertex otherwise.*

Example 2 *Suppose we want to get all the employees whose manager is Harry, who are in a desk whose number is 2, and their office. Then we apply the selection $\sigma_{\$4='Harry'}(G_e)$, giving the following set of CGs:*

Remark 2 *The selection can be expressed by a goal. If j_k is a marker then it is replaced in the right concept vertex in G, and if j_k is a vertex, then the i_kth and the j_kth concept vertex are merged (see example of cartesian product). The selection in the previous example is equivalent to the extension of the following goal:*

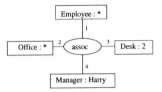

4.2.3   Cartesian product

Let G' be another conceptual graph goal with only one relation vertex r'.

Definition 7 *The cartesian product of G_e and G'_e, denoted $G_e \times G'_e$, returns a set of CGs that contain all possible sets of $n + m$ concept vertices, linked by a new relation vertex rr' of arity $n + m$, such that the n first concept vertices linked in the same order to a relation vertex r form a CG that belongs to G_e, and the m last concept vertices linked in the same order to a relation vertex r' form a CG that belongs to G'_e.*

Example 3 *Let G' be the following goal, which means "give all the managers with their car":*

Let G'_e be the set containing the following CG, which are the solutions to the goal:

Remember the goal G of example 1. Suppose we want to get all the employees who are in a desk whose number is 2, their office and manager and besides the cars of the managers. Then we apply the query $\sigma_{\$4=\$5}(G_e \times G'_e)$, giving the following set of CGs:

$G_e \times G'_e$:

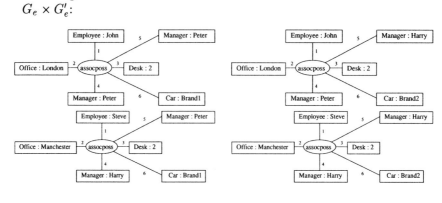

$\sigma_{\$4=\$5}(G_e \times G'_e)$:

Remark 3 *The cartesian product can be expressed by a CG rule and a goal. The query in the previous example is equivalent to the following rule, in which we construct a new conceptual graph which contains a new relation vertex rr' of arity $n + m$, the n concept vertices of G linked to the n first position of rr' according to the order defined on r, and the m concept vertices of G' linked to the m last positions of rr' according to the order defined on r'. and G'.*

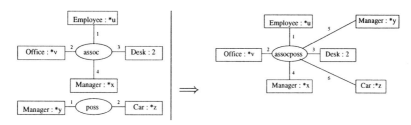

The goal to be asked is:

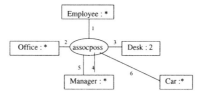

4.2.4 Union

Let G and G' have the same arity.

Definition 8 *The union of G_e and G'_e, denoted $G_e \cup G'_e$, return the union of the extensions of G_e and G'_e.*

Example 4 *Suppose we have a concept type EmpNotMan for the employees that are not managers. Let G'' be the following goal, which means "give all the employees, which are not managers, with their car":*

Let G''_e be the set containing the following CG, which are the solutions to the goal:

Suppose we want to get all the cars and their owners which are employed, that is which are either employee or manager. Then we apply the query $G'_e \cup G''_e$, giving the following set of CGs:

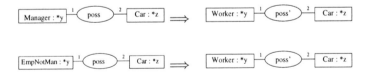

Remark 4 *The union can be expressed by two CG rules and a goal. The query in the previous example is equivalent to the following rules, in which we construct a new CG with a new relation vertex poss'.*

Remark 5 *The goal to be asked is:*

4.3 The CG-SQL query language

Now that the algebra is defined, CG-SQL is a syntactic translation.

The core statement is:

EXT(G)

which corresponds to asking a simple goal and returns the extension of G by an inference process of the model (forward or backward chaining).

The select statement is of the form :

SELECT $i_1, \ldots, i_n$ FROM EXT(G^1),...,EXT(G^p) WHERE F,

and can be expressed in the algebra as $\pi_{i_1,\ldots,i_n}(\sigma_{F'}(G_e^1 \times \ldots \times G_e^p)$, where F' is a formula obtained from F by replacing the symbol $\wedge$ by the keyword AND.

Example 5 *The query of example 1 $(\pi_{1,2}(G_e))$ is expressed by:*

SELECT \$1,\$2 FROM EXT(G)

Example 6 *The query of example 2 $(\sigma_{\$4='Harry'}(G_e))$ is expressed by:*

SELECT * FROM EXT(G) WHERE \$4='Harry'

Example 7 *The query of example 3 is expressed by:*

$G_e \times G'_e$:   SELECT * FROM EXT(G),EXT(G')
$\sigma_{\$4=\$5}(G_e \times G'_e)$:   SELECT * FROM EXT(G),EXT(G')
                 WHERE \$4=\$5

Example 8 *The query of example 4 $(G'_e \cup G''_e)$ is expressed by:*

SELECT * FROM EXT(G')
UNION
SELECT * FROM EXT(G")

Example 9 *A more complex example. We need the following goal, G'''' which means "give all the employees with their car":*

Note that this time, employees can be managers. Indeed, Remember that in the support, $manager \in T_C$ and $employee \in T_C$ and we have $manager \leq$

employee (Every manager is an employee). Thus a manager also has a desk, an office and a manager (who can be himself). Consider the following query: give a list that contains the employees whose desk number is 2, whose manager is Harry and who have a car of the same brand as Harry, and the employees whose desk number is 2, whose manager is Peter and who work in the same desk as Harry. The corresponding algebraic expression is:

$$\pi_1\left(\sigma_{\$1=\$7\wedge\$6=\$8}\left(G_e''' \times \sigma_{\$4='Harry'\wedge\$4=\$5\wedge\$6=\$8}(G_e \times G_e')\right)\right)$$
$$\cup\pi_1\left(\sigma_{\$3=\$7\wedge\$1='Harry'\wedge\$8='Peter'}(G_e \times G_e)\right)$$

Example 10 *This query is expressed in CG-SQL by:*

```
SELECT $1
FROM EXT(G"'),   (SELECT *
                 FROM EXT(G),EXT(G')
                 WHERE $4='Harry' AND $6=$8 AND $4=$5)
WHERE $1=$7
                 UNION
SELECT $1
FROM EXT(G),EXT(G)
WHERE $3=$7 AND $1='Harry' AND $8='Peter')
```

This query is equivalent to the following set of CG rules that should have been added to the knowledge base in order to formulate the query by mean of a goal:

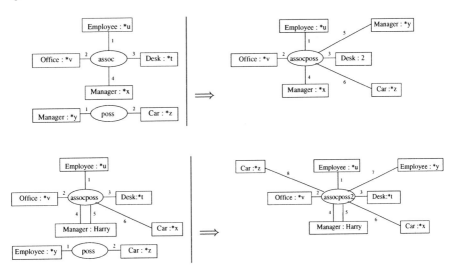

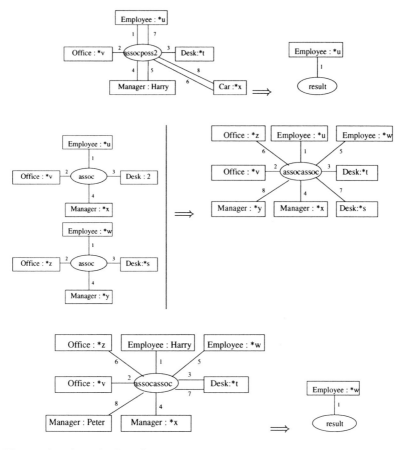

The goal to be asked is then:

In this example we can clearly see that using CG-SQL provides an advantage over the goal-based language which requires adding alot of rules to the knowledge base.

4.4 Completeness of the algebra

We have shown that every algebraic expression is expressible by mean of CG rules. To obtain the completeness of the algebra, we have to show that every CG rule is expressible by mean of an algebraic expression. In fact, we can not express every CG rule, but we can express all nonrecursive sets of rules, in which every concept vertex in conclusion of a rule is co-referenced, because the introduction of recursiveness leads to the problem of the transitive closure that is known to be inexpressible in relational algebra. The need for co-reference links is explained by the undecidable nature of CG inferences. Indeed if we want to keep a decidable process, we need to respect this condition. Therefore, the notion of completeness refers to these kind of rules that we call *safe* rules.

Lemma 1 *Let Ω be a set of safe CG rules. For each relation vertex, there is an algebraic expression that computes the extension of the graph in which it appears.*

Proof 1 (Sketch) *Safe CG rules can have more than one relation vertex in their conclusion. It is shown in [10] that a rule can be split into as many rules as pieces in its conclusion. As every concept vertex in conclusion is co-referenced, there are as many pieces as relation vertices. So we can split a safe rule into several other safe rules with only one relation vertex and the concept vertices associated with it. By construction, safe CG rules are equivalent to a set of safe nonrecursive Datalog rules. Therefore, the proof is similar to that of the existence of a relational algebra expression for each relation of a safe nonrecursive Datalog program [12]. Note that these kind of rules lead to a decidable process, because Datalog is decidable. A difference lies in the selection in which the only operator here is equality: as the model of CG can handle only strings (markers) and no operators like $<, >, \geq, \geq, \neq$, the only operator allowed is $=$, which triggers identification of two symbols within a rule. The other difference is the presence of concept vertices within the CG rules. If the type of a concept vertex does not change between the hypothesis and the conclusion of a rule, the proof is totally reducible. If it happens to change, then this information is redundant in the support, and thus can be ignored.* $\square$

Theorem 4 *Let Ω be a set of safe CG rules. Then the extension of any graph that can be expressed by Ω is expressible by mean of an algebraic expression.*

Proof 2 (Sketch) *As already stated, by construction, safe CG rules are equivalent to a set of safe nonrecursive Datalog rules. Therefore the proof is similar to that of the existence of a relational algebra expression for each fonction from relations to relations that can be generated by safe nonrecursive Datalog program [12], but using the previous lemma. We conclude that the extension of any graph that can be deduced from Ω can be expressed by mean of an algebraic expression.* $\square$

Remark 6 *The model of CG can handle rules that lead to a semidecidable process. Therefore we can not express all CG rules by mean of an algebraic expression. Nevertheless, we can express the decidable part of the CG calculus. This does not mean that our algebra forces the model to have the same expression as Datalog: CG rules which lead to a semidecidable process can still be present in the knowledge base.*

5 Concluding remarks

In this paper, we proposed an algebra for the CG model which allows the expression of complex queries with four operators. We can of course define more operators which are derivable from these four, like equijoin, natural join, and semijoin. The algebra extends the goal-based query language and keeps all the expressive power of the CG model. The associated language, CG-SQL is complete with respect to the decidable part of the CG calculus, that is, every set of safe rules can be expressed by mean of an algebraic expression. Nevertheless, this does not prevent the presence of non safe rules within the knowledge base, because extension of goals are calculated by CG inference mechanisms anyway. But these inferences may never stop, which is inherent to the CG model.

This work enables us to study some perspectives:

5.1 Views

As in classical database systems, we are now able to create views on CG knowledge base by mean of an extension of CG-SQL. Indeed, large algebraic expressions are hard to write down correctly at first time, and may need to be split into several expressions, thus giving view expressions. By giving names to these expressions, they can be reused within queries. Evaluation of views is delayed until a query is asked. An extension of CG-SQL could be:

CREATE VIEW V AS $< SELECT\ statement >$, to create a view,

DROP VIEW V, to delete a view.

The execution of a query that uses the view V replaces it by its corresponding algebraic expression before evaluation. An example of query using a view is:

$G_e \times V$: SELECT * FROM EXT(G),V

5.2 Query optimization

The problem of query optimization arises naturally when we use declarative languages. Indeed, the user does only specify the knowledge he wants to extract from the knowledge base, and the inference mechanism is responsible for choosing the right strategy. To do that, we need to adapt some query optimization techniques which already exist for relational databases [1]. The optimizer generates execution plans of a query and chooses the most efficient one. Execution plans are obtained by modifying the execution tree of a query, which corresponds to applying rewriting techniques to the algebraic expression.

Acknowledgement. The author is grateful to the conceptual graphs research group at LIRMM and to Thérèse Libourel for fruitful discussions.

References

[1] S. Abiteboul, R. Hull, and V. Vianu. *Foundations of Databases*. Addison-Wesley, Reading, Mass., 1995

[2] C. Boksenbaum, B. Carbonneill, O. Haemmerlé, and T. Libourel. Conceptual graphs for relational databases. In *Proceedings of the First International Conference on Conceptual Structures (ICCS-93)*, p. 142-161, LNAI 699, Springer-Verlag, Berlin, 1993

[3] B. Carbonneill and O. Haemmerlé. Standardizing and interfacing relational databases using conceptual graphs. In *Proceedings of the Second International Conference on Conceptual Structures (ICCS-94)*, p. 311-330, LNAI 835, Springer-Verlag, Berlin, 1994

[4] M. Chein and M.-L. Mugnier. Représenter des connaissances et raisonner avec des graphes. *Revue d'Intelligence Artificielle*, vol. 10(1), p. 7-56, 1996

[5] A. Colmerauer. Prolog in 10 figures. *Communications of the ACM*, vol. 28(12), p. 1296-1310, 1985

[6] S. Coulondre and E. Salvat. Piece resolution: Towards larger perspectives. In *Proceedings of the Sixth International Conference on Conceptual Structures (ICCS-98)*, p. 179-193, LNAI 1453, Springer-Verlag, Berlin, 1998

[7] J. Fargues, M.-C. Landau, A. Dugourd and L. Catach. Conceptual graphs for semantics and knowledge processing. *IBM Journal of Research and Development*, vol. 30(1), p. 70-79, 1986

[8] B. C. Ghosh and V. Wuwongse. A direct proof procedure for definite conceptual graph programs. In *Proceedings of the Third International Conference on Conceptual Structures (ICCS-95)*, p. 158-172, LNAI 954, Springer-Verlag, Berlin, 1995

[9] O. Haemmerlé and B. Carbonneill. Interfacing a relational database using conceptual graphs. In *Proceedings of the 7th International Conference and Workshop on Database and Expert Systems Applications (DEXA-96)*, p. 499-505, IEEE-CS Press, Zurich, 1996

[10] E. Salvat and M.-L. Mugnier. Sound and complete forward and backward chainings of graph rules. In *Proceedings of the Fourth International Conference on Conceptual Structures (ICCS-96)*, p. 248-262, LNAI 1115, Springer-Verlag, Berlin, 1996

[11] J. F. Sowa. *Conceptual Structures: Information Processing in Minds and Machines*. Addison-Wesley, Reading, Mass., 1984

[12] J. D. Ullman. *Principles of Database and Knowledge-Bade Systems. Volume I: Classical Database Systems*. Computer Science Press, 1988

Constraint-based Knowledge Acquisition and Verification for Planning

R. Barruffi, E. Lamma, M. Milano, R. Montanari
DEIS, Università di Bologna
Viale Risorgimento 2, 40136 Bologna, Italy
{rbarruffi,elamma,mmilano,rmontanari}@deis.unibo.it

P. Mello
Dipartimento di Ingegneria, Università di Ferrara
Via Saragat, 44100 Ferrara, Italy
pmello@ing.unife.it

Abstract

Traditional planners build goal-oriented plans of actions by reasoning on a representation of the handled objects; this representation is assumed to be complete and static. On the other hand, planning needs to deal with the problem of incomplete and dynamic information when applied to real environments. The fields of network and security management are typical examples where it is really unrealistic making the assumption of complete and static world. In this paper, we present an intelligent support system performing planning tasks in the security management field. In such a context, a mechanism for dynamically acquire knowledge during the computational process is needed. Our approach is based on a definition of the planning problem as a Constraint Satisfaction Problem (CSP). We extended the CSP paradigm in order to deal with incomplete knowledge. Traditional CSPs work exclusively with completely known variable domains, while, in our solution, some variables can range on partially or completely unknown domains. The acquisition of domain values is performed by means of *Interactive Constraints* (IC), during their propagation. It is worth noting that only consistent information for the planner is retrieved so as to simplify further propagation steps.

1 Introduction

Many Artificial Intelligence applications solve problems by using knowledge-based systems. They are based on a description (model) of the real world representing the application domain. Knowledge-based systems applied to complex and dynamic domains have to deal with the problem of incomplete knowledge and changes. Several approaches to this problem focus on the knowledge base updates, when an event is triggered. The update is transparent to the intelligent agent that uses the knowledge base itself. Our approach is based on an "on-demand" knowledge acquisition and consequent update of the knowledge base according to the agent needs. Particularly, our agent has planning capabilities and is applied for the synthesis of plans of actions necessary to recover from attacks detected by an Intrusion Detection System. In such a domain a huge amount of data needs to be handled, thus the knowledge model is typically incomplete and highly dynamic.

Traditional *generative* planners which are based on the unrealistic assumption of omniscience [16] are not appropriate in this domain [4]. There is need to relax this assumption and find a mechanism to plan with incomplete and changing knowledge.

Our planner is a Partial Ordered Planner (POP) [16] which exploits Constraints Satisfaction techniques [6] to augment its search efficiency. Constraint Satisfaction (CS) techniques [6] have been widely used in the past for modelling and solving planning problems [16, 8, 12]. We adopt a Constraint-based approach and we extend it to deal with incomplete knowledge.

We map the planning problem into a CSP, where some constraints, called *Interactive Constraints* (IC) [11], may result in a knowledge acquisition process and a consequent propagation. In fact, we consider that the planner is not aware of all the true facts of the real world. Thus, when the planner tries to verify if a precondition is already satisfied in the initial state, if the available information is not enough, it needs to acquire knowledge from the underlying system. Interactive constraints act as both usual preconditions and constraints when they work on variables ranging on known domains. Otherwise, they perform knowledge acquisition in order to retrieve variable domain values. It is worth noting that in this way the knowledge acquisition process is transparent to the planner which does not need to take into account declarative sensing actions; on the other hand knowledge acquisition can be driven by ICs in order to retrieve only values consistent with the constraint itself, so that the agent works with significantly smaller domains and avoids most time consuming pruning steps.

The hypothesis of static world is another unrealistic assumption of traditional planners, since most of the real domains are typically highly dynamic. The problem of dynamic world is due to the facts that (i) typically the planner is not the only agent that causes changes on the system; (ii) often changes are not deterministic. This can lead to a failure of the plan execution, either because action preconditions are no longer verified at execution time, or because action effects are not those expected because of a non deterministic behaviour of the system during the action execution. A typical approach is to avoid to model volatile information, thus falling into the above described problem of incomplete knowledge. Generative planners tackle the problem by delaying the verification of unknown information until execution. Thus, they base their choice on assumptions or simply do not take any decision and build conditional plans; reactive planners interleave planning and execution so that they can acquire, during execution, the information needed to continue planning and verify action effects. All these planning techniques are based on sensing performed either during execution or during the planning process. We exploit the Interactive CS framework to cope also with dynamicity. Basically, we argue that the interactive constraint propagation mechanism can be used not only to retrieve new information, but also for verifying action preconditions before execution and action effects after execution.

Thus, our agent is based on a "2-phase" planning algorithm: during the first phase, called "generative" phase, the planner builds a plan schema which will be refined during execution, by the second phase, called "reactive" phase. During this phase a IC-driven verification of the executed actions is also performed. In this way, we can monitor the system behaviour and check if it corresponds to that expected by the planner.

Work in progress regards a repair mechanism and a replanning activity that should support the cases in which one or more wrong actions are executed.

As application domain we have choosen the field of network security management. Particularly we focus on those situations where a recovery plan of actions has to be built every time an attack is detected by an Intrusion Detection System(IDS) [10]. Moreover, when the attack is due to a wrong configuration of the system, the planner provides the proper configuration, thus supporting the system manager work.

The aim of this paper is to describe the Interactive CSP (ICSP) framework and how our knowledge-based planning agent benefits from it. Finally we show how this planner works with an example describing the synthesis of a plan necessary to recover from an attack to the e-mail service.

2 Background

Planners making the Open World Assumption (OWA) [4] are based on the hypothesis that anything not indicated into the list of the known facts is unknown and can be retrieved by means of sensing mechanisms. Some OWA-based planners perform *off-line* knowledge acquisition after the planning process, i.e., during execution, and others perform *on-line* acquisition during the planning process.

Following the first approach (i.e., *off-line*), it is possible (see [14]):

1. Planning for all contingencies.
   Some planners build conditional plans [13], i.e., plans with different alternative branches selected at run time according to the response of the corresponding sensing action. This can lead to a computational explosion of the planning process when many alternatives have to be considered since the planner needs to analyse all the interactions of different branches. It might be appropriate when the same plan will be used many times with potentially different sensor values in each execution or when time does not allow execution time planning (either deferred planning or replanning in case of wrong assumption) and finally when an error costs more than extra planning.

2. Making assumptions.

   Some planners base their planning decisions on assumptions made on unknown facts [4] which will be verified during execution by means of sensing actions previously introduced into the plan. In case of wrong esteem, the agent needs to replan. Planning with assumptions is computationally less expensive than conditional planning, but when errors occur replanning is necessary and part of the planning effort is wasted. This approach is appropriate when it is possible to stop execution while replanning occurs, or when the criticality of plan errors is low (i.e., actions are reversible...), or finally when a particular result for a sensor reading is more likely than any of the others.

3. Deferring planning decisions.

   Other planners [14] defer planning decisions until knowledge is available. With deferred planning approach, the planner completes only the parts of the plan for which it has enough information. Since the plan is incomplete, it is the possible to miss important dependencies and constraints. This can require backtracking steps on executed actions with the problems seen above. This approach is appropriate when it is possible to stop execution while planning continues and the cost of failure is low.

4. Embedding contingencies into the action definition.

   Other approaches shift the complexity from the planning process to the action definition activity, by embedding into action descriptions every possible alternative in which a situation can occur [3]. This approach can be suitable when a limited number of possible alternatives is given, otherwise many advantages of planning activity could be lost.

Planners performing *on-line* knowledge acquisition gather information in a dynamic way during the planning process. Those planners interleave planning and execution of sensing actions [5] needed to retrieve information *on demand* and go on in planning.

Note that most of the mentioned OWA-based planners make use of *sensing actions*. Sensing actions are explicitly defined in the action domain; thus, they are defined similarly to causal actions in a declarative formal language by pre and post conditions so that the planner automatically inserts sensing action instances into the plan, each time an information is required.

The main drawbacks of sensing actions mainly concern the facts that: (i) sensing actions have to be explicitly defined in the action domain; (ii) they retrieve the whole state of the underlying system in a systematic way, leaving to the planner the task of selecting information consistent with the case under consideration; (iii) often there may be plans containing many instances of the same sensing action thus resulting in *sensor abuse*.

Our challenge is to provide the planner with a sensing mechanism which mostly overcomes these limits. The solution we propose is suitable both for "off-line" knowledge acquisition and for an "on-line" approach. However, we argue that its capabilities are better exploited if applied to an agent that follows the latter approach as our planner does.

3   Interactive CS Techniques

CS techniques are widely used in many AI applications, to augment the search efficiency by avoiding failures instead of recovering from them, thus reducing computationally heavy backtracking steps [16, 8, 12]. A traditional Constraint Satisfaction Problem (CSP) is defined on a set of variables $\{v_1, v_2, \ldots, v_n\}$ ranging on a completely known domain $\{d_1, d_2, \ldots, d_n\}$ of values. Variables are linked by constraints $c(v_{1_i}, \ldots, v_{k_i})$ that define the combinations of values that can appear in a consistent solution. A solution to a CSP is found when all the variables are instantiated in a consistent way with all the constraints of the problem. For instance, the constraint $logged(User, Machine)$ links variables $User$ and $Machine$ which is satisfied if the $User$ is logged on the given $Machine$. Both variables can be associated with a domain of possible values. Generally speaking, the $User$ domain represents all users in the system, while the $Machine$ domain contains all machines available in the networked system. The constraint $logged(User, Machine)$ prunes variable domains in order to remove inconsistent values.

In order to exploit this feature, we have to map the planning problem into a Constraint Satisfaction Problem (CSP). Many approaches to planning as CSP have been proposed. Particularly, some of them exploit CS techniques for temporal reasoning [12, 15], resource allocation [12, 15], conflict resolution [9, 17, 8] and open condition achievement [8].

We model the planning problem as a CSP whose variables are those appearing in the pre and post conditions of action schemata instances introduced into the plan. Preconditions act as constraints on those variables which are associated with a domain that can be reduced during the computation thanks to constraint propagation.

However classical CS approaches [6] need all the information on variable domains at the beginning of the computation. Thus, we extend the CSP framework in order to apply CS techniques to domains where, given the incompleteness of the knowledge model, there is need of interaction between the low level system and the data processing module, which is a constraint solver in our case. In [11] we introduce a method to dynamically acquire the information from the real world during the computational process. In addition the CSP system itself drives the information gathering process. This general framework can be used in many applications, particularly in all the applications where a low level system provides a large amount of constrained data to be processed, as for instance a vision system used for extracting visual features of objects from an image [11]. We tailor this general solution to planning problems.

Thus, we define an *Interactive CSP* framework where variables range on partially or completely unknown domains. We associate an information gathering procedure with most of the predicates, appearing as preconditions in the basic actions definition, without need to define further declarative actions. When these preconditions are tested, they behave as *Interactive Constraints*; that is, they behave both as usual preconditions and constraints when they work on variables ranging on known domains. Otherwise, knowledge acquisition is performed in order to acquire domain values.

Operationally ICs behave as follow:

Given a binary constraint $IC(c(X, Y))$

- if both variables are associated with a partially or completely unknown domain, suspend the constraint;

- else, if both variables range on a completely known domain, propagate the constraint as in classical CSPs;

- else, if variable X (resp. Y) ranges on a fully known domain and Y (resp. X) is associated with a partially or fully unknown one, knowledge acquisition for variable Y (resp. X) is performed, driven by X.

These constraints are awaked, during the planning process, when some variables are instantiated or their domain pruned.

A solution to the ICSP is an assignment of values to variables which is consistent with constraints.

4   An ICSP-based Planning Architecture

We propose an integrated architecture (see figure 1) based on Interactive Constraint Satisfaction (ICS) techniques. It combines the problem solving ability of *generative* planning in charge of producing a plan schema, and the capability of *reactive* planning to acquire information on demand from the real world. Knowledge acquisition is performed in both phases of the planning algorithm: first in order to provide the generative planner with the information it needs and then to refine the plan at execution time.

The generative phase of the planning algorithm is represented by a Partial Order Planner (POP) whose kernel is similar to the UCPOP algorithm [16]. As in UCPOP algorithm, our planner starts by generating the *NullPlan* with the dummy actions *Init* and *End*. *Init* has no precondition and its postconditions consist of a set, called *InitialState* (*IS*). *IS* contains the knowledge of the underlying system that the planner is aware of, while in a traditional generative planner it represents all the true facts in the real world.

Knowledge is retrieved and organised in a data base according to the class of object to which the information is referred. For example, as far as an instance of the object `network service`, information as *port*, *user*, *path*, *id*, *CPU needs*, *type*, *date*, *time* will be retrieved and recorded. Thus, *IS* is not a static set, but grows continuously according to the new information retrieved by the planner. Note that as soon as the knowledge is gathered and modelled the planner reasons on it as if it were static. Further work is under way in order to deal with changing information. The *End* action has no effect, and its preconditions are

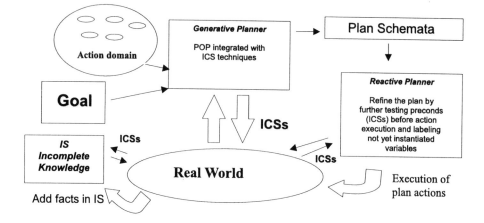

Figure 1: An integrated architecture

the conjunction of the goals of the planning problem. All these conjuncts are initially put into an *Agenda* representing the set of subgoals the planner has to satisfy. During the planning process, as soon as a new action is introduced into the plan, its preconditions are added to *Agenda*. Since the planner treats preconditions as constraint, as soon as it selects one item from the *Agenda*, it will put it into the constraint store.

These constraints are called 'Interactive Constraints' (IC) since on one hand they represent constraints of the plan (precisely they represent constraints between the variables of the predicate itself), on the other hand they are "interactive" because they treat also the case in which the domains of these variables are not yet completely defined into the planning problem, (i.e., the IS set does not contain all the information on the variables of the precondition itself). In these cases, such constraints run low level functions that work as access modules to the real world which will retrieve the values of the variable domain satisfying the constraint represented by the predicate under consideration. The retrieved knowledge is always referred to the initial state since the execution of the plan has not already been performed. Domain values are retrieved either by inferring the information required from the facts contained in IS or, when necessary, by running a low level function which works as access module to the real world.

One of our main purposes is to reduce as much as possible the interaction of the planner with the real system so as to avoid *sensor abuse* [4], by providing it with a mechanism to know when to stop sensing. This mechanism allows the agent to avoid to run low level functions when all the possible values have been already retrieved. We explicit the fact that IS already contains all the information regarding a specific resource by adding an `all` annotation to that item. This reasoning methodology is based on the Local Closed World (LCW) assumption described in [4, 5].

There are predicates representing no logical preconditions [16] with no associated information gathering activity (domain independent constraints) which will be treated in a uniform way as the other constraints on the plan. For instance, the precondition $X \geq Y$ checks domain values with no need to perform any knowledge acquisition procedure.

4.1 The Generative Phase of the Planning Algorithm

We give now a description of the main steps of the generative phase of the planning algorithm. Note that the input parameters $\langle A, O, L \rangle$ represent, respectively, the set A of the actions of the current plan, the set of ordering constraints O and the set L of causal links [16].

$PLAN(\langle A, O, L \rangle)$::

1. *Termination.* If the *Agenda* is empty then return $\langle A, O, L \rangle$.

2. *Goal selection.* Choose a pair $\langle Q, A_k \rangle$ from the *Agenda* where A_k belongs to the set A of actions already instantiated and Q is a precondition of A_k.

3. *Action selection.* Call the Interactive Constraint associated with Q (IC(Q)) in order to verify Q in the initial state:

      if   IC(Q) fails, (i.e., *Init* does not satisfy Q)
      then non-deterministically choose an action A_j (different from *Init*)
              which can be consistently ordered prior to A_k and whose
              effects contain a conjunct R that unifies with Q in a
              consistent way with other constraints:

           if A_j is a newly instantiated action
           then Update A: $A = A \cup \{A_j\}$,
                  $\forall\, Q_i$ precondition of A_j: $Agenda = Agenda + \langle Q_i, A_j \rangle$;
           else if $A_j \subset A$
               then Unify Q with R;
           else fail;
         else $A_j = Init$;

4. *Update L and O*

5. *Update the goal set.* $Agenda = Agenda - \langle Q, A_k \rangle$

6. *Causal link protection.*

7. *Recursive invocation of* $PLAN(\langle A, O, L \rangle)$.

Note that this planning phase return a plan schema.
In a traditional CSP, when no further propagation is possible and a variable domain contain more than one value, a non deterministic instantiation of those variables (i.e., labelling step) is performed. Instead, we do not want

$PLAN(\langle A, O, L \rangle)$ to return a single final solution, i.e., variables might be associated with a domain containing more than one value since the labelling step does not take place in the generative algorithm itself. The reason of our choice is based on the consideration that solutions consistent for the generative planner can be inconsistent when executed in the real world, since we assume that the underlying system can change and non deterministic effects can take place when executing an action.

4.2   The Reactive Phase of the Planning Algorithm

The "reactive" phase of the planning algorithm is performed at execution time. It is devoted to verify, before execution, whether action preconditions are still true and, after action execution, whether action effects have been properly executed.

Moreover, when variable domains contain more than one value a search process is performed at execution time, in order to choose, at run time, a (still) consistent solution, if any, among the possible alternatives. (See figure 1).

This can be realised by an interactive constraint propagation which checks the satisfiability of the precondition in the real world. Obviously, if precondition variables are already instantiated, the interaction with the underlying system returns a boolean value, while if those variables are associated with a domain, the domain can be pruned in order to remove values which are no longer consistent with the current state of the system. For instance, suppose that, during the planning process a printer needs to be selected to print a job. Suppose, also, that at the end of the first phase of the planning algorithm, after constraint propagation, the printer domain still contain 2 printer objects $p1$ and $p2$. If during this phase, the algorithm, no deterministically, selected one of the three printers, it might happen that, at execution time the selected printer is not available anymore and the plan would fail. On the other hand, if we delay the commitment of the *printer* variable until execution no failure would occur.[1]

The effect verification mechanism checks if the corresponding action has been properly executed. For this purpose, again, we can use the interactive constraint propagation mechanism by associating with each action effect an interactive constraint whose goal is to query the underlying system and check whether the action has achieved the desired effect. Note that in this case variables appearing in action effects are already ground and the effect verification results in a boolean value. Thus, the interaction with the real world results in a consistency checking more than proper knowledge acquisition which is computationally less complex. If the verification succeeds, the execution of the plan goes on by selecting the next action. Otherwise, a backtracking mechanism is performed in order to select an alternative plan execution. The planner has to support backtracking steps over causal actions and repair activity for dealing with irreversible actions. In this paper we make the assumption that all the

---

[1]Note that this mechanism allow to avoid failure regarding changes of the available resource. At the moment our agent is not able to treat other kinds of dynamicity.

actions are backtrackable. We are currently working on a repair mechanism able to deal with irreversible actions.

We describe now the main steps of this second phase of the algorithm performed at execution time: the generative planner produces a set of alternative (possibly inconsistent) plans which are passed along with the domain variables to the executive module in charge of refining the plan during its execution. Note that the plan refinement results only in action schemata variables instantiation in order to find the most appropriate values according to the current situation of the real system. A total order among plan actions has been already committed by $PLAN(\langle A, O, L \rangle)$.

$EXEC(\langle A, O, L \rangle)$::

1. *Termination.* If the set A is empty then return success.

2. *Action selection.* Select the first action instance $A_i \in A$ (following the order inferred by the set of constraints O)

3. *Constraint checking and propagation.* For each P_j precondition of A_i call $IC(P_j)$ where P_j are variables associated with the domains acquired in the previous phase of planning:

   if $IC(P_j)$ fails (no domain value is any longer consistent)
   then perform backtracking of the last action executed A_j,
        go back to step 3.
   else:

4. *Action execution.* Perform the labelling of not yet instantiated variables and execute the action A_j

5. *Effects verification.* Verify the effects of the action on the real world: for each E_j effect of A_j call $IC(E_j)$:

   if $IC(E_j)$ fails
   then perform backtracking of the last action executed A_j,
        go back to step 3.

With regards to the example described above $PLAN(\langle A, O, L \rangle)$ is returned without instantiating *Printer*. It will be the *Executive phase* to commit to a final choice so as if in the meanwhile either $p3$ or $p2$ is no longer available it will not fail. Finally, each effect is verified after execution by means of Interactive Constraints associated with the predicates. If something goes wrong, a repair mechanism is triggered as described in $EXEC(\langle A, O, L \rangle)$ algorithm.

5 The Application Domain

The configuration and maintenance of distributed systems require relevant complex tasks to be performed. Now that security has become a primary concern, the task of maintaining the system in the desired state is even more complex; an attack, in fact, can significantly alter the state of a system in a way that is not predictable. In this context, the maintenance cycle consists in two steps: the detection of an attack from the network, and the transition to bring the system back to a desired state. Particularly we focus on the second phase of the cycle. Thus we suppose to have an Intrusion Detection System (IDS) recognizing an attack and triggering a recovery planning process.

Recovery from an attack can be an inherently complex task, so that it might require a lot of interaction with the system administrator for a step-to-step flow control of the repair process. On the other hand, many modern systems allow automatic repair mechanisms at the price of writing complex procedural scripts, one for each situation that is likely to happen. We believe that in a complex system such an approach is not feasible since the complexity of the managed objects leads to a combinatorial explosion in the number of possible combinations and interactions between the actions to be considered. Not only does this approach require long development time, but also it is not flexible enough to cope with unexpected situations like those due to security attacks. These cases would enormously benefit from some level of automation in the script generation. If an automated planner is on place, this can be achieved by simply writing the elementary building blocks and using a declarative approach to specify the re-configuration goals that, given a detected attack, need to be satisfied in order to go back to a consistent (safe) state of the system.

Moreover note that the diagnosis of the problems caused by an attack represents a big issue. In fact, even when an attack is detected, it is not trivial to understand which effects it actually provoked on the network.

Typically a planning agent can be defined as an "intelligent assistant which enables the human user to state what he wants accomplished" [2] and not "how" o "where" to satisfy it which will be stated dynamically by the agent itself.

In our domain it is enough to model each attack and state the set of conditions that need to be satisfied at the end of the repair activity. This can be done independently of the fact that they might be already satisfied in the initial state since they might represent unviolated resources.

The planner starts to build the "recovery" plan of actions given the set of goals, the current situation of the system, the set of performable basic actions and the set of policies of the system.

Our planner lends itself to this sort of applications since it is able to retrieve information about the current situation of the system by directly interacting with the real world through ICs. Thus, for each conjunct of the final goal it will first verify if it is already satisfied otherwise it will choose an action which achieves that goal and so on iteratively.

6   An Example of Recovery Plan

In order to see how our planner works, we present an example in the field of security management. We consider the case of the so called "e-mail spamming" attack; it affects all platforms that accept e-mail from the Internet and damages the e-mail service by reducing its availability. When an IDS, configured to detect any anomalous e-mail traffic, signals the attack, a recovery plan is triggered.

We consider a UNIX platform and *sendmail* as e-mail server program. *Sendmail* is a daemon always listening for incoming *SMTP* (Simple Mail Transfer Protocol) connections. It delivers e-mails according to its configuration file *sendmail.cf*; the e-mails not yet delivered are queued in the default file. The occurrence of the email spamming attack means that the *sendmail.cf* is not properly configured to prevent it. Thus, the goals of the plan are:

- to re-establish the availability of the e-mail service with a correct configuration of the *sendmail.cf* so as to prevent any further e-mail spamming;

- to deliver the high number of e-mails accumulated in the default queue file because of the attack.

Let's suppose the domain theory contains the following action schemata:

Action *Kill(process : Process)*
Preconditions
not status(Process, off)
Postconditions
status(Process, off), not using(Process, file)

The goal of this action is to kill a given process.

Action *MvFile(file : F1, F2)*
Preconditions
not using(process, F1), exists(F1), not exists(F2), data(F1, D)
Postconditions
not exists(F1), exists(F2), data(F2, D)

The above action is devoted to rename a file $F1$ to $F2$. $F2$ data will be the same of $F1$. In order this action to succeed, no application must be using $F1$. In this example the planner will use this action to move the accumulated e-mails from the default queue to a temporary one that we call recovery queue.

Action *OnProcessSendMail(file : RQueue)*
Preconditions
exists(RQueue)
Postconditions
status(sendmailProcess, on), using(sendmailProcess, RQueue)

This action is specific to activate a single sendmail process (i.e., not running as a daemon). The task of this process is to deliver all the e-mails previously moved in the recovery queue (*RQueue*). This allows the e-mail service to be immediately restarted without waiting for all the queued e-mails to be delivered.

Action *OnDaemonSendMail(file : DQueue)*
Preconditions
in(sendmail.cf, antiSpamRules), status(sendmailDaemon, off), not exists(DQueue)
Postconditions
status(sendmailDaemon, on), using(sendmailDaemon, DQueue), exists(DQueue)

The action above reactivates the sendmail daemon with a proper configuration. With "proper configuration" we mean that the sendmail.cf file contains specific antispamming rules.

Action *AddStrings(file : File, string : String)*
Preconditions
not in(File, String)
Postconditions
in(File, String)

This last action is necessary to add new strings to a file. In this example, we need it to insert the antispamming rules in the sendmail configuration file.

The final goal's conjuncts are:

- *status(sendmailDaemon, on)*,

- *using(sendmailDaemon, defaultQueue)*,

- *status(sendmailProcess, on)*,

- *using(sendmailProcess, recoveryQueue)*,

- *data(recoveryQueue, Data)*,

- INITIALLY *data(defaultQueue, Data)*

Note that the planner interprets the goal conjuncts with INITIALLY annotation as conditions that can only be satisfied from the initial state [4]. No other actions can be used to satisfy them.

Suppose the initial real situation is the following:

- the *sendmailDaemon* is stalled as detected by the IDS;

- the *sendmail.cf* does not contain the antispamming rules.

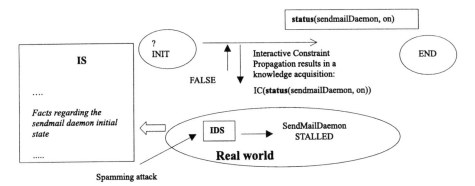

Figure 2: Example of Recovery Plan Synthesis

We assume that the the recovery queue file (absolute) name is "recoveryQueue" and the default queue file (absolute) name is "defaultQueue".
Let's follow the main steps of the plan synthesis process:

- Suppose the planner chooses, first, the $status(sendmailDaemon, on)$ goal conjunct. It will call the associated Interactive Constraint $IC(status(sendmailDaemon, on))$. Its propagation results in an acquisition from the real world of the information regarding the sendmail daemon. This information is added to IS. In particular, the condition $status(sendmailDaemon, on)$ is not verified in the initial state because after the "spamming" attack the sendmail daemon is stalled. See figure 2.

- Thus the planner chooses an action from the action domain whose effects satisfy that condition, i.e., $OnDaemonSendMail(file : DQueue)$. See figure 3. Its preconditions are added to the set $Agenda$ of Goal conjuncts that need to be satisfied. That action also satisfies the condition $using(sendmailDaemon, defaultQueue)$ with $DQueue$ instantiated to the value "defaultQueue".

- When $IC(in(sendmail.cf, antiSpamRules))$ is called, it returns FALSE; then the planner chooses the $AddStrings(file : F, string : String)$ action to satisfy this condition.

- Note that the interactive constraint $IC(status(SendmailDaemon, off))$ infers the information regarding the initial status of the sendmail daemon (i.e., STALLED) from IS since it has been previously retrieved. An action that satisfies $status(SendmailDaemon, off)$ is needed. The planner chooses $Kill(process : Process)$.

- We will see later how the planner will satisfy the last open condition of this partial plan, i.e., $not\ exists(Dqueue)$.

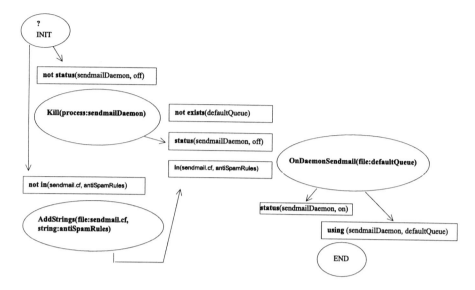

Figure 3: Example of Recovery Plan Synthesis (2)

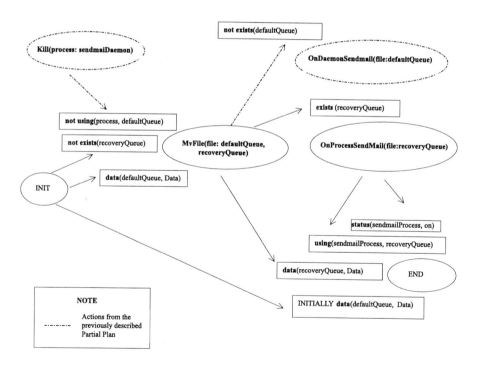

Figure 4: Example of Recovery Plan Synthesis (3)

- The same reasonings can be applied to the synthesis of the partial plan that satisfies the still open goal conjuncts. See figure 4.

- As previously mentioned, the "INITIALLY $data(defaultQueue, Data)$" conjunct needs to be satisfied from the initial state; thus, the variable $Data$ can be only bound to an initial state's value. This value is represented by the data initially contained in the default queue file.

- A $MvFile(file : F1, F2)$ action is needed to satisfy the open condition $data(recoveryQueue, Data)$. The variables $F1$ and $F2$ will be respectively bound to "defaultQueue" and "recoveryQueue".
  At the same time it satisfies the preconditions $not\ exists(defaultQueue)$ of the action $OnDaemonSendMail(file : defaultQueue)$ and $exists(recoveryQueue)$ of action $OnProcessSendMail(file : recoveryQueue)$.

7 Conclusion and Future Work

We presented a Constraint-based solution which allows a planning agent to deal with the problem of incomplete knowledge apart from improve its efficiency during the plan. Particularly the solution is based on an extension of the Constraint Satisfaction (CS) paradigm called Interactive CS (ICS) which allows a data processing module, in our case a planner, to interact directly with the real world and acquire information on demand. We described how the same techniques can be exploited to cope with dynamic knowledge when resource allocation is needed and to verify the effects of the plan execution on the system domain.

This features make possible the applicability of planning techniques in those domains where a huge amount of objects and resources need to be handled. In particular we consider the security management field as application domain; i.e., we deal with those situations in which an attack is detected by an Intrusion Detection System (IDS) and a recovery action plan is needed to bring the system in a correct state.

The implementation of this architecture is being carried out by using the finite domain library of ECL^iPS^e [1] properly extended to cope with the interactive framework. ECL^iPS^e is a Constraint Logic Programming (CLP) [7, 6] system merging all the features and advantages of Logic Programming and Constraint Satisfaction techniques. CLP on Finite Domains, CLP(FD), can be used to represent planning problems as CSPs.

We are currently working on a repair mechanism necessary to treat the cases of failure of the plan execution. The main problem is related with backtracking of irreversible actions. We want to provide the planner with $Backup$ actions to insert into the plan each time one irreversible action is instantiated. The effects of $backup$ actions will then be used in charge of synthesising a repair plan that will retract the effects of the failed action.

Moreover we are considering the possibility to introduce a monitoring activity able to dynamically update the already retrieved information in a transparent way to the planner. In this context the planner can always work with "fresh" information, thus reducing the number of possible failures during execution.

A long term goal is to embed the planner into a fully integrated IDS architecture able to react both reactively in case of detected attack and proactively in case of alarm (i.e., when a dangerous trend is recognised).

8 Acknowledgments

Authors' work has been partially supported by: Hewlett Packard Laboratories of Bristol - UK (Internet Business Management Department), the italian "Centro Nazionale di Ricerca" (CNR) - Committee 12 on Information Technology (Project SCI*SIA) and the italian "Ministero dell'Università e della Ricerca Scientifica e Tecnologica" (MURST).

References

[1] ECRC. *ECL^{i}PS^e User Manual Release 3.3*, 1992.

[2] O. Etzioni, H. Levy, R. Segal, and C. Thekkath. Os agents: Using ai techniques in the operating system environment. Technical report, University of Washington, 1993.

[3] R.J. Firby. *Adaptive Execution in Complex Dynamic Worlds*. PhD thesis, Yale University, 1989.

[4] K. Golden. *Planning and Knowledge Representation for Softbots*. PhD thesis, University of Washington, 1997.

[5] K. Golden and D. Weld. Representing sensing actions: The middle ground revisited. In *Proceedings of 5th Int. Conf. on Knowledge Representation and Reasoning*, 1996.

[6] P. Van Hentenryck. *Constraint Satisfaction in Logic Programming*. MIT Press, 1989.

[7] J. Jaffar and M.J. Maher. Constraint logic programming: a survey. *Journal of Logic Programming - Special Issue on 10 years of Logic Programming*, 1994.

[8] D. Joslin and M. Pollack. Passive and active decision postponment. In *Proceedings of European Workshop of Planning*, 1995.

[9] S. Kambhampati. Using disjunctive orderings instead of conflict resolution in partial order planning. Technical report, Department of Computer Science and Engineering Arizona State University, 1996.

[10] S. Kumar and E.H. Spafford. A software architecture to support misuse intrusion detection. In *Proceedings of the 18th National Information Security Conference*, 1995.

[11] E. Lamma, M. Milano, R. Cucchiara, and P. Mello. An interactive constraint based system for selective attention in visual search. *Proceedings of the ISMIS*, 1997.

[12] J. Lever and B. Richards. parcplan: a planning architecture with parallel actions, resources and constraints. In *Proceedings of 8th ISMIS*, 1994.

[13] M.Peot and D. Smith. Conditional nonlinear planning. In *Proceedings of 1st Int. Conf. on Principles of Knowledge Representation and Reasoning*, 1992.

[14] D. Olawsky and M. Gini. Deferred planning and sensor use. In *Proceedings DARPA Workshop on Innovative Approaches to Planning, Scheduling, and Control*, 1990.

[15] A. Tate, B. Drabble, and J. Dalton. Reasoning with constraints within o-plan2. Technical report, AI Applications Institute Univeristy of Edinburgh, 1994.

[16] D.S. Weld. An introduction to least commitment planning. *AI Magazine*, 15:27–61, 1994.

[17] Q. Yang. A theory of conflict resolution in planning. *Artificial Intelligence*, 58:361–392, 1992.

Coping with Poorly Understood Domains: The Example of Internet Trust

Andrew Basden
The Centre for Virtual Environments, University of Salford.

John B. Evans, David W. Chadwick, Andrew Young
Information Technology Institute, University of Salford.

Abstract

The notion of trust, as required for secure operations over the Internet, is important for ascertaining the source of received messages. How can we measure the degree of trust in authenticating the source? Knowledge in the domain is not established, so knowledge engineering becomes knowledge generation rather than mere acquisition. Special techniques are required, and special features of KBS software become more important than in conventional domains. This paper generalizes from experience with Internet trust to discuss some techniques and software features that are important for poorly understood domains.

Keywords: Internet trust, knowledge-based tools, knowledge elicitation, knowledge-poor domains, knowledge refinement, knowledge generation, Istar.

1. Introduction

1.1 Knowledge Generation

The traditional view of knowledge acquisition is linear (Fig. 1a), in which a knowledge engineer extracts pieces of knowledge from a source and then represents them by symbols in the knowledge representation language. But such an approach assumes the pieces of knowledge already exist in more-or-less finished form and merely need uncovering. When this view is applied to tacit knowledge (1) its explication is seen in terms of merely clearing away the layers that hide the knowledge until it is brought to light.

But in many domains this view is inappropriate. Knowledge is not just extracted but also generated, created, formed by the process of knowledge acquisition and knowledge representation. The process gains a circular element, Fig. 1b, in which the act of representing the knowledge stimulates the thinking of the knowledge engineer and even the expert to think of new pieces and to refashion existing pieces.

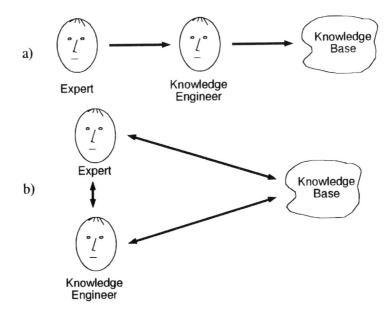

Fig. 1. Linear and Circular Knowledge Acquistion

This process has been discussed in some depth (2), showing it to be different to the conventional process in many ways; there the two approaches are called 'assembly' and 'creative design'. These differences, which are summarised in Table 1, are fundamental, not just small variations in technique, and thus require a rethinking of knowledge acquisition techniques.

They also mean that the software features found in KBS software are seen in a different light, with different criteria becoming important. Traditionally, such things as expressive power have been assumed to be the most important features; in domains where knowledge is poorly understood and must be generated, expressive power takes second place to whether the use of the software is 'proximal' or 'distal' (3) and how easy it is for the knowledge engineer to change knowledge rather than merely add to it. Features that aid interpretation of ill-defined concepts, both by knowledge engineer and by the end user, assume an importance far greater than in many conventional knowledge domains.

In this paper we discuss the attempt to construct a knowledge based system in such a poorly understood domain, that of Internet trust. After a brief description of the project, we discuss four different sources of the need for knowledge generation, then describe our experiences during the project. The discussion then generalises these, and yields two lists of tentative recommendations for knowledge acquisition methodology and for software features needed for exercises of this kind.

116

TABLE 1. Comparison of knowledge engineering paradigms

Paradigm	**Assembly**	**Creative design**
KBS purpose	Advice-giving Training	Knowledge Refinement
Knowledge source	External	The process itself
KR Tool users	Single	Group
KR Tool purpose	Representation only	Communication Clarification Representation
Nature of kg. eng.	Monotonic increment	Non-monotonic reinterpretation
	Planned or situated actions Evolutionary	Continuous process Revolutionary
Prime symbol level task	Add pieces of knowledge	Change knowledge
Style of user action	Discrete user tasks Predefined goals Means to end	Continuous activity Often no task goals Means and ends not separated
	'How' unimportant Actions result in internal changes	'How' important Some actions without internal result
Tool-user Relationship	Distal	Proximal
Quality criteria	Learnability Standardization	Proximality Lack of interruption
Style of user interface	Object Oriented	Holistic

1.2 The Intelligent Computation of Trust (ICT) Project

In order to perform important (e.g. commercial) transactions over the Internet it is essential that the parties are sure of each other's true identity. Clearly before anyone would be prepared to invest time, effort and possibly resources into a transaction it would be wise to firstly ensure that the other party is genuine. The first step is to consider the problem of ascertaining the authenticity of a remote party. Commercial reality would demand that the identity should reference an entity that could be sued in court, if necessary.

Not only do we need to know that the document has come from a reliable source (authentication) we also need to know that no-one other than authorised recipients can access the information of the transaction. Encryption is usually used to ensure this confidentiality, involving public keys, but the problem then lies in the secure exchange of the key between the parties. The problem then becomes one of authentication again, i.e. of the public key of an identified entity.

The basic relationship being investigated is a tripartite one where an entity, an individual person or person acting for a commercial company, is assessing the authenticity of (the public keys of) another on the basis of communication over the Internet. The entity turns to a Certification Authority (CA) or Trusted Third Party (TTP) to aid this process. A CA is responsible for authenticating the identity of a subscriber, and for securely binding this identity to the subscriber's public key, through a process known as certification. A relying party can then obtain the certified public key of a subscriber, and providing s/he trusts the binding carried out by the CA, can trust that this really is the public key of the subscriber, and can then with confidence enter into a secure communication with the subscriber.

But it is felt that not all CAs (and there are many of them) are equally good in performing their task. Many CAs have broad responsibilities; besides issuing the keys for encoded communication they will also provide an Internet service as a commercial package. Not only may some be slipshod in their acceptance of subject entities' bona fides, but some may be prone to subversion from either inside the organisation or from hacking operations carried out from the outside. To guard against this a CA publishes a CPS (certification practice statement) which amounts to a statement of the means by which the CA will perform its various duties including the verification of subscribers. Regular compliance audits are made to ensure that the high standards of checking are maintained.

The multifaceted nature of trust leads us to devise a knowledge based system (KBS) to evaluate the claims and attributes of such CAs based on the statements in their CPSs. The main task of such a KBS is to examine (or to guide the user in examining) the CPS published or referenced by the CA to try to estimate the degree of trust a relying party may place upon the recommendations of any particular CA. The approach is to build a model, based on Chokhani and Ford's (4) general framework for CPSs, and then consider to what extent a given CPS measures up to it.

There is, however, very little established high level expertise of what contributes to trust in such a system. It is a highly interpretive notion, highly context dependent and highly volatile in its meaning. Therefore knowledge for such a KB is not ready to hand, and must be generated rather than extracted.

2. Types of Knowledge Generation

When knowledge generation occurs the expert's or user's knowledge is refined and enhanced in such a way that human knowledge increases. Knowledge generation can take place in two ways (5): when using a knowledge based system and when building the knowledge base. Since the ICT KB has not yet been used, this paper discusses the latter. Four types of knowledge generation have been reported.

2.1 Gap-filling

While building an expert system to predict corrosion (6) it was found that during the process of knowledge engineering the expert - a corrosion expert of worldwide renown - would sometimes encounter gaps in his knowledge, which he then filled by performing laboratory experiments. In this way insights gained as a result of the process helped to refine the expert's own knowledge by filling those gaps. Gap filling usually occurs in well established domains like corrosion knowledge; knowledge is probably more refined than generated. An element of this can be found in much knowledge engineering, especially where the domain of knowledge is not well structured.

2.2 Model Contextualisation

Some tasks are not performed routinely, such as crisis management and decision making in emergencies and war time. In such situations, the people who act as knowledge sources might have some general understanding but lack specific experience. There are no experts, and Paul (7) calls such semi-experts 'journs'. He describes the construction of a knowledge base, SARA, by a process of 'knowledge cultivation' which assumes that the existing body of knowledge is incomplete, and proceeds in cycles to build up the knowledge base. Paul calls such domains 'knowledge-poor'.

In these domains the journs often have some model of what should be done, but it lacks detail from the specific context. An important part of the process of knowledge cultivation is therefore the contextualisation of the model by stimulating the journs to consider specific situations (contexts).

2.3 Cognitive Mapping

Strategic group decision making is a third situation in which knowledge generation or refinement is necessary because of knowledge poverty, but the poverty is of a different sort. While many heuristics for decision making are offered by management consultants, each business situation is radically different, as are the participants, so the heuristics often do not apply to any depth and new knowledge has to be developed each time (8).

In these domains a plethora of factors is relevant to the situation, and in each situation a different plethora pertains. So few, if any, real models are available and there is often no previous experience to guide the new situation (or what experience is offered is suspect). A different kind of knowledge base is needed - cognitive maps and influence diagrams (9,10) - which stimulate the participants (often a group) to consider new factors and how they link together in their particular 'plethoric' situation.

2.4 Exploring New Approaches

In the fourth type of knowledge generation, a new knowledge approach is being explored in an established domain. This might occur, for instance, when current practice is being questioned. It is less common than the other types, but was exemplified in the INCA project (2) in which the purpose of the knowledge base was to select clauses for a construction contract. The standard approach to authoring contracts was to make minor amendments to standard forms, but often neither party fully understood the contract and both parties would then seek advantage in an adversarial manner at the end of the construction. The new approach was to author directly from first principles of contract according to what the parties wanted.

When, during knowledge acquisition, the domain experts were asked fundamental questions such as what issues were important in a contract, how to resolve those issues, and how to obtain a balance between the parties to the contract, they could not provide such knowledge, because they seldom considered such questions. What the knowledge engineer was doing was questioning the rationale behind standard procurement methods and standard forms of contract, and little knowledge was available to help him do this.

So the knowledge engineer had to revert to basic principles of the process of procuring a building and of the relationships between actors in the construction process. Once initial principles had been obtained, the knowledge engineer was faced with the tasks of generating knowledge out of those principles, deciding where the links occurred, and generating clausal text for each of the concepts that could be included in contracts. As this progressed, the knowledge itself was frequently refined and modified.

3. The ICT Knowledge Base

3.1 The Domain of Internet Trust

In many ill structured domains, all four of these are present to some extent, but usually one dominates. To build a KB about Internet trust requires some of the fourth type of knowledge generation, but mainly the second type since there is no established body of knowledge and those involved are only 'journs'. Much of what constitutes trust must be worked out from general understanding by considering specific yet hypothetical situations.

3.2 The Istar Software

The Istar software (11) was designed during the INCA project to facilitate the last-mentioned type of knowledge generation: trying a new approach. Its knowledge representation model is reasonably conventional, semantic net with probabilistic inference net, though possessing a rich variety of types of variable. Bayesian variables were the most commonly used in the ICT KB to represent factors that contribute to degree of trust. Each node in the inference net is a variable whose value must be sought from antecedent variables, some of which are questions put to the end user. Variables can either be free variables or attributes of nodes. For an inference session, one or more nodes are designated goals, and a cycle of backward and forward chaining is undertaken until all questions needed to answer the goals have been asked.

Istar's most important characteristic is the highly 'proximal' (3) interface it presents to the knowledge engineer. Donald Norman (12) once remarked,

> "The real problem with the interface is that it is an interface. Interfaces get in the way. I don't want to focus my energies on an interface. I want to focus on the job."

The user interface of Istar was designed to allow the knowledge engineer to "get on with the job", so that using the tool could become an integral part of the thinking process. The knowledge engineer draws knowledge on an 'easel' as a box and arrows diagram to express the nodes and arcs of the inference net, rather than entering it either as text or via dialog boxes. Both boxes and arrows are drawn, moved or redirected, with simple press-drag-release mouse movements, without the cognitive load imposed by point-and-click interfaces and Fitt's Law (13). This made it easy for the user to enter or alter knowledge at the very moment of thinking it, and thus the process of expressing knowledge in new ways became much easier.

Istar was therefore thought to be a good starting point for the ICT project. The technical aim of the project was to investigate, through action research, what features are useful in conceptualizing such knowledge-poor domains and what steps and approaches are useful in knowledge acquisition. We report the findings below.

3.3 Knowledge Base Construction

Knowledge concerning trust is scattered in various forms, including formal documents, books, expert opinion, accepted norms and usages, etc. In our case the main source of knowledge came from a framework document for CPSs (4), supplemented by intense discussions with four partners with expertise in communications security, but who are nevertheless 'journs' as far as trust is concerned. In addition, a small number of international experts were interviewed using a questionnaire devised for the purpose.

Since trustability is the main criterion in the examination of a CPS, we have two goals: **Can Trust** and **Can't Trust**, both Bayesian, whose values are interpreted as indicating the presence of reasons for trusting and distrusting the authenticity of the sending entity. The leaf nodes represent entries in the CA's CPS. Experience has shown that while the absence of some CPS entries or their lax appraisal might signify a lessening of trust and therefore contribute to the **Can't Trust** goal, some safety-related entries would contribute to **Can Trust** though their absence would not necessarily increase **Can't Trust**. As far as possible, the two goals are treated as independent from the point of view of Bayesian inference, and combining them for a final result is carried out by the interpretation of the user. A version of the inference net is shown in Fig. 2, in which inference flows left to right, so that the **Can Trust** and **Can't Trust** goals are shown, respectively, bottom-right and top-right, and the question nodes are all to the left. When the KB is run, a backward chaining cycle starts from the goals to seek unanswered questions, which are then put to the user in sequence. Questions can be grouped into single screen 'forms'.

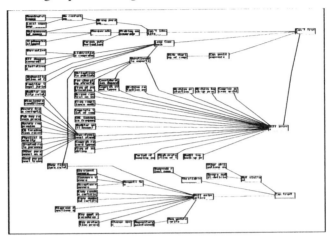

Fig. 2. ICT Inference Net

The result of the assessment of a CA is thus in the form of two scores, each reflecting the degree of affirmation in the two goals. The final judgement, as to whether or not to accept the findings of this particular CA in the current commercial circumstances, is left to the relying party. If there are reasons for both trusting and distrusting, then such reasons are sought by examining the values of other, intermediate, nodes. One advantage of using an inference net is that the syntax of the net matches closely the semantics of the knowledge, so that each node often represents some significant factor in the knowledge domain.

KB construction started in a tentative way, by taking a part of the framework document which would seem to be directly relevant to the trust concept, namely the section on Identification and Authentication, and to consider how this information should be modelled. First instincts suggested that some kind of data structure should be designed to try to capture the kind of details in which the framework document was phrased. This proved quite tricky, largely because the framework does not set out to provide a specific criterion which real CPSs should meet, but to draw the attention of the investigator to areas of certification where a CPS might be weak. For instance, section 4.3.1 of the framework contains a point of concern regarding the

"Authentication requirements for a person acting on behalf of a subject including:
> Number of pieces of identification required;
> How a CA validates the pieces of identification provided;
> If the individual must present personally to the authenticating CA;
> How an individual as an organisational person is authenticated."

Essentially the investigator is being asked various 'how to' questions and satisfactory answers are to be adjudged in the light of other answers. Clearly the number of pieces of identification in itself is hardly indicative of authenticity if they turn out to be easily forged or stolen documents. The 'how to' questions also pose a difficulty in that the total range of responses to the question has to be considered and spelt out, at some stage, in the dialogue. If there is an authentication procedure which is beyond the experience of the KB, then its suitability for trust is problematic.

Rather than proceeding in the direction of a more elaborate data structure, it was decided to initially build a small net involving such identification issues as name forms, uniqueness, use of trademarks and authentication requirements, amongst others. The preliminary KB was then presented to all members of the team who then proceeded to subject it to criticisms, most of which centred at first upon the actual meanings of the concepts involved as they impinged upon this section of the framework. But it was decided that the KB route was a better way to proceed than by building a data structure. At a later stage, once it had been decided which aspects contributed to the **Can't Trust** goal, similarities could be discerned which led to the grouping of the leaf nodes (on the left-hand side on the diagram) into intermediate nodes occupying a more central position. Quite often the corresponding fan-in of inference brought together leaf nodes from separate parts of the framework document. Similar groupings were noted for the **Can Trust** goal.

The change of approach involved a defocusing on the specifics of the framework document and not insisting on a detailed mapping from its contents into the inference diagram. Several problems remain to be ironed out, however. Knowledge about the full range of possibilities that are to be catered for still requires an amount of expert advice, along with the implications of these possibilities as contributing to the goals. One additional software feature which would facilitate this is the 'labelled vertical slider', in which a response could be made on a continuous scale, assisted by various named levels of gradation. Being vertical would enable a considerable amount of text to be displayed alongside each gradation point, to further assist the description of the CPS by the user.

4. Project Findings

The findings of this project are divided into two areas, the first concerned with the knowledge and the acquisition thereof, and the second concerned with software features that facilitate working in knowledge-poor domains.

4.1 Findings Concerning Knowledge and its Acquisition

Effect of Knowledge Source

The type of knowledge source can have a marked effect on the structure of the KB. Working from a hierarchical document like the CPS framework tends to produce a tree-like inference net with only a small number of multiple consequents (Fig. 2). This is because the knowledge is contained within a tightly structured arrangement with a nested hierarchy of sections, paragraphs and subparagraphs. This is unlike the situation in which the knowledge is being elicited from a human expert through interrogation, where one can expect a larger number of cross-linkages and counter argument. The reason is that such documents are often a deliberate simplification of actual expertise for purposes of clarity, memorability or authority. Such simplified expertise alone cannot yield a high quality KB, so it must be 'cultivated' to deeper levels (7) by the knowledge engineer proactively seeking its enrichment through discussion with experts, even when they only 'journs'.

Development of Knowledge Engineer

The knowledge engineer is the recipient of information from a wide variety of knowledge sources, and thus has considerable responsibility for making appropriate interpretations. At the start of the project s/he will usually have only a naïve view of the domain, but in established domains the experts can usually guide such interpretations and gradually the knowledge engineer develops considerable expertise of their own. However, in a domain where expertise has yet to become established this guidance is less effective, and the 'journs' are themselves developing expertise on the fly. Therefore arriving at the most appropriate conceptualization of the domain can take longer - and such conceptualizations often seem obvious in retrospect. An example of this from the ICT project was: the various parties involved were initially lumped together as mere "users" and it took time to recognise that they will have quite different concerns and interests and thus had to be distinguished into relying parties and sending entities.

However, while we may feel happier with a non-tree-like inference topology, closer to the imagined structure of multifacetted human inference, we should be careful of the introduction of the knowledge engineer's views. There are two issues here. One is justification of the knowledge, for instance in a court of law; strict adherence to the knowledge contained in the published work, even though simplified, is easier to justify than a person's interpretation. The other is that discussion with human experts might overly concentrate on particular examples and special cases and thus obscure the true pattern of inference. The broader picture of general inference relationships should be continually brought back into focus.

Structure of the KB

We found the structure of the original inference net was improved by the introduction of intermediate subgoals. This was achieved by taking one of the leafs (framework entry) linked to a goal and asking "Why?" For instance (4) has an entry concerning uniqueness of names, which is deemed relevant to trust. So we ask "Why?" and discover that if two entities with identical trademarks e.g. Apollo, were allowed to use this name as their (non-unique) identifier in a certificate, then genuine confusion between the two certficates could arise, which could lead to either the possibility of sending confidential information to the wrong party. Thus trust in authenticity is lessened.

We also found a "What else?" question useful, both for determining extra antecedents not mentioned by Chokhani and Ford, and also to discern alternate inference paths to the goal. For instance, non-unique names can also make it easier for parties to masquerade as others and, again, trust is lessened.

In this way, using these two questions, which are two of the four questions mentioned by (14), the knowledge from the CPS framework was 'cultivated' (7) and given a more semantic feel. Confidence would be gained by the builder that real understanding was being increased. However, as seen from an interim KB shown in Fig. 2, this process is not complete.

In more complex situations involving choice, it was tempting to set up an enumeration data type to itemise the alternatives available. But it was found that, at least in the initial stages, a close mapping between the entry and such a type was not helpful, because it tended to obscure the inferential patterns being elicited. In the initial stages specific details of type should not be of too much concern. In any case, the particular type of construct to model a certain feature can easily be changed at a later stage, if necessary.

4.2 Findings Concerning KBS Software Features

Since the process of creating knowledge bases in knowledge-poor domains differs from that of assembling knowledge bases in well established domains, we can expect a different set of features in KBS software to be important. Here we identify and discuss what features have been particularly important in the ICT project thus far, not as an authoritative list, but rather to initiate debate.

Surprisingly, few attempts have been made to identify what software features aid knowledge engineering, beyond general statements of the need for such things as expressive power and ease of use. In the proceedings of *Expert Systems '97* not a single paper out of the 39 published had an explicit discussion of this; only (15) moved anywhere near this, listing some features added at the request of the user. This is a notable lack since KBS software should contain features tailored to the process of knowledge engineering as opposed to programming, and it should not be left entirely to the commercial software developers to determine what these features are. It is for this reason that we present an initial, and very incomplete, list of some features that we have found important in handling this kind of knowledge.

Visual Knowledge Representation

As expected, the visual nature of the knowledge representation language proved useful for two purposes, to ease construction and subsequent alteration of the KB, and to gain an holistic view thereof. Istar employs a very simple visual style, even omitting arrows on links and avoiding the display of too much information. As discussed in (16) important information came through tacit conventions like left-to-right inference and through the pattern of links around a box rather than in the explicit symbols. However, one symbolic effect that has proved important in this project was to distinguish visually between links that have a positive effect from those that have a negative one.

The importance of such 'visual cues' in Istar's user interface is one of the issues discussed in (16). Another is the mimimization of cognitive load and the avoidance of interruption of the knowledge engineer's thinking process by carefully 'grading' the load imposed by each operation. We found Istar's user interface appropriate here, though it had been designed for a different type of knowledge generation.

Separate Texts

Because of the importance of human interpretation in ill structured domains of knowledge, Istar offers at least four different texts for each attribute: a label (which is short enough to be displayed in the box representing the node), a meaning (which is a sentence of arbitrary length intended to record precise meanings, and which is shown in a window when the mouse moves over nodes), a question text (which is displayed if the node is put to the user as a question) and explanation text (which augments the question text). The label and meaning texts are shown during KB development and the question and explanation texts during runs with the user. If any text is missing then the next in a defined order of priority is used.

We found that use was made of all four texts, for different purposes. As in the earlier INCA project, the meaning text was important both to force precision in discerning the meaning of each node and also as a record for later use.

We found however that several explanation texts would have been useful during the run because there were several things the user wished to know:

♦ Reference to source document (where appropriate)
♦ Brief statement of what the thing in the question referred to, including its context

♦ Brief statement of what its significance was for the goal
♦ An example.

We found that many of these had to be provided in discussion with experts.

Further, there should perhaps be two versions of some of these texts, one for knowledge-poor experts and one for ignorant users. How to expand Istar to accommodate these is being considered. Cawsey (17) discusses a variety of explanations, differentiating them along three dimensions of role, content and type.

Seeing the Consequence of Questions

In a large, complex inference net, it has proved useful to display parts of the inference net, leaving the remainder hidden, especially the network of antecedents or consequents of a given node. Because for Istar inference takes the form of graph search rather than rule-firing, it has proved relatively easy to implement such facilities, and a second button was added to the user question panel which, when hit, displayed the entire consequent net of the current question. In this way, a display was given of the significance of the current question node in terms of what other nodes it influences, whether directly or indirectly. This feature was particularly impressive during demonstrations.

Exploring the Result

In addition to giving a visual representation to inference, the Istar easel can also be thought of as a guide to giving a reasoned analysis to a result: "Why has this particular goal value resulted in this case?" This type of question can be answered, at least partially, by Istar's facility to show the antecedent net of any node, backtracking along the inference path which led to it and displaying what it finds. However, the facility needs to be made more sophisticated, to indicate the degree and direction that each leaf has on the value of the goal and hence on the degree of trust.

Modifying the KB During Run

During development, four main kinds of modifications to the KBS were encountered: to types and weights, to topological structure, to texts and to the sequence in which questions were put to the user. Few changes to numeric weights were made during the early stages of development, while the structure of the KB was being developed.

Many changes were motivated by demonstrating the KBS inference session to 'tame' experts. We found that what raised most discussion was not the results produced so much as the wording of the questions and of explanation texts. This agrees with the highly interpretive nature of the meaning of trust, in that the running of the KB stimulated the emergence of a variety of interpretations of each question as it appeared. Such discussion led, in the main, to changing of question and explanation texts, less commonly, to label and meaning texts, and occasionally to altering the local structure of the inference net or the type or weight of an node.

We found that it was essential to be able to make the alterations immediately they were suggested, so that ideas are not forgotten or distorted. To do this, without aborting the run, requires the KBS software to be multi-threaded in nature and robust against changes in KB structure. Istar possessed both of these qualities, so that a button could be added to the user question panel to allow access to the KB details and structure, and this new feature was frequently made use of.

Inverting the Meaning

An operation we found was commonly required was to invert the meaning of a node and therefore, with it, of each of its links, as shown in Fig. 3. This was often because the original meaning had been a double negative, which could confuse, so, during discussion, it was decided to reverse its meaning. This involves not only changing the various texts, but also modifying each arc, antecedent and consequent, of the node. At the symbol level at which most KBS software operates this is a cumbersome process and error-prone, but at the knowledge level it is an atomic operation. Therefore it deserves to be made a simple, single-button, action in KBS software.

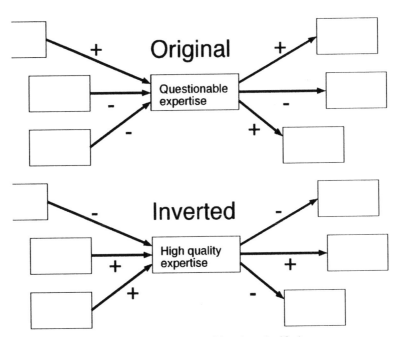

Fig. 3. Inverting the Meaning of a Node

5. Conclusions

Paul (7) and others have discussed 'knowledge-poor' domains, in which there are no true experts because real expertise has yet to build up. Creating a knowledge base for such domains takes the form of knowledge generation, rather than mere acquisition. This paper identifies four types of knowledge generation - gap-filling, model conceptualization, cognitive mapping and exploring new approaches in existing practice. In most of these, the very nature of knowledge engineering changes from what Winograd (18) calls a 'constructor's-eye-view' to a 'designer's-eye-view', and this has significant implications for both techniques and KBS software.

This paper generalises the findings from an attempt to build a knowledge base to calculate trustworthiness of the authenticity of Internet information. The project demonstrated some of the characteristics of knowledge-poor domains, especially of the second type, and the need for techniques tailored to knowledge generation. Not only is there no established body of expertise, but Internet trust is a highly interpretive notion, very context dependent and volatile in its meaning. The knowledge engineer might work from documents, but finds these simplified, or might engage experts in discussion, but finds they are only 'journs' as far as this issue is concerned. So to construct a good knowledge base needs special techniques.

KB construction is no longer a linear sequential activity, but more of a cyclical, continuous process in which both knowledge engineer and experts progress through learning cycles stimulated by the cooperative activity of building the KB. Two questions were found of particular value in this process, "Why?" and "What else?" In such domains one can expect each piece of knowledge to be reinterpreted at least once if not several times during KB construction and thus to be subject to modification of both its weights and its semantic structure.

To support such a fluid, iterative, unpredictable process the KBS software must become 'proximally' (3) part of the knowledge engineer, so that it does not interrupt the flow of thinking and reinterpretation and so that it makes it as easy as possible for the structure of the inference net to accurately reflect the structure of the relevant knowledge. Surprisingly, few have commented on what features should be provided in KBS software to meet the requirements of such knowledge engineering, but we have found the following to be important:

a) The main medium for both building and understanding the KB should be visual, so that the KB is 'drawn' (in the form of a diagram of nodes and arcs) rather than programmed.

b) The style of user interface is crucially important, as it must reduce to a minimum the cognitive load on the user, especially when knowledge is changed; as discussed in (16), conventional point-and-click styles of user interface are deeply flawed and new 'proximal' styles must be devised.

c) Unlike programming or traditional knowledge representation, where expressive power is of prime importance, and syntactic and semantic constraints are applied in the hope of reducing the incidence of programming errors, in this kind of knowledge engineering constraints must be kept to a minimum and expressive power is less important than flexibility.

d) The phases of building and running the KB are merged, and it must be possible to explore and even modify the KB during the run - that is, as soon as the participants make a reinterpretation. To modify inference structure during a run demands a special robustness of the software! A variety of explanations is needed for exploration, especially toplogical searches.

More work is needed. Fig. 2 shows certain nodes with high fan-in, which indicates intermediate nodes might be missing; so methods must be found to identify them. Special inference procedures may be needed, and ways to control more precisely the order in which questions are asked. And we intend to allow the KBS software to seek input from across the Internet as well as from the user, and so the inference cycle must be made asynchronous. The project continues.

Acknowledgements

We wish to thank Steve McGibbon (Lotus Developments) and Tim Dean (DERA) for their input during discussions of the knowledge base. This project is funded by the EPSRC under grant number GR/L 54295.

References

1. COLLINS H.M. The TEA-Set: Tacit knowledge and scientific networks, Science Studies, 1974, v.4, pp. 165-186.
2. BASDEN A., HIBBERD P.R. User interface issues raised by knowledge refinement, International Journal of Human Computer Studies, 1996, v.45, pp.135-155.
3. POLANYI M. The Tacit Dimension, 1967, (Routledge and Kegan Paul).
4. CHOKHANI S., FORD W. Internet Public Key Infrastructure, Part IV: Certificate who wizardPolicy and Certification Practices Framework, an Internet-draft of the Internet Engineering Task force, July 1997.
5. BASDEN, A. On the application of Expert Systems, International Journal of Man-Machine Studies, 1983, v.19, pp.461-477.
6. HINES J.G., BASDEN A. Experience with the use of computers to handle corrosion knowledge, British Corrosion Journal, 1986, Vol.21, n.3, pp.151-156.
7. PAUL J. Building expert systems for knowledge-poor domains, in Bramer M.A., Macintosh A.I. (eds.), Research and Development in Expert Systems, X, 1993, (IEE BHR Group, London), pp.223-234.
8. EDEN, C. Perish the Thought, Journal of the Operational Research Society, 1985, v.36(9), pp.809-819.

9. MOORE E.A., AGOGINO A.M. INFORM: an architecture for expert-directed knowledge acquisition, International Journal of Man-Machine Studies, 1987, Vol.26, pp.213-230.

10. EDEN C. Using cognitive mapping for strategic options development and analysis (SODA), in Rosenhead J. (ed.), Rational analysis for a problematic world: problem structuring methods for complexity, uncertainty and conflict, 1989, (John Wiley, Chichester, UK).

11. BASDEN, A., BROWN, A.J. Istar - a tool for creative design of knowledge bases, Expert Systems, 1996, v.13(4), pp.259-276.

12. NORMAN, D.A. Why interfaces don't work, in Laurel B (ed.), The Art of Human-Computer Interface Design, 1990, (Addison-Wesley), pp.209-219.

13. CARD S.K., MORAN T.P., NEWELL A. The Psychology of Human-Computer Interaction, 1983, (Lawrence Erlbaum Associates, Hillsdale, NJ, USA).

14. BASDEN, A., WATSON, I.D., BRANDON, P.S., Client Centred: an approach to developing knowledge based systems, 1995, (Council for the Central Laboratory of the Research Councils, UK).

15. SUGDEN, R.C., HUME, S.J., Developing a common knowledge authoring tool for heterogeneous target systems in the PRODIGY project, in Macintosh A, Milne R (eds.), Applications and Innovations in Expert Systems V, 1997, (SGES Press, ISBN 1 899621 19 9), pp.71-82.

16. BASDEN A., BROWN A.J., TETLOW S.D.A., HIBBERD P.R. The design of a user interface for a knowledge generation tool, International Journal of Human Computer Studies, 1996, v.45, pp.157-183.

17. CAWSEY, A. Explanation and Interaction: The Computer Generation of Explanatory Dialogues, 1992, (Bradford Books, MIT Press, London, UK).

18. WINOGRAD, T. From programming environments to environments for designing, Communications of the ACM, 1995, v.38(6), pp.65-74.

SESSION 3: CLASSIFIERS

Pruning Boosted Classifiers with a Real Valued Genetic Algorithm

Simon Thompson[1]
University of Portsmouth

Abstract

Ensemble classifiers and algorithms for learning ensembles have recently received a great deal of attention in the machine learning literature because of their perceived advantages [1],[2],[3],[4],[5],[6]. In particular boosting has received a great deal of attention as a mechanism by which an ensemble of classifiers that has a better generalisation characteristic than any single classifier that can be discovered. In this paper we examine and compare a number of techniques for pruning a classifier ensemble which is overfit on its training set and find that a real valued GA is at least as good as the best heuristic search algorithm for choosing an ensemble weighting.

1. Introduction

Ensemble learning systems such as boosting [1] are able to improve the generalisation ability of machine learning algorithms [5]. Unfortunately, it is our experience that they tend to suffer from over-fitting. That is, that for a number of iterations the ensemble exhibits improved generalistion properties but then, with the addition of extra members of the ensemble, generalisation accuracy declines often falling below the generalisation accuracy of the initial member of the ensemble. Other authors have also reported this behaviour [4],[7].

Clearly such properties are undesirable in a machine learning algorithm, and must be addressed before we are able to use them to construct a practical learning and classification system. Although it might be possible for an experienced investigator to tune their algorithm in such a way that a crash of this sort becomes unlikely for a particular data-set it would be better if a practical algorithm or heuristic could be found that could be automatically applied.

However, given an ensemble of classifiers to be combined using a weighted majority vote which exhibit crashing characteristics (ie. there is a subset of classifiers which have a better combined generalisation performance than the whole ensemble) there

---

[1]Email:sgt@sis.port.ac.uk

must be a set of weightings that perform as least as well as the weightings for the best subset.

A trivial proof of this is:

Consider x classifiers combined in a weighted majority vote to give a generalisation accuracy of α

if there exist $y \subset x$ which can be combined to give a generalisation accuracy of χ

and $\chi > \alpha$ then the classifiers in x can be combined under a weighted majority vote to form a classifier with generalisation accuracy χ simply by weighting the classifiers in x that are not present in y with 0

2. Related work

There are two papers on pruning classifier ensembles in the public domain.

In [8] Prodromidis et al present methods for pruning classifiers in a distributed meta-learning system. They select a subset of classifiers from an ensemble which are then combined by a meta-learned combiner (see [9] for details of meta-learning). They call their technique *pre-training pruning*. They evaluate two different methods of doing this, choosing a diverse set of classifiers and choosing a set based on the coverage of the base classifiers across a hold-out set (they used 3 different ways of doing this, looking at true positives - false positives, a cost model adjusted heuristic and a combined class speciality metric)

Pre-training pruning appears to give good results, allowing a significant reduction in the size of the ensemble to be meta-learned, and therefore achieving the goals of reduced learning time and increased classification throughput that Prodromidis etal set in their paper. Diversity based pre-training pruning is reported to give better results than the coverage based heuristics.

In [7] Margineantu and Deitterich introduce a number of pruning heuristics for pruning a boosted classifier. They examine the effects of *early-stopping, kl-divergence pruning, kappa pruning, kappa convex hull pruning* and *reduced-error pruning with backfitting*. They compare the performance of these methods over ten data-sets, and find that the kappa pruning and reduced-error-with-backfitting pruning perform best (they also find good results for kappa convex hull pruning, but reject it because it requires a set size for the pruned ensemble).

3. Approach

We decided to investigate the performance of the algorithms from the literature over ensembles of classifiers learned by a boosting algorithm using C4.5 as the base classifier. We found that many of these classifiers are overfit on the training data that they are derived from so that if ensemble members were removed a better generalisation performance would result.

Both the attempts to prune ensembles of classifiers that we have found in the literature find that diversity based methods appear successful at selecting the constituents of the ensemble (kappa pruning algorithm is based on the kappa statistic κ measure of disagreement between classifiers). Margineantu and Deitterich also conclude that backfitting is an effective method. Because of this we decided to investigate and compare the two methods.

3.1 Backfitting

Margineantu & Dietterich's describe a backfitting algorithm. This involves choosing an additional classifier to add to a set of classifiers by a greedy search and then checking that the each of the other classifiers in the set cannot be replaced by another classifier to produce a better ensemble, this process is known as the backfitting step. The backfitting algorithm used by Margineantu & Dietterich has an interesting starting mechanism

To quote:

"Backfitting proceeds as follows. Like a simple greedy algorithm, it is a procedure for constructing a set of U classifiers by growing U one classifiers at a time. The first two steps are identical to the greedy algorithm. We initialise U to contain the one classifier h_i that has the lowest error in the test set"..."We then add the classifier h_j such that the voted combination of h_i and h_j has the lowest pruning set error" [7] (our underscore).

Underscored is an interesting feature of this algorithm. There are three possible cases when choosing the second classifier in this way. In the first case the classifier h_j has a higher weight than the weight of the most accurate classifier h_i. So $w_i < w_h$. In the second case the weightings are reversed $w_i > w_h$, finally we have the case $w_i = w_h$ (in fact in our experiments we have observed that $w_i \neq w_h$ is almost always true). In case one $h_{i,j}$ the weighted vote of h_i and h_j will always be identical to h_j because h_j will always outvote h_i, In case two the vote will produce results identical to h_i , and in case 3 the vote will be no more accurate than h_i as the best classifier would be to choose h_i when there is disagreement, as h_i is right more often than h_j

Thus we can see that the second step in the give algorithm will always lead to an *arbitrary* choice being made between all the classifiers that have a lower weight than w_i. All the classifiers with a higher weight will be rejected because their votes with h_i will be less good than *any* of the votes made by a $h_{i,j}$ where w_j is lower than w_i.

The algorithm then proceeds by adding another classifier h_k to the ensemble, such that $h_{i,j,k}$ out-performs any other combination of $h_{i,j}$ and h_x where h_x is any other classifier in the ensemble. In order for $h_{i,j,k}$ to be better than h_i $w_i < w_j + w_k$ must hold. This gives h_j and h_k the chance to gang up on h_i and out vote it. This condition can be likened to a hung-parliament in a parliamentary political systen where no party holds an absolute majority.

We can write down some inequalities that must be true if $\alpha_{i,j,k} > \alpha_{i,j}$ where α_n is the accuracy of the classifier h_n over the pruning set, p_s. Given that h_ϕ is the omniscient "god" classifier - ie. it is always right

$$w_j + w_k > w_i \tag{1}^2$$

$$\wedge\ h_\phi(x) = h_j(x) = h_k(x) \neq h_i(x)\ \exists\ x \in p_s \tag{2}^3$$

$$\wedge\ (((h_\phi(x) = h_i(x) = h_k(x)) \vee (h_\phi(x) = h_i(x) = h_j(x)) \forall\ h_\phi(x) = h_i(x)) \tag{3}^4$$

$$\vee\ (\alpha'_{j,k} > \varepsilon'\ )) \tag{4}$$

Where α'_n is the accuracy of a classifier over the set where $h_\phi(x) \neq h_i(x)$ and ε' is the error caused by $h_\phi(x) = h_i(x)$ but $h_\phi(x) \neq h_j(x) = h_k(x)$. (4) states h_j and h_k give a greater advantage over the part of the test set where h_i is wrong than the disadvantage that they generate by voting together incorrectly.

The two venn-diagrams in Figure 1 illustrates the situations where the classifier $h_{i,j,k}$ will out perform $h_{i,j}$

It can be seen that the algorithm presented by Margineantu & Dietterich can find such a region. But since h_j has been chosen arbitrarily from the set of classifiers with a lower weight than h_i it is less likely that the optimal $h_{i,j,k}$ will be found. Even worse than that, because the classifier h_k was chosen with respect to $h_{i,j}$ it is likely that although the backfitting step will remove h_j in favour of a classifier that works better with h_k and h_i we still will not have the optimal set of three classifiers. In order to overcome this difficulty we developed an alternative algorithm that should be tested in conjunction with the algorithm discussed above.

In our variation is as follows:
1. Select the most accurate h_i on the pruning set
2. Select h_j and h_k the optimal pair of classifiers when combined with h_i to form $h_{i,j,k}$
3. Iteratively attempt to find the optimal classifier to add to the ensemble and then backfit on the other members of the ensemble until a certain number of iterations has been made or no improvement in accuracy is achieved.

An alternative would have been to search for the optimal first 3 classifiers in the ensemble, but this is an unacceptably computationally intensive procedure. For our experiments we were searching over ensembles of $m = 50$ classifiers, for our algorithm we were required to check $(m-1.m-1)-(m-1)$ or 2352 combinations of classifiers, if we had tried to find the optimal first 3 directly we would have to have checked $m^3 - 3(m-1)$ or 124853 combinations of the ensemble.

---

[2] or h_k and h_j can never out vote h_i

[3] h_j and h_k must be right when h_i is wrong at least for one example in the pruning set

[4] h_i and h_j must agree, or h_i and h_k must agree for all the occasions where h_i is right.

One of h_j and h_k always votes with h_i when it is correct, but they have regions which don' t overlap with h_i which they out vote it on and where they are correct (indicated with arrows)

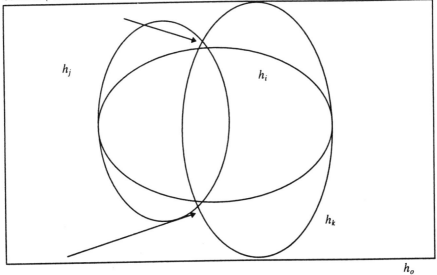

The region where h_i is correct, but is outvoted is smaller than the region where h_j and h_k are both correct and h_i is not.

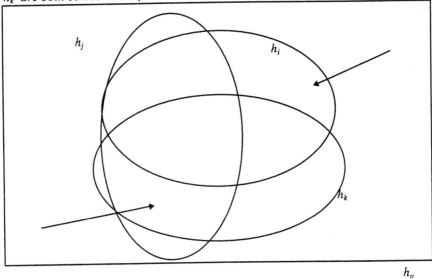

Figure 1. the scenarios in which $h_{i,j,k}$ can be better than $h_{i,j}$

3.2 Diversity

We implemented a diversity based metric to discover how well it would prune the ensemble. The algorithm we used is :
1. Select h_i, the most accurate classifier on the pruning set.
2. Select h_k the most different classifier available from the classifier pool from h_{meta} the current ensemble.
3. Repeat 2 until the maximum number of iterations

Notice in this algorithm there is no early stopping condition. This is because we found that if we allowed the algorithm to stop when no further improvement was being made it suffered from the same sort of problems as the backfitting algorithms that we discussed in the previous section. Also, because pathologically different members of the ensemble are chosen initially the new ensemble performs very badly. We set the number of classifiers permitted to have non-0 weights in the optimised ensemble to 40, which is 80% of the total which was the figure reported by Margineantu & Dietterich to be most effective with this method. We anticipated that this approach would work well on the ensembles that did not exhibit strong overfitting, but poorly on the badly overfit ensembles, because these tended to produce a number of poor classifiers that would be very different from the most accurate classifier and would tend to be included in the ensemble for that reason.

3.3 The Genetic Algorithm.

We implemented a real-valued GA [10] to attempt to optimise the weights for the classifier.

There were two reasons why we thought that a real-valued GA could be useful for this purpose.

1) We are dealing with a set of real numbers that is too large (approximately 50 members) to be exhaustively searched.

2) A low cost fitness function can be developed for this task.

3.3.1 Genetic Algorithms, a short overview

Genetic Algorithms are a class of iterative parallel search procedures [11]. They were inspired by the process of natural selection in Evolution, but do not model it particularly closely, for instance most GA's implement only one string of genetic material as the information carrier from generation to generation while most natural systems implement a two string, or diploid approach. This means that most GA's do not model in any way the action of dominance of genes in gene pairs on evolution.

In recent years it has been reported that GA's or similar algorithms have performed better than any other algorithm for a number of significant problems which have previously been the subject of considerable research attempting to develop other more traditional solutions. It has also been reported that some new problems appear to be tractable to GA's where no alternative mechanism has yet been developed.

The generic genetic, or evolutionary algorithm [12] is:

1) Initialise a population of examples in some way. For instance generate a set of hypothesis at random.

2) Assess the utility of the hypothesis against some "fitness function" which measures how well (or badly) a hypothesis solves your problem. For instance calculate the amount of material required to make a number of garments if the layout pattern represented by a particular hypothesis is used.

3) Select a subset of hypothesis which will be used to generate the next population

4) Generate the next population using the selected hypothesis. Selected hypothesis are "crossed over" and "mutated" to generate new hypothesis. In practice cross-over is done by mixing some of the values representing each of the parent hypothesis to form a new set of values, and mutation by varying values in the new hypothesis at random.

5) Repeat 2 to 4 until some stopping condition is reached. For instance repeat 50 times, or until a solution that scores 100% emerges.

There are a large number of variations on this generic algorithm, for an authoritative survey on the subject the reader is directed to "A Genetic Algorithm Tutorial" [13].

3.3.2 The Real-Valued GA for Ensemble weighting optimisation

We developed a GA to optimise the weightings of the ensemble classifiers we have developed. The basic scheme that we used is shown in Figure 2 below. We used a real-valued GA [11] to optimise the weights of the ensemble of classifiers. This can be done efficiently because we can obtain the classifications made by each of the members of the ensemble on the items of data in a hold-out set (a partition of the nodes training set reserved for this purpose), and then estimate the utility of the weightings by just calculating the weighted majority vote using the evolved weights and the stored classifications. The algorithm we developed is as follows:

1) Generate a population of strings of floating point numbers of length n using the weights estimated during re-sampling as a seed, or just at random where n is the number of classifiers in the ensemble

2) Obtain the classifications for all items in the hold-out set given by all n of the classifiers in the ensemble. Store these results.

3) Estimate the generalisation accuracy for the meta-classifier generated by the weighted majority vote of the classifiers using each of the sets of weights represented by the individuals in the population, and the stored classifications.

4) Use a tournament selection procedure to generate new individuals, estimate the generalisation for each individual as it is generated and only introduce it into the population if it has better fitness than one of its parents. Mutate the new individuals by adding a floating point number generated by a Gaussian random number generator (the return value of a call to the java.util.Random nextGaussian() function is divided by 20 and added to the current value. If the result is negative then it is subtracted from 0 to make a positive). Repeat this until $(n \cdot m)$ individuals have been generated where n is the number of individuals in the initial population and m is a number representing the number of "generations" that we are willing to run (and therefore the computation time we are willing to expend on this procedure).

In the parlance of the evolutionary algorithms research community this is a steady-state real-valued GA that uses two-point cross-over and tournament selection, with the original population seeded by a pre-existing solution generated by conventional methods.

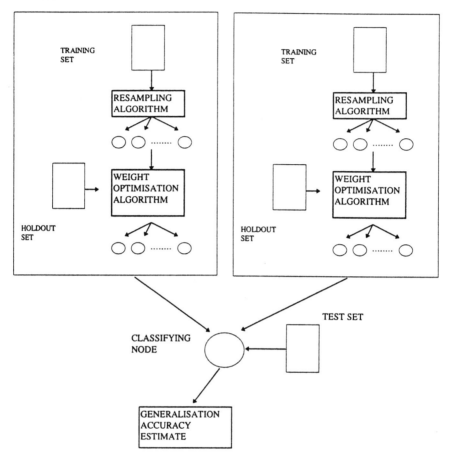

Figure 2. A scheme for optimising ensemble weights using a G.A.

We implemented two variations on this theme.

Our first variation that we have called randInit is as above, except that rather than use the weights that are given by the boosting algorithm it generates a set of starting weights using a pseudo-random number generator.

The second variation that we called newMute is identical to our original algorithm but it uses a different mutation heuristic. This works by simply switching off a member of the ensemble by setting its voting weight to 0.

4. Experimental Work

We conducted a number of experiments to compare the performances of the pruning algorithms on datasets drawn from the UCI repository [14].

Our setup was as follows. We first split each data-set into four cross-validation sets using 75/25 training test splits. Then we derived eight sub-training sets from each of the training sets. Each of the sub-training sets was then used as the input to a boosting classifier using the Ada-Boost algorithm developed by Freund and Shapire [5]. Each booster was run for 50 iterations producing 50 ensemble members.

We combined the ensembles in two different ways. Using the weighted vote by boosted hypothesis (WVBH) rule we calculated the weights of the classifiers on each node that had voted for the majority class. These were then used as the basis for a weighted majority vote of the boosted classifiers. Using the single weighted majority gate (SWMG) rule we combined the votes of all the ensemble members generated from all the subsets using a simple weighted majority vote.

In table 1-6 we give the results for the performances of the classifier ensembles after pruning. In the column best we have record the best performance of an ensemble derived from one of the sub-training sets. In the column worst we have recorded the worst performance of an ensemble derived from one of the sub-training sets. In the column labelled ave the average performance of the sub-training set is given, and their standard deviation is given in SD. The performance of the meta-classifiers created by voting over all the classifier ensembles generated from a particular training set is given in SWMG and WVBH. All results are given as an advantage over results obtained from four fold cross validation of C4.5.

diversity						
	Best	Worst	AVE	SD	SWMG	WVBH
letter	4.14	-49.29	-37.61	16.38	4.64	-8.6
adult	0	-0.46	-0.29	0.14	0.11	0.07
satimage	0	-52.63	-37.93	8.97	1.19	-16.01
nursery	6.36	-53.87	-28.05	18.27	-6.42	-17.55
car	10.44	2.55	5.98	2.06	8.12	7.66
mushroom	0	-52.12	-25.03	21.41	8.53	-27.3
splice	0	-23.95	-16.09	6.43	-2.86	-8.29
waveform	0	-13.21	-10.91	2.95	9.52	2.8
musk	0	-32.65	-9.8	8.68	-4.25	-5.76
yeast	3.7	0.72	1.84	0.97	2.34	3.7

Table 1 generalisation advantage of ensembles pruned using the diversity based algorithm

randInit					
	Best	Worst	AVE	SD	SWMG	WVBH
letter	5.34	-0.4	1.61	1.59	5.82	5.57
adult	0	-0.61	-0.33	0.19	0.18	0.04
satimage	5.19	1.69	2.89	1.16	4.59	4.34
nursery	0	-20.53	-9.81	4.07	-7.71	-7.75
car	10.21	5.34	6.64	1.59	6.73	6.73
mushroom	20.97	5.14	14.54	4.2	14.19	14.14
splice	0.16	-2.48	-0.92	0.86	1.17	0.92
waveform	7.76	4.56	5.74	0.99	10.48	9.36
musk	0	-2.92	-1.95	0.48	-0.93	-1.23
yeast	3.15	-1.16	0.89	1.27	2.61	2.61

Table 2 generalisation advantage of pruning using the randInit G.A. (see Section 3.3.2)

new_mute					
	Best	Worst	AVE	SD	SWMG	WVBH
letter	5.67	-82.14	-67.37	27.69	2.77	-31.86
adult	0	-0.45	-0.23	0.14	0.17	0.15
satimage	0	-63.34	-53.57	10.02	-0.1	-32.67
nursery	0	-53.87	-37.91	16.19	-6.88	-23.44
car	9.75	0.23	6.03	2.52	7.89	7.66
mushroom	0	-52.12	-42.16	17.81	-20.47	-52.17
splice	0.29	-36.07	-12.76	10.93	-3.24	-4.37
waveform	3.2	-42.43	-28.78	18.21	5.6	-12.32
musk	0	-11.8	-10.91	1.22	-8.84	-11.68
yeast	4.24	0.45	1.74	1.13	2.61	2.61

Table 3 generalisation advantage of pruning using the new_mute G.A. (see section 3.3.2)

margineantu					
	Best	Worst	AVE	SD	SWMG	WVBH
letter	0	-82.37	-25.85	32.63	2.12	2.44
adult	0	-2.23	-1.34	0.48	0.0	-0.06
satimage	4.09	-0.85	1.18	1.71	5.79	5.79
nursery	0	-38.64	-16.3	12.9	-8.27	-8.31
car	6.03	3.02	4.61	1.15	5.34	5.34
mushroom	12.3	5.14	7.12	2.14	5.9	5.85
splice	0	-69.65	-19.49	28.97	0.03	0.16
waveform	4.4	-4	-1.03	2.28	7.28	6.48
musk	0	-11.8	-3.38	3.22	0.21	0.15
yeast	0	-7.38	-4.98	1.48	1.26	0.72

Table 4 generalisation advantage of ensembles pruned using the algorithm given in [7]

new-backfit						
	Best	Worst	AVE	SD	SWMG	WVBH
letter	4.94	-7.53	-4.06	4.08	6.04	5.72
adult	0	-1.64	-1.22	0.23	0.14	-0.03
satimage	3.64	-1.2	0.46	1.6	5.39	5.39
nursery	0	-38.64	-12.19	9.99	-8.07	-8.07
car	8.35	2.55	5.34	1.86	7.19	7.19
mushroom	12.3	5.9	8.63	2.89	5.9	5.85
splice	0	-5.89	-2.58	1.86	0.67	0.79
waveform	6.32	-2.24	2.84	2.92	9.76	8.8
musk	0	-11.8	-3.01	3.48	0.75	0.57
yeast	0	-4.67	-3.29	0.97	1.8	1.53

Table 5 generalisation advantage of pruning with the backfitting algorithm (see Section 3.1)

genetic						
	Best	Worst	AVE	SD	SWMG	WVBH
letter	5.69	-77.84	-8.81	26.15	5.97	5.37
adult	3.52	-1.88	2.35	1.65	2.86	3.03
satimage	4.44	-63.34	-51.84	21.44	-0.3	-41.12
nursery	0	-53.87	-38.06	15.91	-6.46	-23.44
car	9.05	5.57	6.64	1.08	8.35	7.89
mushroom	8.91	-52.12	-33.4	25.52	-3.51	-52.17
splice	0.54	-3.36	-2.07	1.19	0.41	-0.08
waveform	7.44	2	4.03	1.57	9.92	9.12
musk	0	-26.91	-9.69	7.31	-4.25	-5.04
yeast	4.24	0.72	1.77	1.15	2.88	2.07

Table 6 generalisation advantage of ensembles pruned using an optimising genetic algorithm that takes the ensemble weights estimated by ADA-BOOST as a starting point for search.

The results of these experiments summarised in Table 7 below. As well as showing the results for each of the pruning algorithms over the SWMG combination rule we have included a column "best" which gives the cross-validated results for the highest observed generalisation rates obtained by the SWMG classifiers before they over-fitted, in other words the advantage that would be obtained if the booster was stopped after it produced the last classifier that did not reduce the ensembles generalisation abilities. The column "unpruned" shows the relative performance of the boosting algorithms after 50 iterations of boosting.

We have highlighted results that show an improvement.

Data-set	diversity	randInit	newMute	margineantu
letter	4.64	5.82	2.77	2.12
adult	0.11	0.18	0.17	0.0
satimage	1.19	4.59	-0.1	5.79
nursery	-6.42	-7.71	-6.88	-8.27
car	8.12	6.73	7.89	5.34
mushroom	8.53	14.19	-20.47	5.9
splice	-2.86	1.17	-3.24	0.03
waveform	9.52	10.48	5.6	7.28
musk	-4.25	-0.93	-8.84	0.21
yeast	2.34	2.61	2.61	1.26
	newbackfit	genetic	Unpruned	Best
letter	6.04	5.97	1.7	6.17
adult	0.14	2.86	0.09	0.17
satimage	5.39	-0.3	2.84	4.43
nursery	-8.07	-6.46	-6.46	-6.49
car	7.19	8.35	0.61	1.85
mushroom	5.9	-3.51	-8.04	14.18
splice	0.67	0.41	-1.35	0.91
waveform	9.76	9.92	6.96	11.13
musk	0.75	-4.25	-7.09	0.94
yeast	1.8	2.88	2.62	3.43

Table 7 advantage (%) over C4.5 of pruned meta-classifiers using SWMG combination rule.

Figure 3 is a histogram of the average improvement given by each method over C4.5.

5. Discussion

In this section we will attempt to draw some conclusions from the results shown in table 7.

Our first conclusion is that these results confirm the results of previous investigators and show that it is possible to prune ensemble of classifiers.

Secondly we note that the pruning algorithm that worked best was the randomly initialised GA, in fact it did almost as well as early stopping ("best"). This was a major surprise to us, because it was our hypothesis based on our previous knowledge of GA's that the GA which had its population initialised from the weights estimated by the boosting algorithm would out-perform the randomly initialised one.

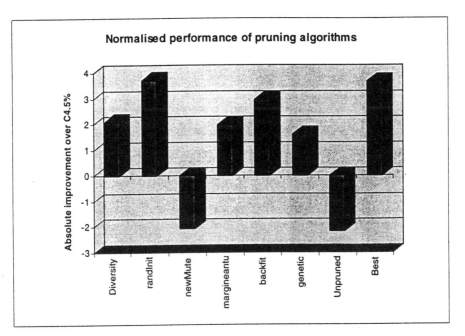

Figure 3. The comparative performance of the pruning methods tried normalised over the 10 datasets.

This behaviour could be explained if the weights that are estimated by the boosting algorithm are in a different local minima in the search space from the global minima. Looking again at table 7 makes us suspicious that this is in fact what is going on. None of the algorithms achieves the best accuracy for all data-sets making us think that their are many different local minima across this search space.

The third conclusion that we draw is that our variation on the backfitting procedure given by Margineantu & Dietterich is superior on the letter, splice, waveform, musk, yeast car and (marginally) adult datasets and inferior on the satimage data-set. We expected that this would be the case, but it is worth noting that our procedure is more computationally intensive than theirs.

In terms of computational cost the backfitting procedures seem to be slightly more efficient than the GA's. We used a population size of 100 for 50 generations or about 5000 calls to the objective function for both of the GA's, but they generally converged and terminated at about 25 generations. The backfitting procedures typically terminated after approximately 15 iterations, since they made approximately 100 calls to the objective function per- iteration as did the GA this would appear to be more efficient. However, the initial search for the new-backfitting procedure requires approximately 2500 calls to the objective function for a 50 member ensemble making it some-what less efficient than the GA.

6. References

1. Shapire,R.E. "The Strength of Weak Learnability" *Machine Learning,* 1990 5(2): pp 197-227

2. Cesa-Bianchi,N., Freund,Y., Haussler,D., Helbold, D.P. Schapire,R.E. & Warmuth, M.K. "How to use Expert Advice" In: *Proceedings of the Twentyfifth Annual ACM Symposium on the Theory of Computing*, 1993, pp 382-391

3. Breiman, L. "Bias, Variance and Arcing Classifiers". Technical Report 460, Statistics Department, University of California, Berkeley, CA., 1996

4. Quinlan J.R. "Boosting First Order Learning" *Proceedings of the 14th International Conference on Machine Learning,* Italy 1997

5. Freund, Y. and Schapire, R.E. "Experimenting with a New Boosting Algorithm" *In: Proceedings of the Thirteenth International Conference on Machine Learning ICML96.* Bari, Italy, July 3-6 1996 pp148-157

6. Sharkey, A.J.C. and Sharkey, N.E, "Combining diverse neural nets", *The Knowledge Engineering Review,* 1997, 12:3, pp231-247

7. Margineantu, D.D. & Dietterich, T.G. "Pruning Adaptive Boosting" In: ICML-97: *Proceedings of the Fourteenth International Conference on Machine Learning.* 1997, San-Franciso, CA. Morgan Kaufmann

8. Prodromidis, A.L., Stolfo,S. & Chan, P.K. "Pruning Classifiers in a Distributed Learning System" Pre-print of paper submitted to KDD-98.

9. Chan,P. & Stolfo,S.J. "Shared Learned Models among Remote Database Partitions by Local Meta-Learning", *Proc. Second Intl. Conf. On Knowledge Discovery and Data Mining*, 1996, pp2-7

10. Wright, A.W. "Genetic Algorithms for real-parameter optimization", In Rawlings, R.E. (ed) *Foundations of Genetic Algorithms*, 1990, pp 205 -220, Morgan-Kaufmann

11. Goldberg, D.E. "Genetic Algorithms for Search, Optimisation and Machine Learning", Addison-Wesley Publishing Company Inc, 1989

12. Greffenstette J.J. "Deception considered harmful" In: Whitley,D. (ed) *Foundations of Genetic Algorithms 2* ,1991, pp 75-91, Morgan-Kaufmann

13. Whiltey, D "A Genetic Algorithm Tutorial", *Statistics and Computing,* 1994, 4, pp 65-85, 1994

14. Merz, C.J., & Murphy, P.M. UCI Repository of machine learning databases [http://www.ics.uci.edu/~mlearn/MLRepository.html]. Irvine, CA: University of California, Department of Information and Computer Science, 1998.

On Rule Interestingness Measures

Alex A. Freitas

CEFET-PR (Federal Center of Technological Education), DAINF
Av. Sete de Setembro, 3165. Curitiba - PR, 80230-901, Brazil
alex@dainf.cefetpr.br
http://www.dainf.cefetpr.br/~alex

Abstract

This paper discusses several factors influencing the evaluation of the degree of interestingness of rules discovered by a data mining algorithm. The main goals of this paper are: (1) drawing attention to several factors related to rule interestingness that have been somewhat neglected in the literature; (2) showing some ways of modifying rule interestingness measures to take these factors into account; (3) introducing a new criterion to measure attribute surprisingness, as a factor influencing the interestingness of discovered rules.

1 Introduction

A crucial aspect of data mining is that the discovered knowledge should be somehow interesting, where the term interestingness arguably has to do with surprisingness (unexpectedness), usefulness and novelty [Fayyad et al. 96].

Rule interestingness has both an objective (data-driven) and a subjective (user-driven) aspect. This paper focus on the objective aspect of rule interestingness. For a discussion about subjective aspects of rule interestingness, the reader is referred e.g. to [Liu et al. 97]. It should be noted that, in practice, both objective and subjective approaches should be used to select interesting rules. For instance, objective approaches can be used as a kind of first filter to select potentially interesting rules, while subjective approaches can then be used as a final filter to select truly interesting rules.

This paper is organized as follows. Section 2 presents a review of several rule interestingness criteria. Section 3 presents a case study on how a popular rule interestingness measure can be extended to take into account several rule interestingness criteria in an integrated, combined fashion. Section 4 introduces a new criterion for rule interestingness measures. Finally, section 5 summarizes and concludes the paper.

2 A Review of Rule Interestingness Criteria

2.1 Rule Interestingness Principles

For the purposes of this paper, a classification rule is a knowledge representation of the form A => B, where A is a conjunction of predicting attribute values and B is the predicted class. When evaluating the quality of a rule, three common factors to be taken into account are the coverage, the completeness and the confidence factor of the rule, defined as follows. The coverage of the rule (i.e. the number of tuples satisfied by the rule antecedent) is given by |A|. The rule's completeness (or proportion of tuples of the target class covered by the rule) is given by |A&B| / |B|. The rule's confidence factor (or predictive accuracy) is given by |A&B| / |A|.

[Piatetsky-Shapiro 91] has proposed three principles for rule interestingness (RI) measures, as follows.

1) RI = 0 if |A & B| = |A| |B| / N.

2) RI monotonically increases with |A&B| when other parameters are fixed.

3) RI monotonically decreases with |A| or |B| when other parameters are fixed.

The first principle says that the RI measure is zero if the antecedent and the consequent of the rule are statistically independent. The second and third principle have a more subtle interpretation. Note that Piatetsky-Shapiro was careful to state these principles in terms of *other parameters*, which is a phrase general enough to include any other parameter that we can think of. Let us assume for now that the rule parameters referred to by these principles are the terms |A|, |B|, and |A&B|, which are the terms explicitly used to state the principle. Note that this is an implicit assumption in most of the literature. However, we will revisit this assumption later in this section.

With the above assumption, principle 2 means that, for fixed |A| and fixed |B|, RI monotonically increases with |A&B|. In terms of the above mentioned rule quality factors, for fixed |A| and fixed |B|, the confidence factor and the completeness of the rule monotonically increase with |A&B|, and the higher these factors the more interesting the rule is.

Principle 3 means that: (1) for fixed |A| and fixed |A&B| (which implies a fixed coverage and a fixed confidence factor) RI monotonically decreases with |B| - i.e. the less complete, the less interesting the rule is; and (2) for fixed |B| and |A&B| (which implies a fixed rule completeness) RI monotonically decreases with |A| - i.e. the greater the coverage, the smaller the confidence factor, and the less interesting the rule is.

[Major & Mangano 93] have proposed a fourth principle for RI measures (which does not follow from the first three principles), namely:

4) RI monotonically increases with |A| (rule coverage), given a fixed confidence factor greater than the baseline confidence factor (i.e. the prior probability of the class).

In passing, we mention that [Kamber & Shinghal 96] have proposed a fifth principle for rule interestingness, but this principle is mainly oriented for characteristic rules, which are beyond the scope of this paper.

It should be noted that the above principles were designed mainly for considering the widely-used rule quality factors of coverage, completeness and confidence factor. Another widely-used rule quality factor is rule complexity. Although these factors are indeed important when evaluating the quality of a rule, they are by no means the only ones. In this paper we draw attention to five other factors related to rule quality and particularly to rule interestingness. These additional factors are discussed in the next subsections.

Note that, in theory, Piatetsky-Shapiro's principles still apply to rule interestingness measures considering these additional factors, as long as they remain fixed. (As mentioned before, the principles were carefully defined with the expression "fixed *other* parameters".) The problem is that, in practice, these additional factors do not remain fixed. These additional factors will probably vary a great deal across different rules, and this variation should be taken into account by the rule interestingness measure.

2.2 Disjunct Size

A rule set can be regarded as a disjunction of rules, so that a given rule can be regarded as a disjunct. The size of a disjunct (rule) is the number of tuples satisfied by the rule antecedent, i.e. |A|.

Thus, small disjuncts are rules whose number of covered tuples is small, according to some specified criterion (e.g. a fixed threshold, or a more flexible criterion). At first glance, it seems that small disjuncts are undesirable, and indeed most data mining algorithms have a bias favoring the discovery of large disjuncts.

Unfortunately, however, prediction accuracy can be significantly reduced if all small disjuncts are discarded by the data mining algorithm, as shown by [Holte et al. 89]. This is a particularly serious problem in domains where the small disjuncts collectively match a large percentage of the number of tuples belonging to a given class [Danyluk & Provost 93]. The main problem is that a small disjunct can represent either a true exception occurring in the data or simply noise. In the former case the disjunct should be maintained, but in the latter case the disjunct is error prone and should be discarded. Unfortunately, however, it is very difficult to tell which is the case, given only the data.

[Holte et al. 89] suggested that one remedy for the problem of small disjuncts was to evaluate these disjuncts by using a bias different from the one used to evaluate large disjuncts. Hence, they proposed that small disjuncts be evaluated by a maximum-specificity bias, in contrast with the maximum-generality bias (favoring the discovery of more general rules – i.e. larger disjuncts) used by most data mining algorithms. [Ting 94] further investigated this approach, by using an instance-based learner (as far as we can go with the maximum-specificity bias) to evaluate small disjuncts.

From a rule interestingness point of view, the lesson is that small disjuncts and large disjuncts should be evaluated in different ways – i.e. with different evaluation biases - by a rule interestingness measure.

2.3 The Imbalance of the Class Distribution

A class distribution is imbalanced if tuples belonging to one class are either much more frequent or much rarer than tuples belonging to other classes. To simplify our discussion, let us consider the common case of two-class problems.

Other things being equal, a problem where the two classes have the same relative frequency (or prior probabilities) is more difficult than a problem where there is a great difference between the relative frequencies of the two classes. In the latter case, it is relatively easy to discover rules predicting the majority class, but it is difficult to discover rules predicting the minority class. The smaller the relative frequency of the minority class, the more difficult it is to discover rules predicting it, and thus, intuitively, the more interesting are the rules predicting the minority class and the less interesting are the rules predicting the majority class. This point if often ignored by data mining algorithms.

[Kononenko & Bratko 91] have proposed an information-theoretic measure for evaluating the performance of a classifier by taking into account the problem of imbalanced class distributions, and their measure has some interesting properties. However, their approach was designed to evaluate a classifier as a whole - mainly to compare the performance of different classifiers in the same domain or the performance of a classifier in different problem domains - rather than to compare the interestingness of different rules discovered by the same classifier, which is the focus of this paper.

Note that the problem of imbalanced class distributions interacts with other problems discussed in this paper. For instance, consider the interaction between the problem of imbalanced class distributions and the problem of small disjuncts. Let r_1 and r_2 be two small disjuncts (rules) of the same size (i.e. the same number of covered tuples), where r_1 predicts the minority class and r_2 predicts the majority class for a new tuple. Then r_1 tends to have a much smaller prediction accuracy than r_2 [Quinlan 91].

Finally, note that using a rule interestingness measure which takes into account the relative class frequencies is not the only approach to cope with the problem of imbalanced class distributions. For instance, another approach to address this problem consists of selectively removing tuples from the majority class, so that the class distribution becomes less imbalanced [Kubat & Matwin 97]. In this paper however, we are interested only in modifying the rule interestingness measure used by the algorithm, leaving the data being mined intact.

2.4 Attribute Costs

Most rule interestingness measures consider the rule antecedent as a whole, without paying attention to the individual attributes occurring in the rule antecedent. In this sense, these measures are coarse-grained. However, two rules with the same value of a coarse-grained rule interestingness measure can have very different degrees of interestingness for the user, depending on which attributes occur in the rule antecedent.

In this section we consider one situation where the notion of attribute interestingness is crucial and is related to the issue of attribute costs. In section 4 we will propose a new criterion to measure the interestingness of individual attributes occurring in a rule antecedent.

In order to classify a new tuple with a given rule, it is necessary to match the rule conditions against the tuple's predicting attributes (i.e. attributes other than the class one). Hence, the algorithm must access the values of the new tuple's predicting attributes. In some application domains, different attributes might have very different "costs" to be accessed. The typical example is medical diagnosis. For example, it is trivial to determine the gender of the patient, but some health-related attributes can only be determined by performing a very costly examination. In this case attribute costs must be taken into account when evaluating a rule. Continuing with our example, suppose that the antecedent ("if part") of a discovered rule r_1 involves the result of an exam e_1 costing, say, $200, while the antecedent of a discovered rule r_2 involves instead the result of another exam e_2 costing, say, $20. All other things (including prediction accuracy) being equal, we would rather use rule r_2 for diagnosis. In other words, the smaller the cost of the attributes occurring in the rule, the more interesting (the more useful, the less costly) the rule is. Some data mining algorithms that take into account attribute costs are described in [Nunez 91], [Tan 93], [Turney 95].

2.5 Misclassification Costs

In some application domains, different misclassifications might have very different costs. For instance, in the domain of bank loans, the cost of erroneously denying a loan to a good client (who is likely to pay it back) is usually considerably smaller than the cost of erroneously granting a loan to a bad client (who is unlikely to pay it back). In this case the data mining algorithm must be modified to take misclassification costs into account [Provost & Fawcett 97], [Roberts et al. 95], [Michie et al. 94], [Breiman et al. 84]. This implies that the rule interestingness measure should take misclassification costs into account. We will revisit the issue of misclassification costs in section 3.2.1.

We must make here a comment similar to the one made in the section on imbalanced class distributions. Using a rule interestingness measure which takes into account misclassification costs is not the only approach to cope with this problem. For instance, another approach to address this problem consists of adjusting the relative proportions of each class in the data being mined. Once more in this paper, however, we are interested only in modifying the rule interestingness measure used by the algorithm, leaving the data being mined intact.

2.6 Asymmetry in Classification Rules

It should be noted that classification is an *asymmetric* task with respect to the attributes in the database. Indeed, we want to discover rules where the value of the predicting attributes determine the value of the goal attribute, not vice-versa. Hence, intuitively a rule interestingness measure should be asymmetric with respect to the rule antecedent and the rule consequent.

It is interesting to note that statistical measures of association, such as the popular χ^2 (chi-squared) measure, which is widely used in data mining systems, were not designed for classification tasks. Rather, they were designed for measuring the association (or dependency) between two attributes in a *symmetric* way, i.e. none of the two rule terms (antecedent and consequent) being analyzed is given special treatment when computing the χ^2 value.

We note in passing that an additional problem associated with the use of statistical significance tests in data mining, as pointed out by [Glymour et al. 97], is that these tests were designed to evaluate a single hypothesis, whereas data mining algorithms typically have to evaluate many alternative hypothesis.

3 A Case Study on the Applicability of Additional Rule Interestingness Factors

The above subsections 2.2 through 2.6 have identified five factors that should be involved in measuring the interestingness of a rule, but that have often been somewhat ignored in the literature on rule interestingness. We now discuss how these factors can be applied to define a rule interestingness measure.

There are several rule interestingness measures proposed in the literature. As a case study, we will focus on one of the most popular ones, introduced by [Piatetsky-Shapiro 91] as the simplest measure satisfying the three principles discussed in subsection 2.1. This measure, hereafter called PS (Piatetsky-Shapiro's) measure, is defined as:

$$PS = |A\&B| - |A||B|/N. \quad (1)$$

The remaining of this section is divided into two parts. Section 3.1 discusses how the PS measure addresses the additional rule interestingness factors discussed in subsections 2.2 through 2.6. Section 3.2 shows how this measure can be extended to better address some of those rule interestingness factors.

3.1 Analyzing the PS Rule Interestingness Measure

We now discuss how the PS measure, given by formula (1), addresses the rule quality factors of disjunct size, imbalance of the class distribution, attribute costs, misclassification costs and the asymmetry of classification rules.

Disjunct size - The PS measure takes into account the size of the disjunct, since formula (1) contains the term |A|. However, this measure treats small disjuncts and large disjuncts in the same way, with the same bias, which is undesirable, as discussed in section 2.2.

Imbalance of the Class Distribution - The PS measure takes into account the relative frequency (prior probability) of the class predicted by the rule, since formula (1) contains the term |B|. Other things being equal, the larger the value of |B|, the smaller the value of PS, so that the PS measure has the desirable property of favoring rules that predict the minority class.

Attribute Costs - The PS measure does not take into account attribute costs, neither any other measure of attribute interestingness. Actually, this measure considers the rule antecedent as a whole only, without paying attention to individual attributes of the rule antecedent.

Misclassification Costs - The PS measure does not take into account misclassification costs.

Asymmetry of Classification Rules - The PS measure is symmetric with respect to the rule antecedent and the rule consequent. We consider this an undesirable property of this measure, given the asymmetric nature of the classification task.

To summarize, out of the five factors influencing rule interestingness discussed in subsections 2.2 through 2.6, the PS measure takes into account only one of them (imbalance of the class distribution).

3.2 Extending the PS Rule Interestingness Measure

To render our case study more concrete, we will consider how to extend the PS rule interestingness measure in the context of a medical diagnosis application, where the goal is to predict whether or not the patient has a given fatal disease. We will make the realistic assumption that our application domain has two important characteristics, which will influence our design of an extended PS measure, namely varying misclassification costs and varying attribute costs. The next two subsections will discuss these two characteristics and how a rule interestingness measure can be extended to take them into account.

3.2.1 Varying Misclassification Costs

Different misclassification have different costs. The cost of predicting that a patient does not have a disease, while (s)he in reality does, is very high, since it can lead to the death of the patient due to lack of proper treatment. On the other hand, the cost of predicting that a patient has a disease, while (s)he in reality does not, is relatively smaller – see also section 2.5. Hence, in our example application domain, the PS measure must be modified to take misclassification costs into account. A simple way of doing this is to multiply formula (1) by a new term called MisclasCost, defined as:

$$\text{MisclasCost} = 1 / \sum_{j=1}^{k} \text{Prob}(j)\text{Cost}(i,j), \quad (2)$$

where Prob(j) is the probability that a tuple satisfied by the rule has true class j, class i is the class predicted by the rule, Cost(i,j) is the cost of misclassifying a tuple with true class j as class i, and k is the number of classes.

Assuming a two class problem, a natural estimate for Prob(j) would be

$$\text{Prob}(j) = |A\&\sim B|/|A|, \quad (3)$$

where ~B denotes the logical negation of the rule consequent B. One problem with this estimate is that, if the rule covers few tuples, this estimate is not reliable. In other words, there is an interaction between the rule interestingness criteria of misclassification costs and disjunct size. Unfortunately, these criteria are usually considered independently from each other in the literature. In order to take into account the interaction between these two criteria, the reliability of the above probability estimate can be improved by using the Laplace correction [Roberts et al. 95], so that the estimate for Prob(j) in formula (3) would be given by

$$\text{Prob}(j) = (1 + |A\&\sim B|) / (2 + |A|). \quad (4)$$

(This correction can be easily generalized to an n-class problem by replacing the "2" in the denominator with n.) Note how the Laplace correction improves the reliability of a probability estimate for small disjuncts without significantly affecting this reliability for large disjuncts.

3.2.2 Varying Attribute Costs

Different attributes have different costs of testing – see section 2.4. In our example application domain, attributes can represent several different kinds of predicting variables, including the patient's physical characteristics – e.g. gender, age, etc. – and the results of medical exams undergone by the patient – e.g. X-rays, blood tests, etc. Let us assume that each attribute has a well-defined cost, which represents the cost of determining the value of that attribute. Hence, attributes referring to the patient's physical characteristics have a minimum (virtually zero) cost to have their values determined, while attributes referring to the result of medical exams have much more significant costs to have their values determined.

Hence, in our example application domain, the PS measure must be modified to take attribute costs into account. A simple way of doing this is to multiply formula (1) by a new term called AttUsef (Attribute Usefulness), defined as the inverse of the sum of the costs of all the attributes occurring in the rule antecedent, that is:

$$\text{AttUsef} = 1 / \sum_{i=1}^{k} \text{Cost}(A_i), \quad (5)$$

where Cost(A_i) is the cost of the i-th attribute occurring in the rule antecedent, and k is the number of attributes occurring in the rule antecedent.

Note that this formula has the side effect of penalizing "complex" rules, i.e. rules with many attributes in their antecedent. In some cases, however, the number of attributes in the rule is already being taking into account by another term of the rule interestingness measure, such as an explicit measure of rule complexity. In this case, to avoid that a rule be penalized twice for its high complexity, AttUsef can be simply defined as the inverse of the arithmetic average of the costs of all the attributes occurring in the rule antecedent, that is:

$$AttUsef = 1 / (\sum_{i=1}^{k} Cost(A_i) / k), \quad (6)$$

where $Cost(A_i)$ and k are as defined above.

To summarize, in our example application domain, the PS measure must be extended to take into account both misclassification costs and attributes costs, and a simple way of doing this is to multiply formula (1) by formulas (2) and (6). Notice that this extension also has the effect of rendering the PS measure asymmetric. It is easy to see that in other application domains the PS measure should be extended in other ways, depending on the particular characteristics of the application. Hence, a rule interestingness measures is a bias and, as any other bias, has a domain-dependent effectiveness [Schaffer 94], [Rao et al. 95], [Michie et al. 94]. The challenge is to define a rule interestingness measure that is the most suitable for the target application domain.

4 A New Criterion for Rule Interestingness Measures: Attribute Surprisingness

Sections 2.4 and 3.2.2 discussed attribute costs as a kind of rule interestingness factor. In the literature, this seems to be the only rule interestingness factor defined on a "fine-grain, predicting-attribute level" - i.e. directly based on individual attributes occurring in a rule's antecedent - rather than being defined on a "coarse-grain" level, considering a rule antecedent as a whole. This section proposes a new rule interestingness criterion defined on the predicting-attribute level. Instead of focusing on attribute costs, which are related to rule usefulness, our new criterion focuses on the aspect of rule surprisingness. (Recall that rule interestingness involves several aspects, including both usefulness and surprisingness.)

Hence, we introduce a new term to measure rule surprisingness, called AttSurp (Attribute Surprisingness). In principle, any rule interestingness measure can be extended to take this term into account. For instance, the PS measure defined in formula (1) can be extended by multiplying that formula by the new term AttSurp. We propose that AttSurp be defined by an information-theoretic measure, based on the following idea.

First, we calculate the information gain of each attribute, defined as the class entropy minus the class entropy given the value of the predicting attribute. Attributes with high information gain are good predictors of class, when these attributes are considered individually, i.e. one at a time. However, from a rule interestingness point of view, it is likely that the user already knows what are the best predictors (individual attributes) for its application domain, and rules containing these attributes would tend to have a low degree of surprisingness (interestingness) for the user.

On the other hand, the user would tend to be more surprised if (s)he saw a rule containing attributes with low information gain. These attributes were probably considered as irrelevant by the users, and they are kind of irrelevant for classification when considered individually, one at a time. However, attribute interactions can render an individually-irrelevant attribute into a relevant one. This phenomenon is associated with surprisingness, and so with rule interestingness. Therefore, all other things (including prediction accuracy, coverage and completeness) being equal, we argue that rules whose antecedent contain attributes with low information gain are more interesting (more surprising) than rules whose antecedent contain attributes with high information gain. This idea can be expressed mathematically by defining the term AttSurp in the rule interestingness measure as:

$$AttSurp = 1 / (\sum_{i=1}^{k} InfoGain(A_i) / k), \quad (7)$$

where $InfoGain(A_i)$ is the information gain of the i-th attribute occurring in the rule antecedent and k is the number of attributes occurring in the rule antecedent.

5 Summary and Discussion

This paper has discussed several factors influencing the interestingness of a rule, including disjunct size, imbalance of class distributions, attribute interestingness, misclassification costs and the asymmetry of classification rules. These factors are often neglected by the literature on rule interestingness, which often focuses on factors such as the coverage, completeness and confidence factor of a rule.

As a case study, we focused on a popular rule interesting measure, defined by formula (1). We have shown that this measure takes into account only one of the five rule quality factors discussed in this paper, namely imbalanced class distributions. Then we discussed how this measure could be extended to take into account the other four factors. In particular, the extended rule interestingness measure has the form:

$$(|A\&B| - |A| \, |B| / N) * AttUsef * MisclasCost, \quad (8)$$

where the term AttUsef measures attribute usefulness - computed e.g. by formula (5) or (6) - and the term MisclasCost measures the misclassification cost - computed e.g. by formulas (2) and (4). Finally, the problem that formula (1) is symmetric, whereas classification rules should be asymmetric, was solved by adding the asymmetric terms AttUsef and MisclasCost to the extended formula (8).

The main goal of this paper was not to introduce yet another rule interestingness measure. Rather this paper had the main goals of: (1) drawing attention to several factors related to rule interestingness that have been somewhat neglected in the literature; (2) showing some ways of modifying rule interestingness measures to take these factors into account, which will hopefully inspire other researches to do the same; (3) introducing a new criterion to measure attribute surprisingness, as a factor influencing the interestingness of discovered rules. In particular, we believe that this new criterion is quite generic, and can be used in a large range of different application domains, so that it is a promising factor to take into account when designing a rule interestingness measure.

We cannot overemphasize that a rule interestingness measure is a bias, and so there is no universally best rule interestingness measure across all application domains. Each researcher or practitioner must adapt a rule interestingness measure (or invent a new one) to his/her particular target problem.

One limitation of this paper is that we have, implicitly, largely focused on how to measure the interestingness of different rules discovered by the same data mining algorithm, mining the same data. An open problem is how to extend our arguments for comparing the interestingness of different rules discovered by different data mining algorithms, or discovered from different data sets. Another limitation is that our discussion has not taken into account the interaction between rules in the induced rule set. In principle, however, the issue of rule interaction is somewhat orthogonal to the issue of individual rule interestingness, in the sense that the measure of rule interaction (typically a measure of rule overlapping) is often independent of the measure of individual rule interestingness. The reader interested in rule selection procedures taking into account rule interaction is referred to [Gebhardt 91], [Major & Mangano 93], [Major & Mangano 95].

References

[Breiman et al. 84] L. Breiman, J.H. Friedman, R.A. Olshen and C.J. Stone. *Classification and Regression Trees.* Pacific Groves, CA: Wadsworth, 1984.

[Danyluk & Provost 93] A.P. Danyluk & F.J. Provost. Small disjuncts in action: learning to diagnose errors in the local loop of the telephone network. *Proc. 10th Int. Conf. Machine Learning*, 81-88, 1993.

[Fayyad et al. 96] U.M. Fayyad, G. Piatetsky-Shapiro and P. Smyth. From data mining to knowledge discovery: an overview. In: U.M. Fayyad, G. Piatetsky-Shapiro, P. Smyth and R. Uthurusamy. (Eds.) *Advances in Knowledge Discovery and Data Mining*, 1-34. AAAI/MIT Press, 1996.

[Gebhardt 91] F. Gebhardt. Choosing among competing generalizations. *Knowledge Acquisit.*, 3, 1991, 361-380.

[Glymour et al. 97]. C. Glymour, D. Madigan, D. Pregibon and P. Smyth. Statistical themes and lessons for data mining. *Data Mining and Knowledge Discovery* 1(1), 11-28. 1997.

[Holte et al. 89] R.C. Holte, L.E. Acker and B.W. Porter. Concept learning and the problem of small disjuncts. *Proc. Int. Joint Conf. AI (IJCAI-89)*, 813-818.

[Kamber & Shinghal 96] M. Kamber & R. Shinghal. Evaluating the interestingness of characteristic rules. *Proc. 2nd Int. Conf. Knowledge Discovery & Data Mining*, 263-266. AAAI, 1996.

[Kononenko & Bratko 91] Information-based evaluation criterion for classifier's performance. *Machine Learning 6*, 1991, 67-80.

[Kubat & Matwin 97] M. Kubat and S. Matwin. Addressing the curse of imbalanced training sets: one-sided selection. *Proc. 14th Int. Conf. Machine Learning*, 179-186. Morgan Kaufmann, 1997.

[Liu et al. 97] B. Liu, W. Hsu and S. Chen. Using general impressions to analyze discovered classification rules. *Proc. 3rd Int. Conf. Knowledge Discovery & Data Mining*, 31-36. AAAI, 1997.

[Major & Mangano 93]. J.A. Major and J.J. Mangano. Selecting among rules induced from a hurricane database. *Proc. AAAI-93 Workshop on Knowledge Discovery in Databases*, 28-44. July/93.

[Major & Mangano 95]. J.A. Major and J.J. Mangano. Selecting among rules induced from a hurricane database. *J. Intel. Info. Systems* 4(1), Jan./95, 39-52.

[Michie et al. 94] D. Michie, D.J. Spiegelhalter and C.C. Taylor. *Machine Learning, Neural and Statistical Classification*. Ellis Horwood, 1994.

[Nunez 91] M. Nunez. The use of background knowledge in decision tree induction. *Mach. Learn.* 6, 231-250.

[Piatetsky-Shapiro 91] G. Piatetsky-Shapiro. Discovery, analysis and presentation of strong rules. In: G. Piatetsky-Shapiro and W.J. Frawley. (Eds.) *Knowledge Discovery in Databases*, 229-248. AAAI, 1991.

[Provost & Fawcett 97] F. Provost & T. Fawcett. Analysis and visualization of classifier performance: comparison under imprecise class and cost distributions. *Proc. 3rd Int. Conf. Knowledge Discovery & Data Mining*, 43-48. AAAI, 1997.

[Quinlan 91] J.R. Quinlan. Improved estimates for the accuracy of small disjuncts. *Machine Learn.* 6(1), 93-98.

[Rao et al. 95] R.B. Rao, D. Gordon and W. Spears. For every generalization action, is there really an equal and opposite reaction? Analysis of the conservation law for generalization performance. *Proc. 12th Int. Conf. Mach. Learn.*, 471-479. 1995.

[Roberts et al. 95] H. Roberts, M. Denby and K. Totton. Accounting for misclassification costs in decision tree classifiers. *Proc. Intelligent Data Analysis Conf. (IDA-95)*. 1995.

[Schaffer 94] C. Schaffer. A conservation law for generalization performance. *Proc. 11th Int. Conf. Machine Learning*, 259-265. 1994.

[Tan 93] M. Tan. Cost-sensitive learning of classification knowledge and its application in robotics. *Machine Learning* 13, 1993, 7-33.

[Ting 94] K.M. Ting. The problem of small disjuncts: its remedy in decision trees. *Proc. 10th Canadian Conf. Artificial Intelligence*, 91-97. 1994.

[Turney 95] P.D. Turney. Cost-sensitive classification: empirical evaluation of a hybrid genetic decision tree induction algorithm. *Journal of Artificial Intelligent Research*, 2, Mar./95, 369-409.

MVC - A Preprocessing Method to Deal with Missing Values

Arnaud Ragel

Bruno Crémilleux

GREYC CNRS UPRESA 6072

Université de Caen

14032 Caen Cedex, France

{ragel, cremilleux}@info.unicaen.fr

Abstract

Many of analysis tasks have to deal with missing values and have developed specific and internal treatments to guess them. In this paper we present an external method, MVC (Missing Values Completion), to improve performances of completion and also declarativity and interactions with the user for this problem. Such qualities will allow to use it for the data cleaning step of the KDD[1] process[6]. The core of MVC, is the RAR[2] algorithm that we have proposed in [15]. This algorithm extends the concept of association rules[1] for databases with multiple missing values. It allows MVC to be an efficient preprocessing method: in our experiments with the c4.5[13] decision tree program, MVC has permitted to divide, up to two, the error rate in classification, independently of a significant gain of declarativity.

keywords: Association rules, Missing Values, Preprocessing, Decision Trees.

1 Introduction

The missing values problem is an old one for analysis tasks[9] [12]. The waste of data which can result from casewise deletion of missing values, obliges to propose alternatives approaches. A current one is to try to determine these values [10],[4]. However, techniques to guess the missing values must be efficient, otherwise the completion will introduce noise. With the emergence of KDD for industrial databases, where missing values are inevitable, this problem has become a priority task [6] also requiring declarativity and interactivity during treatments. At the present time, treatments are often specific and internal to the methods, and do not offer these qualities. Consequently the missing values problem is still a challenging task of the KDD research agenda [6].

To complete missing values a solution is to use relevant associations between the attributes of the data. The problem is that it is not an easy task to discover relations in data containing missing values. The association rules algorithms [2] [1] are a recent and efficient approach to extract quickly all the associations out

---

[1] Knowledge Discovery in Databases
[2] Robust Association Rules

of large databases but they are unable, like the majority of analysis methods, to work when missing values are embedded in the data [15]. We have proposed in [15] the RAR algorithm to correct this weakness. It is fully compatible with the core of the fast association rules algorithms [2]. The efficiency of RAR to mine databases containing multiple missing values, allows to use it for the missing values problem. This is what we propose in this paper with the MVC (Missing Values Completion) method. MVC uses the association rules, discovered with RAR, to fill the missing values, independently of any analysis tasks, during a preprocessing, declarative and interactive process with the user. This approach also allows to correct some faults of usual completion methods and so performances of analysis tasks are increased: the error rate of the classification software c4.5[13] can be divided by two in our experiments if MVC is used rather than the missing values treatment of c4.5.

In this paper, we focus on the missing values problem for decision trees but we will see that MVC can be interesting for any analysis tasks. Section 2 briefly reviews usual approaches to deal with missing values in decision trees and points out problems. In Sect. 3 we present the RAR algorithm[15] and show in Sect. 4 its interest for the missing values problem in MVC. In Sect. 5 we present experiments using MVC for classification tasks with the decision tree program c4.5[13] and conclude in Sect. 6, on the possibility with MVC to control the noise that may be introduced during the completion step.

2 Missing Values and Decision Trees

A decision tree is a divide and conquer classification method: it is either a leaf node containing a classification or an attribute test, with a branch to a decision tree for each value of the attribute. The main problem of the missing values in decision tree is to know in which branch we should send a case with an unknown value ? Considering all possible trees, to avoid the missing values problem, is computationally infeasible [7], and deleting data with missing values may cause a huge waste of data. Consequently, a current approach is to fill them [10], [14].

For no having universal and independent method to deal with missing values, many programs used specific and internal treatments that we will briefly review here.

A current approach is to fill the missing values with the most common value. This value can be chosen either in the whole dataset either in datasets constructed for the classification task. For example, if in a dataset the known values for an attribute X are a for 70% of the cases, b for 10% of the cases and c for 20% of the cases, missing values for X will be filled with a. An important critic which can be said is that the common value is chosen in datasets constructed to decide the class variable and not to decide the missing values. Thus such treatments may be irrelevant. There are other variants, like c4.5[13], where missing values are sent in each subset, with a weight proportional to the known values in the subset. In this case, it is equivalent to fill missing values with several weighted values. The precedent critic can be done also for c4.5.

Another technique, proposed by Breiman et al. in [3], is to use a surrogate split to decide the missing value for an attribute. The surrogate attribute is the one with the highest correlation with the original attribute. If this method uses more information than the precedent ones, its efficacy depends on the possibility to find correlations between two attributes. Looking for more associations have been proposed by Quinlan and Shapiro in [11] where they use a decision tree approach to decide the missing values for an attribute. If S is the training set and X_1 an attribute with missing values, the method considers the subset S', of S, with only cases where the attribute X_1 is known. In S' the original class is regarded as another attribute while the value of attribute X_1 becomes the class to be determined. A classification tree is built using S' for predicting the value of attribute X_1 from the other attributes and the class. Then, this tree can be used to fill the missing values. Unfortunately it has been shown that difficulties arise if the same case has missing values on more than one attribute[10]: during the construction of a tree to predict X_1, if a missing value is tested for an attribute X_2 another tree must be constructed to predict X_2 and so on. So this method cannot be used practically. More recently, in 1996, K. Lakshminarayan et. al proposed in [8] a similar approach where they use machine learning techniques (Autoclass[5] and c4.5[13]) to fill missing values. They avoid the problem of multiple missing values on a same data using the internal missing values treatments of c4.5 or Autoclass. Consequently, a declarative and association approach is only used to decide missing values for one attribute: missing values of the others attributes are treated with the missing values treatment of c4.5 or the one of autoclass.

With this brief overview of missing values treatments for decision trees, which can be extended to other analysis methods, we see that the main difficulty is to find declarative associations between data in presence of multiple missing values, which are relevant to guess missing values. In the next section, we present a method which can be used for this task.

3   The Robust Association Rules Algorithm

The RAR algorithm, that we have proposed in [15], corrects a weakness of usual association rules algorithms: a lot of relevant rules are lost by these algorithms when missing values are embedded in databases. We briefly recall principles of association rules and we point out the main characteristics of the RAR algorithm.

3.1   Association Rules

An association rule[1] is an expression of the form $X \longrightarrow Y$, where X and Y are sets of items, and is evaluated by a support and a confidence. Its support is the percentage of data that contains both X and Y. Its confidence is the percentage of data that contains Y among those containing X. For example, the rule *fins=y and tail=y* $\longrightarrow$ *hairs=n* with a support of 13% and a confidence of 92% states that 13% of animals have fins, tail and no hairs and that 92% of animals with fins and tail have no hairs. The problem of mining rules is to find all rules that satisfy a user-specified minimum support and minimum confidence.

One of the reason of the association rules success is that there are fast algorithms [2] [16] which allow to explore quickly very large databases with a minimum number of pass on data: supports are calculated using an efficient construction of pertinent itemsets of size k from pertinent itemsets of size k-1. Confidences are calculated using valid supports previously found, without new passes on the datasets.

Association rules have been firstly developed to mine transaction databases (basket data analysis). In these databases the missing values problem do not exist in practically, which explain that this problem has not been considered of interest by the fast algorithms. The RAR algorithm corrects this fault, to discover association rules in databases containing multiple missing values.

3.2 The RAR algorithm

In order to avoid the collapse of fast association rules algorithms when a database has missing values, a key point of RAR is to discover rules in valid databases rather than in the whole database. A valid database (vdb) is defined for an itemset X as the largest sub database without missing values for this itemset.

Id	X1	X2	X3	X4
1	?	a	a	c
2	a	a	b	?
3	a	b	c	c
4	a	b	d	c
5	?	b	e	d
6	b	b	f	?
7	b	c	g	d
8	b	c	h	d

VDB 1

Id	X1	X2	X3	X4
1	Disabled			
2	a	a	b	?
3	a	b	c	c
4	a	b	d	c
5	Disabled			
6	b	b	f	?
7	b	c	g	d
8	b	c	h	d

VDB 2

Id	X1	X2	X3	X4
1	?	a	a	c
2	Disabled			
3	a	b	c	c
4	a	b	d	c
5	?	b	e	d
6	Disabled			
7	b	c	g	d
8	b	c	h	d

VDB 3

Figure 1: RAR approach for dealing with missing values

For example in the Fig. 1, if the first left database is the whole database it is also the vdb of the itemsets {X2}, {X3} and {X2, X3} because there is no missing value of X2 and X3. The second one is the vdb of itemsets {X1}, {X1,X2}, {X1,X3}, {X1,X2,X3} and the third one is a vdb for {X4}, {X2,X4}, {X3,X4}, {X2,X3,X4}.

To be fully compatible, without increasing the complexity, with the core of the fast association rules algorithms[2], some modifications for support and confidence calculations have been to be done (see [15] for more information).

If ignoring missing values often leads to a huge waste of data, it is not the case for the RAR algorithm: the association rules approach is an exhaustive research so ignoring missing values does not lead to definitively reject data contrary to methods using heuristics, e.g decision trees. For example, in the Fig. 1, data 1 is not used to evaluate support of $\{X1, X3\}$ but it is used to evaluate support of $\{X2, X4\}$. In a decision tree, if X1 is the root attribute, data 1 would have been rejected, and as it is impossible to construct all the trees (NP-complete problem [7]), this data would be definitively rejected from the analysis task. We have shown in [15] that this approach, which avoid to use a treatment to complete, gives satisfying results for association rules.

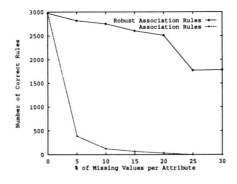

Figure 2: Robust Association Rules Performances

Figure 2 depicts the results of an experiment comparing performances between the RAR algorithm and the main fast algorithm[2]: a reference ruleset is constructed from a database, 2000 data and 8 attributes, with no missing values. Then missing values are randomly introduced with a rate of 5% at first and 30% to finish with an increment of 5% on each attribute of this database. The number of correct rules (include in the reference ruleset) retrieved with the two different approaches are shown by the curves in Fig 2. We see that the number of retrieved rules is clearly larger with RAR, especially when the number of missing values increases.

4 Interest of RAR for Missing Values

4.1 Presentation of MVC

The efficiency of RAR, to find all the association rules quickly in a database with missing values, allows us to propose the MVC method. This method works as in the Fig 3, where it first extracts rules and then uses them to fill missing values, with a possible interaction with the user.

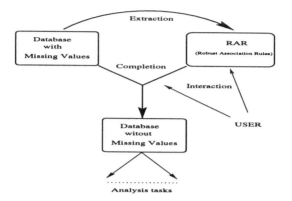

Figure 3: The MVC Process

For the completion, the rules matching a data and concluding on a missing attribute are used to decide its value. Two situations are possible:
1- All the matching rules indicate the same conclusion, then it is used.
2- Several matching rules conclude on different values. In this case the confidence measure and the number of rules concluding on a same value are used to solve the conflict automatically. Of course, the user can intervene. This approach is simple but, in our experiments, there is always a clear preference, in number of rules, for one value rather than the others.

We show below an example of completion for a data from the Zoo database[3].
data: **aquatic=y, tail=y, hairs=?, legs=0, fins=?**
with use of *Rule 1: aquatic=y, and, legs=0 $\longrightarrow$ fins=y (sup[4]: 17%, conf[5]: 97%)*
becomes: **aquatic=y, tail=y, hairs=?, legs=0, fins=y**
with use of *Rule 2: fins=y and tail=y $\longrightarrow$ hairs=n (sup: 13%, conf: 92%)*
becomes: **aquatic=y, tail=y, hairs=n, legs=0, fins=y**

In this example, we can see that recursion is permitted with MVC. However, to avoid series of wrong completions, only rules with a high confidence value (more than 95%) are used for the recursion. With this intuitive treatment the user can easily intervene in the completion process: he can visualize the ruleset, remove, change or add new rules. Furthermore the confidence of a rule can be a good indication of the correctness of the treatment: the rule with a confidence of 97%, in the previous example, indicates that 3% of noise may

---

[3]UCI Machine Learning Repository, http://www.ics.uci.edu/ mlearn/MLRepository.html
[4]support
[5]confidence

be introduced. It is always possible to find matched rules, to complete, if we allow the use of rules with a low support and a low confidence. This point can appear as a weakness of our approach because a low confidence may implicate noise in data. As a matter of fact, this critic can apply to any method which completes the missing values, like the ones presented in Sect. 2. But, as they cannot give a value like confidence to measure the noise, it does not point out. We will consider this point in our conclusion.

As MVC is a preprocessing method, it comes within the data cleaning step in the KDD process. Another important point is that MVC corrects some weaknesses of usual missing values treatments.

The first one is, as we have seen in Sect. 2, that multiple missing values and computational time prevent usual methods from finding relevant associations to fill missing values. In RAR, the use of the association rules concept, which is designed to explore quickly large databases, allows to construct a ruleset especially for the missing values problem. Thus when a missing value occurs, all the available information of the ruleset is used by MVC to fill it.

Another problem is due to internal treatments, e.g for c4.5 or CART. In this case when a missing value is not correctly filled, the resulting noise will perturbate the treatment of the remaining missing values: if an example E, is sent in a wrong subset because of an incorrect determination of a missing value, all the following subsets will be falsified by the presence of E. Consequently missing values treatments, using information in these subsets, will be falsified too. In MVC such a situation does not appear because rules are discovered in a first step, before any completion. Furthermore during the completion step, the recursion can be controlled.

In the next section we will show that such properties allow MVC to be a declarative and independent treatment but also more efficient.

5 Results

In this section, we try to evaluate the contribution of MVC for classification tasks and compare the ability of treatments (MVC and the internal method of a decision tree program c4.5) to treat missing values. c4.5[13] is one of the most used decision tree program and it can handle missing values by sending them to each subset, with a weight proportional to the known values in the subset. As the missing values treatment of c4.5 is automatic, for scientific exactness, MVC has been used without interaction with the user.

5.1 Introduction of multiple missing values

For this experiment we take a database with no or few missing values, to have a reference database, and we randomly introduce missing values for each attribute (rate 5% to 20% by increment of 5%). Two studies are then realized. The first one is made running MVC and comparing the returned complete database with the reference one. We will see then the capacity of MVC to preprocess data. A second study is made running c4.5 twice on these databases: firstly, using its own treatment to deal with missing values and secondly using MVC to preprocess the missing values. We will compare results in classification using MVC or the missing values treatment of c4.5. Two databases, coming from the UCI Machine Learning Repository has been used for these experiments. The Vote database which has 435 data and 17 attributes and the Credit Card database which have 690 data and 15 attributes[6].

Table 1: Power of Completion with MVC

MV[a]	Vote Database		Credit Card Database	
	Percentage of Completion	Correct Completion	Percentage of Completion	Correct Completion
5%	100%	99.00%	100%	98.56%
10%	100%	98.00%	100%	96.70%
15%	100%	96.70%	100%	95.68%
20%	100%	95.50%	100%	94.13%

[a]Percentage of Missing Values

Tab. 1 gives the results of the first study to show the power of completion of MVC. We can see that MVC has succeed to complete all the missing values, introducing only a low noise rate: for example, in the vote database with 15% of missing values on each attribute, the noise introduced by the completion step is 3.3%.Let us remember that it is impossible to make a such experiment with the c4.5 approach because the completion of a missing value is not unique (a missing values is filled by a distribution of values).

Tab. 2 gives the results of classification with c4.5 using either his own missing values treatment or either MVC. We can see that classification error rate using MVC is lower: it can be divided up to two. Another result is that the more we introduce missing values in the credit card database the better are the results. Such a result may be explained by the fact that some unexpected values for data (e.g noise) may be set to unknown with this experiment and then are filled by MVC with typical ones.

5.2 Real world applications

In this experiment we use 2 databases, from real world, with missing values at origin:

1. OERTC database: This database is used, for classification tasks, in collaboration with the lymphome group of the O.E.R.T.C (European Organization of Research and Treatment of Cancer). We have used the

---

[6]some with missing values

Table 2: Average Results over ten trials with multiple missing values

MV[a]	Use of MVC	Unpruned Tree			Pruned Tree			
		Size Tree	Err.[b] (train)	Err. (test)	Size Tree	Err. (train)	Err. (test)	Err. (predic.)
Vote Database								
(Ref. Result[c])		29.2	1.9%	4.8%	16	2.6%	4.4%	5.7%
5%	no	42.4	2.5%	7.8%	13.9	4.2%	6.7%	7.6%
10%	no	57.7	3.2%	9.2%	10.6	7.1%	8.3%	9.8%
15%	no	51.1	4.1%	8.0%	8.8	9.1%	10.1%	11.8%
20%	no	64.6	4.6%	9.7%	11.2	10.8%	12.9%	14.4%
5%	yes	35.5	2.5%	8.0%	6.1	4.6%	5.5%	6.5%
10%	yes	30.7	2.6%	6.2%	6.1	4.3%	5.3%	6.2%
15%	yes	37.6	2.6%	7.6%	8.8	4.5%	6.0%	6.7%
20%	yes	46.6	2.6%	8.5%	10.0	4.9%	6.7%	7.4%
Credit Card Database								
(Ref. Result)		162.4	7.4%	16.5%	21.9	11.2%	13.2%	14.4%
5%	no	200.8	7.8%	16.8%	13.2	12.4%	13.5%	16.1%
10%	no	190.4	8.8%	17.9%	14.9	13.2%	13.8%	17.4%
15%	no	182.5	9.1%	18.0%	11.4	14.3%	15.1%	19.0%
20%	no	206.8	8.9%	16.8%	15.2	15.9%	17.8%	21.6%
5%	yes	141.5	7.4%	16.5%	23.3	11.3%	14.6%	14.9%
10	yes	134.1	6.5%	13.9%	39.9	9.6%	13.8%	14.6%
15	yes	155.1	6.3%	15.8%	22.1	11.0%	13.9%	14.3%
20	yes	145.6	5.6%	13.9%	15.4	10.0%	12.0%	12.4%

[a]Percentage of Missing Values
[b]Percentage of Errors.
[c]Reference Result

H7 protocol which has 832 cases (1988-1993) and 27 attributes. Eleven of them have missing values with the following proportions: 52%, 43%, 88%, 84%, 39%, 8%, 6%, 7%, 2%, 6% and 6.5%.

2. Auto insurance database: it comes from the UCI Machine Learning Repository and has 205 cases with 25 attributes[7]. Six of them have missing values with the following proportions: 20%, 0.97%, 1.95%, 1.95%, 0.97%, 0.97%, 1.95%.

Tab. 3 gives the results. In the OERTC database results are significatively increased using MVC. An interesting point is that MVC has made to emerge an attribute not used otherwise. With it, qualities of the tree seem to be better (a predicted error of 6.8%). In the Auto database, results are the same but, the low rates of missing values and the few cases, cannot really decide if MVC could be useful. However MVC has completed missing values with an unique value, contrary to c4.5, which is better for the understanding.

[7]numeric attributes have been discretized for this experiment

Table 3: Average Results over ten trials on real world applications with c4.5

Use of MVC	Unpruned Tree			Pruned Tree			
	Size Tree	Err.[a] (train)	Err. (test)	Size Tree	Err. (train)	Err. (test)	Err. (predic.)
	OERTC Database						
no	91.4	4.4%	8.5%	41.3	6.2%	7.3%	10.0%
yes	89.7	2.2%	5.6%	40.4	3.5%	6.5%	6.8%
	Autos Database						
no	152.1	4.0%	16.6%	88.3	8.3%	19.5%	30.0%
yes	149.2	4.3%	16.0%	83.4	8.3%	18.5%	29.9%

[a]Percentage of Errors.

5.3 Conclusion on Results

With MVC, results seem to be noticeably improved in classification when there are many missing values. Otherwise, results are at least as good with the preprocessing. Unlike c4.5 approach, another advantage is that the completion is made with only one value which allows the user to understand and react about it.

6 Conclusion

Contrary to previous approaches reviewed in Sect. 2, the ability of RAR to discover associations in missing values databases has permitted to propose an efficient method to fill missing values. The latter, MVC, uses RAR to guess the missing values in databases. Such an approach leads to a significant gain of performances: the error rate in classification, with c4.5[13], can be divided up to two, if MVC is used rather than the classical missing values treatment of c4.5. But the main advantage of MVC is to be a preprocessing method, independent of any analysis tasks, which offers a more understandable treatment of the missing values and a possible interaction with the user. Such qualities, rarely available as far as we know for the missing values problem, may enable MVC to become a tool for the data cleaning step of the KDD process [6].

At the present time, we are working on several points to improve the use of rules in MVC. One of them, is a definition of a new rule score, specially designed for the completion problem: it will combine several criteria rather than only the use of the confidence measure. A second point is to try to determinate an optimum completion threshold: we think that there is a threshold for which the noise, introduced by the missing values completion, could become a more important problem than the remaining missing values. As MVC can evaluate the completion of missing values (using the confidence measure) a such study is possible and should be interesting.

References

[1] R. Agrawal, T. Imielinski, and A. Swami. Mining association rules between sets of items in large databases. In Proc. of the ACM SIGMOD Conference on Management of Data,p 207-216, Washington, USA, 1993.

[2] R. Agrawal, H. Mannila, R. Srikant, H. Toivonen and A. I. Verkamo. Fast Discovery of Association Rules. In Advances in Knowledge Discovery and Data Mining, p 307-328, MIT Press, 1996.

[3] L. Breiman, J.H Friedman, R.A Olshen, C.J Stone. Classification and Regression Trees, The Wadsworth Statistics/Probability Series, 1984.

[4] G. Celeux. Le traitement des données manquantes dans le logiciel SICLA. Technical reports number 102, INRIA, France, December 1988.

[5] P. Cheeseman, J. Kelly, M. Self, J. Stutz, W. Taylor and D. Freeman. Bayesian Classification. In Proc. of American Association of Artificial Intelligence (AAAI), p. 607-611, San Mateo, USA, 1988.

[6] U.M Fayyad, G. Piatetsky-Shapiro, and P. Smyth. From data mining to knowledge discovery: An overview. In Advances in Knowledge Discovery and Data Mining, p. 1-36, MIT Press, 1996.

[7] L. Hyafile and R. Rivest. Constructing optimal binary decision trees is np-complete. Information Processing Letters number 5, p. 15-17, 1976.

[8] K. Lakshminarayan, S.A Harp, R. Goldman and T. Samad. Imputation of missing data using machine learning techniques. In Proc. of the Second International Conference on Knowledge Discovery and Data Mining (KDD-96), MIT Press, 1996.

[9] R.J.A Little, D.B Rubin. Statistical Analysis with Missing Data, Wiley series in probability and mathematical statistics, John Wiley and Sons, USA, 1987.

[10] W.Z Liu, A.P White, S.G Thompson and M.A Bramer. Techniques for Dealing with Missing Values in Classification. In Second Int'l Symposium on Intelligent Data Analysis, London, 1997.

[11] J.R Quinlan. Induction of decision trees. Machine learning, Vol 1, p. 81-106, 1986.

[12] J.R Quinlan. Unknown Attribute Values in Induction, in Segre A.M.(ed.), In Proc. of the Sixth Int'l Workshop on Machine Learning, p. 164-168, Morgan Kaufmann, Los Altos, USA, 1989.

[13] J.R Quinlan. C4.5: Programs for Machine Learning, Morgan Kaufmann, San Mateo, USA, 1993.

[14] A. Ragel: Traitement des valeurs manquantes dans les arbres de décision. Technical reports, Les cahiers du GREYC, number 2, University of Caen, France, 1997.

[15] A. Ragel and B. Crémilleux. Treatment of Missing Values for Association Rules. In Proc. of The Second Pacific-Asia Conference on Knowledge Discovery and Data Mining (PAKDD-98), volume 1394 of Lecture Notes in Artificial Intelligence, p. 258-270, Melbourne, Australia, 1998.

[16] H. Toivonen. Sampling large databases for association rules. In Proc. of the 22nd Int'l Conference on Very Large Databases (VLDB'96), p. 134-145, Morgan Kaufmann, India, 1996. [available on the web from http://www.informatik.uni-trier.de/ ley/db/conf/vldb/Toivonen96.html]

SESSION 4: NEURO-FUZZY APPROACHES

Alarm Analysis with Fuzzy Logic and Multilevel Flow Models

Fredrik Dahlstrand
Department of Information Technology
Lund Institute of Technology
Box 118, SE-221 00 Lund, Sweden
Phone: +46 46 222 95 10
Fax +46 46 222 47 14
E-mail: fredrikd@it.lth.se

Abstract

This paper presents one method for combining Multilevel Flow Models (MFM) alarm analysis and fuzzy logic. The already existing MFM alarm analysis algorithm, which is using discrete logic, has several problems when confronted with uncertainty such as noise or signals close to a decision limit. The new result presented in this paper is a fuzzy MFM alarm analysis algorithm, which is more reliable when faced with uncertainties.

1 Introduction

In many large industrial processes a simple alarm situation may turn into a complex one due to the huge amount of information that is presented to a human operator. The difficulty, when performing alarm analysis, is not to obtain the information but rather to sort out which information is important in a certain alarm situation.

One way to reduce the amount of information presented is to model the causality of the process, that is, to describe which components depend on each other. With such a model it is possible to determine the root cause of an alarm situation because it is possible to find out which alarms are consequences of other alarms. Professor Morten Lind has introduced a way to model consequential dependencies in a process: Multilevel Flow Models [6], from now on referred to as MFM.

MFM is used to model the intentions of a man-made (technical) process and the means by which these intentions are achieved. Further work by Larsson has introduced a reliable method to perform an alarm analysis [2, 3]. MFM alarm analysis has three main advantages:

1. It is a relatively easy task, compared to expert systems, to build, update and maintain the knowledge base, this due to the graphical nature of MFM. Furthermore, the high level of abstraction requires less detailed knowledge of the system.

2. With the already existing alarm analysis algorithm it is possible to accurately measure the worst-case execution time.
3. The already existing MFM algorithm is very fast. The worst case execution time for the Guardian model [5], which corresponds to 374 backward chaining rules, is about 7000 diagnoses per second. The test was performed on a 200 MHz Pentium Pro running the Windows NT operating system.

MFM fault diagnosis and alarm analysis have successfully been tested on real world processes. Larsson [2] describes how MFM was tested on the Steritherm process. The Steritherm process is used to sterilise liquid food products, for example, milk. In the Guardian project [5], MFM was used to monitor the human body, and more specifically, to monitor a patient in an intensive care unit. In an ongoing project several solutions to combine MFM with quantitative and probabilistic methods are investigated.

This method has however one drawback, it does not handle uncertainties in the process, such as signals close to decision limit, noisy signals, missing data, etc. The already existing algorithm uses crisp logic with two or three distinct values, for example, the flow through a pipe may either be described as too low, too high or normal. A situation, as described in Figure 1, may cause a burst of random alarms. The signal is likely to be within limits (the horizontal lines show the desired interval) but due to noise the alarm analysis switches chaotically between failed and working states.

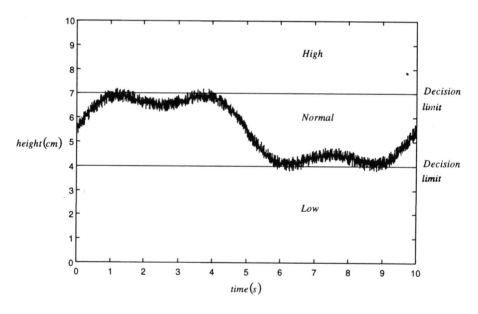

Figure 1: *A noisy signal close to decision boundaries. The desired signal level is between the two horizontal lines.*

Ideally, in a situation as the one in Figure 1, the algorithm should not indicate an alarm but rather indicate that the signal is close to a decision limit.

This paper shows one approach to combine the concept of MFM alarm analysis and fuzzy logic to produce a more reliable alarm analysis.

2 Multilevel Flow Models

MFM models are graphical representations of the goals and functions of technical systems. The goals describe the purposes of the system, and the functions describe the capabilities of the system. MFM models describe the functional structure of a system by modelling the flow structures in the system. MFM models are built by using three basic concepts, *goals*, *functions*, and *physical components*.

2.1 Functions

MFM describes the functionality of a system by modelling the flows of *mass*, *energy* and *information*. The mass, energy, and information flows are modelled by using six different flow functions:

- The *source* function is used to model the capability of providing an infinite amount of mass, energy, or information.
- The *sink* function is used to model the capability of receiving an infinite amount of mass, energy, or information.
- The *transport* function is used to model the capability of transporting mass, energy, or information.
- The *barrier* function is used to model the capability of preventing mass, energy, or information transport.
- The *storage* function is used to model the capability of storing mass, energy, or information.
- The *balance* function is used to model the capability of forking and combining different flows of mass, energy, or information. The flows must be of the same basic type.

Beside these six functions, information flows may be modelled using three more functions:

- The *observer* function is used to model the capability of monitoring the state of a physical component and translate this into a flow of information.
- The *actor* function is used to model the capability of altering the state of a physical component.
- The *decision* function is used to model the capability of decision making. Decisions may be made either by control algorithms or by human operators.

There exists one more function, the *manager*, which is used to model the capability of resource management and control. The manager is used to describe a system that is intended to manage a certain task. The graphical representations of the MFM functions are shown in Figure 2.

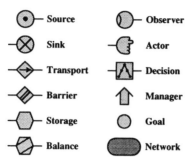

Figure 2: *The graphical representation of functions, goals, and networks.*

Functions may be connected to each other into flow paths. However, the flow functions may not be connected to each other in an arbitrary manner. The legal MFM connections are shown in Figure 3. For example, the storage must be connected to either a transport or a barrier at each connection point. A balance must be connected to at least one transport or barrier at each end. The observer, sink, source, and actor have only one connection point, thus acting as the end or the beginning of a flow structure.

Figure 3: *All legal MFM function to function connections. In this figure the functions have been place so that a function may only be connected to functions to the left or to the right, but not to functions above or below.*

2.2 Relations

The goals, functions, and physical components in an MFM model are dependent on each other. To model this, four different types of relations are used:

- An *achieve* relation is used to connect a group of MFM functions that work together to fulfil the connected goal.
- An *achieve-by-management* relation is the same as an *achieve* relation with the extension that the goal is fulfilled by management of resources. The management is done by, for example, human operators or PID-controllers.
- A *condition* relation is used to model that the connected goal must be fulfilled to allow for the connected function to be available.

- A *realise* relation is used to connect the physical components to the functions. This is normally not shown in an MFM model.

The graphical representation of these relations is shown in Figure 4.

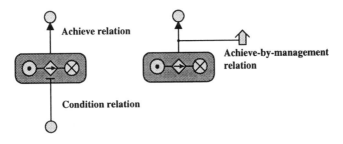

Figure 4. *The MFM relations.*

2.3 An Example of an MFM Model

The following example, the heat exchanger in Figure 5, is a part of the Steritherm [2] process. Water is pumped through a steam injector, where it is heated with steam. The heated water is then transported through a plate heat exchanger and heats the product to the desired temperature.

This process has three goals:

G1   Heat the product to desired temperature.
G2   Bring product to heat exchanger.
G3   Bring water to heat exchanger.

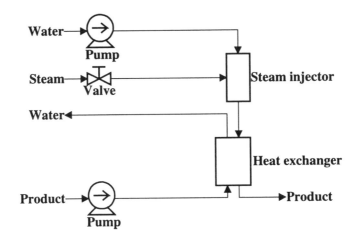

Figure 5: *Process schematics of a heat exchanger.*

G1 is the primary goal of the process. G2 and G3 are subgoals, which are required in order to achieve G1.

Even though the process is rather small there are many functions present, as seen in Table 1.

	Function	The function is realised by
F1	Provide thermal energy.	The steam system.
F2	Transport thermal energy.	The steam valve.
F3	Provide thermal energy.	The water tank.
F4	Transport thermal energy.	The water tank.
F5	Transport thermal energy.	The steam injector.
F6	Transfer thermal energy between media.	The heat exchanger.
F7	Receive thermal energy.	The product.
F8	Provide steam.	The steam system.
F9	Transport steam.	The steam valve.
F10	Provide water.	The water tank.
F11	Transport water.	The water pump.
F12	Mix water and steam.	The steam injector.
F13	Transport heated water.	The heat exchanger.
F14	Receive heated water.	The water tank.
F15	Provide product.	The product tank.
F16	Transport product.	The product pump.
F17	Receive product.	Another part of the Steritherm process where the packing of the product takes place.

Table 1: *The functions in the Steritherm process.*

The third basic concept of MFM is the physical components. In this process the physical components are:

C1   Product tank.
C2   Product pump.
C3   Heat exchanger.
C4   Water tank.
C5   Water pump.
C6   Steam system.
C7   Steam valve.
C8   Steam injector

The MFM model of the process in Figure 5 is shown in Figure 6. The dots below some of the functions indicate that a sensor in the process monitors those functions' alarm states. F2, F4, and F6 have temperature sensors, which measure the temperature of the steam, the water, and the product respectively. F9, F11, F13, and F16 have flow sensors, which measure the flow of the steam, the water, the steam/water mixture, and the product respectively.

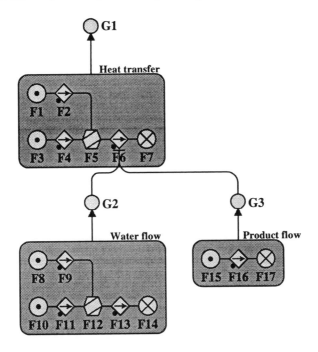

Figure 6: *An MFM model of the heat exchanger in Figure 5.*

2.4 Alarm Analysis

Even though the previously described process is small, it contains several sensors. A single failure may cause consequential failures, for example, if the steam system does not provide enough steam then following alarm situation may occur:

- F9 reports that the flow of steam is too low.
- F2 reports that the temperature of the steam is too low.
- F6 reports that the heated product is not hot enough.

In the situation described above it may not be too hard to figure out which alarm is the root cause. However, in a process with hundreds of sensors, the alarm situation may not be as easily handled. The already existing MFM alarm analysis algorithm introduced by Larsson [2, 3] handles alarm situation by organising the alarms into two classes:

1. *Primary alarms.* These are the alarms that are directly connected to the primary source of the failure.

2. *Secondary alarms.* These alarms may be the consequence of a primary alarm. However, it is also possible that they are hidden primary alarms, that is, primary alarms that are failed in such way that they appear to be caused by another failure.

Each of the MFM functions has a set of alarm states that indicates in which way they have failed. These are described in Table 2.

Alarm state	Description
locap	The inflow, or outflow, is greater than intended for the function.
loflow	The flow through the function is lower than intended.
hiflow	The flow through the function is higher than intended.
lovol	The stored volume in the function is lower than intended.
hivol	The stored volume in the function is higher than intended.
leak	The inflow is greater than the outflow.
fill	The outflow is greater than the inflow.

Table 2: *Description of the MFM alarm states.*

Each function may only be in some of these states. The possible alarm states for each function are enumerated in Table 3. Besides the alarm states each function may be in a normal state, that is, working as expected.

Function	Alarm states
Source	*locap, normalcap*
Transport	*loflow, normalflow, hiflow*
Barrier	*leak, normal*
Storage	*lovol, normalvol, hivol, fill, normal, leak*
Balance	*loflow, normalflow, hiflow, fill, normal, leak*
Sink	*locap, normalcap*

Table 3: *The possible alarm states for the different MFM functions.*

Figure 7 shows a part of the process in Figure 5. Assume that the water pump (F11) transports too much water. Even though the water tank is able to provide as much water as the pump requires, it will eventually run out of water, thus being in a state of *locap*. Since the pump is the cause of the *locap* alarm, the transport (F11) is guessed to be primary, and (F10) is guessed to be secondary.

F10 F11

Figure 7: *An MFM alarm situation.*

This type of intelligent guessing in the MFM alarm analysis algorithm is called *consequence propagation*. Table 4 lists the rules for the consequence propagation used in the example above. The source is denoted by S and the transport is denoted by T. Part A shows the rules for alarm state consequence propagation. Note that this only applies to functions without sensors. Part B shows the rules used to determine the failure state of the source function, and finally part C shows the rules used to classify the alarm. Similar rule sets exist for all legal MFM connections, see Larsson [2, 3].

A	$\neg hiflow(T) \Rightarrow normalcap(S)$
	$hiflow(T) \Rightarrow locap(S)$
B	$normalcap(S) \Rightarrow working(S)$
	$locap(S) \Rightarrow failed(S)$
C	$normalcap(S) \Rightarrow ok(S)$
	$\neg hiflow(T) \wedge locap(S) \Rightarrow primary(S)$
	$hiflow(T) \wedge locap(S) \Rightarrow secondary(S)$

Table 4: *The rules used for the consequence propagation between a transport (T) and a source (S).*

To describe how the flow structure is searched when performing an alarm analysis, the example MFM model in Figure 8 will be used. The dots indicate the functions that are measured (connected to sensors in a process). If the transport (F11) is the most recently changed alarm, then the algorithm starts by searching all possible paths through the flow structure in such a way that every function appears only once in each path. The search ends when a sensor is found, or when a function with only one connection point is reached, that is, a source, an observer, a sink or an actor function.

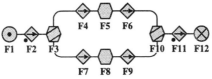

Figure 8: *An example of a MFM alarm analysis situation.*

The tree is traversed according to the following algorithm, the Waltz algorithm [4]:

1. Search downward for a leaf node.
2. If the leaf node is a function with a sensor that reports an alarm, perform the consequence propagation back to the root node.
3. If the root node is now considered a primary alarm for this path then perform the consequence propagation down to the leaf node.
4. Search downward for a new leaf node and repeat from 2 until all paths have been analysed.

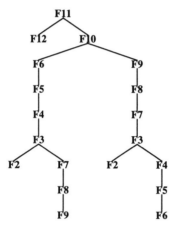

Figure 9: *The tree searched when performing an alarm analysis on the MFM model in Figure 8.*

Using this algorithm, two types of conflicts may occur:

- A function's guessed alarm state may be high based on one path, or low based on another path. This problem is solved by introducing a new guessed alarm state, *hilo*, which indicates that the function's alarm state is either high or low.
- The function at the root may be considered a primary alarm based on one path, or secondary based on another path. This problem is solved by assuming that the function's alarm is secondary, since it is probably caused by another alarm. Even if it actually is primary the definition of a secondary alarm states that it might be a hidden primary alarm.

3 Fuzzy Alarm Analysis

The crisp logic MFM analysis algorithm has some problems when faced with noisy signals, and signals close to a decision limit. Fuzzy logic [7] would be an interesting approach to come to terms with some of the problems concerning the uncertainties in the real world. The following benefits are gained when combining the existing MFM alarm analysis with fuzzy logic:

- The alarm analysis algorithm is more reliable when there are disturbances caused by small and rapid changes.
- It is possible to grade the closeness to a decision limit.
- It is possible to grade the failure, that is, how failed a function is.
- The rules and the algorithm of the already existing MFM alarm analysis algorithm may be used.

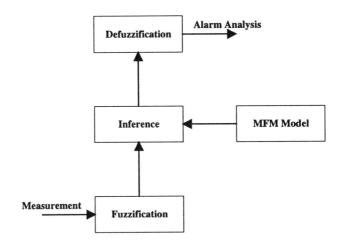

Figure 10: *An architecture for fuzzy MFM alarm analysis.*

Figure 10 shows the architecture used for fuzzy MFM alarm analysis. First the measured process values are fuzzified. Then the connections in the MFM model determine which rules are used by the inference. Finally, the results of the fuzzy alarm analysis are defuzzified back to information, which is presented to the operator or some higher level diagnostic algorithm.

Throughout the remainder of the section the fuzzification, the inference, and the defuzzification stages will be described. To demonstrate the proposed fuzzy analysis algorithm, the following alarm situation is used (see Figure 5 and Figure 6):

- F9 reports that the flow of steam is too low.
- F13 reports that the flow of the steam/water mixture is too low.

Figure 11 shows the search tree for the alarm situation above. To limit the example, the path F9–F12–F13 is the only path that will be analysed.

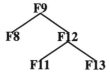

Figure 11: *The search tree for the alarm situation.*

3.1 Fuzzification

To transform the measured value into a fuzzy alarm state, fuzzy sets as those in Figure 12 are used. Figure 12 shows the *loflow, normalflow*, and the *hiflow* fuzzy sets used for the alarm states for transports and balances. For each of the other alarm states similar fuzzy sets exist.

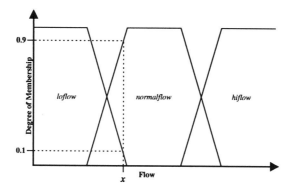

Figure 12: *The fuzzy sets used when determining the alarm state of a transport or a balance.*

Assume that the flow of the steam/water mixture through the heat exchanger (F13 in Figure 6) is x. Then the alarm state of the function belongs to the fuzzy set *loflow* to a degree of 0.1 as shown in Figure 12. The grades of membership to the other fuzzy sets are obtained in the same way, see Table 5. F9's alarm state belongs more to the *loflow* fuzzy set than to the *normalflow* fuzzy set, while F13's alarm state belongs more to the *normalflow* fuzzy set than to the *loflow* fuzzy set.

Function	*loflow*	*Normalflow*	*hiflow*
F9	0.9	0.1	0.0
F13	0.1	0.9	0.0

Table 5: *Degree of membership to the alarm state fuzzy sets for the measured functions.*

3.2   Inference

The inference engine uses the same rules as the already existing discrete logic MFM alarm analysis algorithm, see Table 4. Using the steps of the Waltz algorithm the steps will be:

1. The search starts at F9 and ends at F13 because F13 has a sensor.
2. Since the sensor of F13 reports an alarm the consequence propagation is done according to the consequence propagation rules from F13 to F9. The result is shown in Table 6.

	F13	F12	F9
loflow	0.1	0.1	0.9
normalflow	0.9	0.9	0.1
hiflow	0.0	0.0	0.0
working	0.9	0.9	0.1
failed	0.1	0.1	0.9
ok	0.9	0.9	0.1
primary	0.1	0.0	0.0
secondary	0.0	0.1	0.1

Table 6: *The result of the F13–F12–F9 consequence propagation.*

3. Since the sensor of F13 also is in *normalflow* state, and thus F9 must be a primary alarm, the consequence propagation is done from F9 to F13. The result is shown in Table 7.

	F9	F12	F13
loflow	0.9	0.9	0.1
normalflow	0.1	0.1	0.9
hiflow	0.0	0.0	0.0
working	0.1	0.1	0.9
failed	0.9	0.9	0.1
ok	0.1	0.1	0.9
primary	0.9	0.0	0.0
secondary	0.0	0.9	0.1

Table 7: *The result of the F9–F12–F13 consequence propagation*

Now the results of step 2 and 3 must be merged together. This is done according to the rules in Table 8.

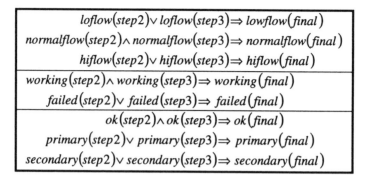

$loflow(step2) \lor loflow(step3) \Rightarrow lowflow(final)$

$normalflow(step2) \land normalflow(step3) \Rightarrow normalflow(final)$

$hiflow(step2) \lor hiflow(step3) \Rightarrow hiflow(final)$

$working(step2) \land working(step3) \Rightarrow working(final)$

$failed(step2) \lor failed(step3) \Rightarrow failed(final)$

$ok(step2) \land ok(step3) \Rightarrow ok(final)$

$primary(step2) \lor primary(step3) \Rightarrow primary(final)$

$secondary(step2) \lor secondary(step3) \Rightarrow secondary(final)$

Table 8: *The rules for merging together step 2 and step 3 of the Waltz algorithm.*

Here, *step2* is the function's calculated fuzzy values in step 2, *step3* is the function's calculated fuzzy values in step 3, and *final* is the result of the consequence propagation. The result of the consequence propagation is shown in Table 9.

	F9	F12	F13
loflow	0.9	0.9	0.1
normalflow	0.1	0.1	0.9
hiflow	0.0	0.0	0.0
working	0.1	0.1	0.9
failed	0.9	0.9	0.1
ok	0.1	0.1	0.9
primary	0.9	0.0	0.1
secondary	0.1	0.9	0.1

Table 9: *The final result of the consequence propagation.*

3.3 Defuzzification

After the alarm analysis has been performed the desired knowledge is "how failed the function is", and whether it is a cause or a consequence, that is, primary or secondary. To obtain this knowledge from the fuzzy values in Table 9 the fuzzy sets in Figure 13 are used. For the consequence state a similar set is used.

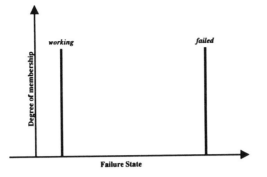

Figure 13: *The fuzzy sets for the failure state.*

The defuzzication is performed by using the centre of gravity method [1]. Figure 14 shows the defuzzication of the consequence state for function F9.

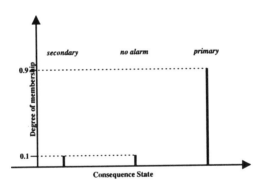

Figure 14: *Example of defuzzication using the result of the consequence propagation in Table 9 and the consequence state fuzzy sets.*

The output from the defuzzifier is presented as two numbers. The first number indicates how failed the function is, and the second number indicates if the alarm is primary or secondary. In this example the value of failure ranges from 0 to 100, where 0 means working, and 100 means that the function is failed. Furthermore, the consequence value ranges from −1 to 1, where −1 means a secondary alarm, 1 means a primary alarm, and 0 means working as expected (no alarm situation). These ranges may be chosen to suit the needs of higher level diagnostic algorithms. Using this gives the final result in Table 10. This shows that the cause of the alarm situation is that the steam valve does not transport enough steam. A failure value of 90 means that F9 and F12 are "very failed". A consequence value of 0.7 means that F9 is considered to be a "very primary" alarm. F12 is considered to be a "very secondary" alarm since the consequence value is −0.9. F13 is almost working as expected.

	Failure	Consequence
F9	90	0.7
F12	90	-0.9
F13	10	0.0

Table 10: *The result after defuzzication.*

4 Conclusions

MFM alarm analysis using fuzzy logic may solve some of the problems the already existing discrete logic algorithm would not handle, for example, chaotic switching due to noise and closeness to a decision limit. One possible drawback of the proposed alarm analysis algorithm is that it may be slower than the already existing algorithm, because of the increased computational complexity. However, since the already existing MFM algorithm is very fast, the fuzzy logic algorithm may still be among the fastest algorithms available.

5 Acknowledgements

I would like to thank my supervisor Jan Eric Larsson and my colleague Bengt Öhman at the Department of Information Technology for their support. I would also like to thank Anu Uus for her help with the proof-reading. This project is funded by TFR project no. 96–187.

References

1. Cox, E., Fuzzy Systems Handbook, Academic Press, London, 1994.
2. Larsson, J. E., Knowledge-Based Methods for Control Systems, Doctor's thesis, TFRT–1040, Department of Automatic Control, Lund Institute of Technology, Lund, 1992.
3. Larsson, J. E., "Diagnosis Based on Explicit Means-End Models," Artificial Intelligence, vol. 80, no. 1, pp. 29–93, 1996.
4. Larsson, J. E. and F. Dahlstrand, "New Algorithms for MFM Alarm Analysis", invited paper, Proceedings of the IEEE International Conference on System, Man, and Cybernetics, San Diego, California, 1998.
5. Larsson, J. E. and B. Hayes-Roth, "Guardian: An Intelligent Autonomous Agent for Medical Monitoring and Diagnosis," IEEE Intelligent Systems, vol. 13, no. 1, pp. 58–64, 1998.
6. Lind, M., "Representing Goals and Functions of Complex Systems-An Introduction to Multilevel Flow Modeling," Technical report, 90–D–38, Institute of Automatic Control Systems, Technical University of Denmark, Lyngby, 1990
7. Zadeh, L. A., "Fuzzy Sets," Information and Control, vol. 8, pp. 338–353, 1965.

Learning Full Pitch Variation Patterns

with NeuralNets

Tingshao Zhu   Wen Gao

MOTOROLA-ICT Joint R&D Lab, Institute of Computing Technology,
Academia Sinica, Beijing, 100080. P.R. China

Charles X. Ling

Department of Computer Science, University of Western Ontario
London, Ontario N6A 5B7. Canada

Abstract

Prosodic model is very important for speech synthesis. It includes pitch model, duration model and pause model, and pitch model is the most important. Now most pitch models are constructed by linguistics experts, and they are described qualitatively and with low precise. We consider the pitch models as the mapping between the pitches of isolate syllable and those of the same one in phrase, so neural net can be used to learn the patterns. For acquiring these patterns quantitatively and precisely, BP networks are established to extract pitch and duration variation patterns from large speech database. Since the networks have been trained from actual speech samples, the quality of synthesis speech which is based on the networks can be high. In this paper, the architecture is first specified, then the new time wrapping algorithm and the networks are introduced in detail, and at last results are given too.

1 Introduction

In the field of speech signal process, pitch is one of the most important parameters. Tone is decided by pitch variation, and it denotes different meaning in some languages especially in Chinese [1]. When two or more Chinese syllables combine together, each syllable's tone will be changed. In speech synthesis, prosodic model is very important for improving the intelligibility and naturalness. It includes pitch model, duration model and pause model, and pitch model is the most important one. The pitch models, which are now being used in most speech synthesis applications, are extracted by experts, but these models are described qualitatively and with low precise. Although there are many pitch models, they cannot describe the variation completely, because they are made by people through some statistics on speech samples. These speech samples cannot cover all the speech phenomena. On the other hand, it is difficult to deal with massive speech data.

Wu Zongji[10] has done much research about tone patterns of two-word phrases. He found that when two syllables are combined, their tones tend to be continuous. In addition, he found some qualitative rules about tone changes, for example, when the first one is a rising tone, the tone shape of the second syllable is lower than that of the first one. Other researchers have also done some working about tone variation, such as (Lin, Yan and Sun, 1984) and (Chu, 1995).

Pitch models can be regarded as the mapping between the pitches of isolate syllable and those of the same one in phrase, so neural net can be used to learn the mapping. For acquiring these patterns quantitatively and precisely, BP networks are established to learn full pitch variation patterns from large speech database. Since the networks have been trained from actual speech samples, the quality of synthesis speech which is based on the networks can be high. But because the size of speech database is always very large, it is impossible for people to extract these patterns by hand.

In order to extract pitch variation patterns, we construct neural networks to learn the patterns. A prototype system called SpeechDM has been implemented. In Chinese, the pitches extracted from an isolate syllable differ from those extracted from the same syllable in phrases, and SpeechDM extracts the patterns from the mapping between them.

2 Learning Process

SpeechDM is a prototype system on data mining, and it is designed to deal with speech and find some useful patterns from large speech database. The system consists of data preprocessing, data learning and postprocessing. Figure 1 depicts the process of learning full pitch variation patterns in SpeechDM.

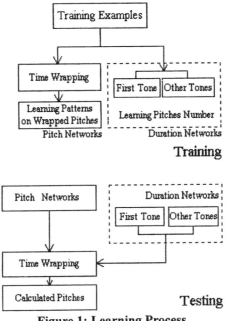

Figure 1: Learning Process.

In order to learn the full pitch variation patterns by neural net, the data should be normalized at first. It is well know that the BP net is trained with fixed input units, that is, the length of each training example must be the same. But in speech, the number of pitches of a syllable differs from each other significantly, so each training example must be wrapped to the equal length to fit for the requirement of BP net.

Two kinds of networks are built to learn the patterns: pitch network and duration network. The first one learns from the wrapped pitches which have the same length, and the second learns the variation patterns of the number of pitches. After the networks have been trained, the testing example should be wrapped to the length of the pitch network's input layer. At the same time the number of the same example is extracted and acts as testing example for duration network. Then the calculated pitches can be wrapped according to the result of duration network.

In Chinese two-word phrases, the first one differs from the same syllable in isolation greatly, so networks are built to learn patterns from the first syllable and the second separately. Chinese is a tonal language, and there are four kinds of tones: first tone, second tone, rising tone and fourth tone, and 1, 2, 3, and 4 can denote them. According to some previous experiments, when the duration network is trained from the examples including all the tones, the results are bad. But when these examples are split into two parts, one includes the examples with first tone and the other includes the examples with other tones, the results are much better. So in training duration network, the examples from the first syllables in phrases are split into two parts, and two networks learn the patterns separately.

3 Data Preprocessing

Data preprocessing mainly deals with the data from speech database directly, which extracts pitch, wraps the duration and normalizes the pitch values to meet the requirement of learning algorithm.

3.1 Data Preparation

The Speech Database that we are using is a Chinese speech synthesis database called CoSS-1. CoSS-1 includes the pronunciation of all isolate syllables, the 2-4 word phrases and some sentences. The number of isolate syllables with tone is 1268, and that of two-word phrase is 640.

CoSS-1 records the speech wave and laryngograph synchronously. The sampling rate is 16000/s, and each sample is stored in two bytes. The two-word phrase covers almost the whole tone collocations in Chinese. It is easy to distinguish each cycle in laryngograph, so the pitches are extracted by annotating each keynote cycling in laryngograph.

We implemented a tool called Pitcher to extract pitch from laryngograph. The period along laryngograph is annotated through signing the beginning and ending point by hand, and the reference cycle within the period should be signed the same way, then pitcher deals with the cycles one by one automatically. Let X_i be the beginning point of one cycle and X_j be the ending point, then the pitch of this cycle should be $16000/(X_j - X_i)$.

3.2 Time Wrapping and Normalization

It is well known that the number of neural net's input units is fixed, but the length of pitch, which acts as the training examples, differs from each other significantly. So the training examples should be wrapped into same length. A new algorithm is designed to wrap the pitches. The algorithm is shown in Figure 2.

```
Time wrapping algorithm:

/* the length and value of pitch which will be wrapped */
Input: float *pitch . int pitchlen,

/* the wrapped pitch and its length */
Output: float *twpitch, int twlen;

For each i between 1 and twlen
{
    Calculate the relative location in   1 – pitchlen
        loc = (float) (pitchlen * i) / (float) twlen;
        intloc = (int) loc
    If loc=(float)intloc then twlen[i] = pitch[intloc];
    If not, get four integers near loc
        calculate the value by the analogy function across them
        twlen[i] = value;
}
```

Figure 2: Time Wrapping Algorithm.

For the speech data we used, the pitches' value domain is between $50 - 260$. In SpeechDM, the following equation is used to normalize the pitch value.

$$\text{Normalized\_Pitch} = (\text{Pitch\_value} - min) / (max - min)$$

Where **max** is the maximum of all pitches' value and **min** is the minimum. **Pitch_value** stores the pitch to be calculated and **Normalized_Pitch** is the normalized value.

4 Neural Network

Neural networks are used to learn the patterns of the pitch variation. Since they are trained from actual speech samples, it is possible to get more accurate results than other methods.

4.1 Network Architecture

There are many kinds of neural networks which can be used for learning. We intend to learn the patterns from the mapping between the pitches in isolate syllable and those in phrase, since backpropagation network has implicit input layer and output layer, and it can also give very good result[6], thus it is chosen to be trained in SpeechDM.

To learn the pitch variation patterns from the mapping, the pitches of the syllable in phrase are extracted firstly, and the pitches of the same syllable but in isolation are extracted too. The pitches from phrase are acted as output and those from isolation as input. In Chinese, when syllables are combined, their pitches are modified according to some rules, so the tones can be regarded as the factors that influence the pitches of the two syllables. The tones of the two syllables are also included in input layer.

Two pitch networks are built to learn the patterns from the first syllables and the second ones of the two-word phrases in CoSS-1. Four duration networks are built to learn the variation patterns of the number of pitches, and they can be split into two groups, two networks are trained by the examples extracted from all the first syllables of two-word phrases, and the other two networks learn all the second syllables. For each group, one is designed to learn the patterns from the examples with first tone, and the other learns from examples with other tones.

4.2 Network Input and Output

Since the tone is important for pitch variation, the input layer of either pitch network or duration network consists of the tones of both syllables. There are only four tones in Chinese, eight units are used to indicate the tones of the first syllable and the second one in phrase. For example: 01001000 indicates the first syllable's tone is second tone and the second syllable's tone is first tone.

For pitch network, input layer consists of not only the units that present two syllables' tones but also the pitches of the syllable in isolation, and the output layer only consists of the pitches in phrases. The length that input training pitches are wrapped into equals to the mean of the number of all isolate syllables' pitches, and for the output layer, the length equals to the mean of number of pitches from all the first syllables or second ones. The hidden layer consists of 100 units and the number can be modified before the training.

For duration network, input layer consists of not only the tones of the two words but also vowel and consonant of each one, and the number of the pitches of the isolate syllable is also included. The output layer only consists of the number of the same syllable in phrase. To normalize the number, it can be divided by 100. The number of the hidden units is 20.

In order to generate training and testing data, you should split the phrase firstly, calculate the pitches, wrap the pitches to the same length and normalize pitches' value. Then the data can be used to train and test neural network. Most of them act as training examples and others as testing.

5 Results

To show the result graphically, a tool is designed to show the test examples. From the graph, it is easy to see whether the calculated pitch coincides with the actual pitch or not, and it can display as much as ten syllables ' pitch at the same time.

For testing, some data are selected from CoSS-1, after processed; some data are extracted randomly to act as testing examples and others for training. Each experiment use different data, despite displaying the calculated pitches in graph, some statistics are also calculated from the results.

Table 1 gives some statistics of the results from one test. The calculations are based on the deduction between the original syllable's pitches in phrase and those calculated by the network, and of course they have been wrapped to the same length. Table 2 gives the results of the duration testing, and the number in phrase and that calculated by network is shown to see the difference between them.

	Phrase	Max	Min	Mean	Variance
F	Chuang1shan4	4	0	-1.477206	4.376950
I	Jin4zhan4	13	0	-0.241210	42.273769
R	Liu2xie4	18	0	-4.525616	15.284344
S	Gong1hui4	15	0	2.656483	10.662880
T	Wang2pai2	9	0	2.016155	7.791716
S	Zhi4xun2	6	0	-0.001093	2.958961
E	Bing3yao4	14	0	-3.638539	23.004646
C	Bao3xian3	7	0	-0.527984	10.082108
O	La1suo3	7	0	0.168661	7.902920
N D	Xiao4you3	19	0	4.453946	24.817568

Table 1: The results of one test.

		Spell	Number in Phrase	Calculated by NetWork
First **Syllable**	First Tone	la1suo3	51	50
		cao1yan3	35	49
		chong1ren4	29	41
		chuan1ma3	36	50
		a1pian4	36	42
	Other Tones	tu2an4	31	30
		chuo4hao4	32	29
		shu4e2	27	29
		cuo4shou3	37	35
		fu3ai4	35	30
Second **Syllable**	First Tone	ta1yang1	50	51
		xiang1Yue1	75	51
		sui2jun1	41	51
		qie4sheng1	40	43
		ban4yin1	50	52
	Other Tones	can2ren3	44	40
		du1fu3	33	36
		wei2ao4	42	37
		yi2zhi4	35	40
		fu2fu2	39	39

Table 2: The results of one test on the number of pitches.

From the results we can see that the calculated pitches match the actual pitch closely, and the duration results for first tone are bad, but those for other tones matches the number in phrase well.

6 Conclusion

Since pitch variation patterns are very important for speech synthesis, we try to use neural network to learn the patterns from actual speech data. SpeechDM is the data mining system that is designed to learn the patterns of pitch variation in Chinese two-word phrase. From the result, we can see that the network has learned the pattern of pitch variation very well. This work is an on-going research, and we intend to use the calculated results in speech synthesis to see whether it can improve the quality of speech. We hope that by learning these patterns from actual speech examples, it is possible to use them to improve the intelligibility and naturalness of Chinese synthesis speech.

REFERENCES

1. Lin Tao, Wang Lijia. Acoustics course of study. Peking University Press, Beijing, 1994.

2. Chu Min. Research on Chinese TTS system with high intelligibility and naturalness. Ph.D thesis, Institute of Acoustics, Academia Sinica, 1995.

3. Usama M.Fayyad, Gregory Piatetsky-Shapiro, Padhraic Smyth, and Ramasamy Uthurusamy. Adavance In Knowledge Dicovery And Data Mining. AAAI/MIT Press, 1996.

4. George H.John. Enhancements to the Data Mining Process. Ph.D thesis, Stanford University, 1997.

5. Yang Xingjun, Chi Huisheng. Speech Signal Digital Process. Publishing House of Electronic Industry, Beijing, 1990.

6. Wang Wei. Principle of Artificial Neural Network ---- rudiment and implement. Beijing University of Aeronautics and Astronautics Press, Beijing, 1995.

7. Kero, B, L. Russell, S. Tsur and W.M. Shen. An Overview of Data Mining Technologies. The KDD Workshop in the 4th International Conference on Deductive and Object-Oriented Databases, Singapore, 1995.

8. Famili. The Role of Data Pre-processing in Intelligent Data Analysis. Proceedings of the IDA-95 Symposium, Baden-Baden, Germany, 1995, pp 54-58.

9. J. Han, Y. Fu, Y. Huang, Y. Cai, and N. Cercone. DBLearn: A system prototype for knowledge discovery in relational databases. Proc. 1994 ACM-SIGMOD Int'l Conf. on Management of Data (SIGMOD'94), Minneapolis, MN, May 1994.

10. Wu Zongji. The tone variation in mandarin. Chinese grammar. No 6, 1982, pp 439-449.

11. Lin Maocan, Yan Jinzu, Sun guohua.: Experiment of the normal accent in Beijing dialect. Dialect. No 1, 1984.

A Neural Network Based Approach to Objective Voice Quality Assessment

R. T. Ritchings[1], G. V. Conroy[1], M. A. McGillion[1], C. J. Moore[2], N. Slevin[3], S. Winstanley[4], H. Woods[4]

[1]Multimedia Signal Processing Group, Department of Computation, UMIST, Manchester, UK

[2]NorthWest Medical Physics, Christie Hospital NHS Trust, Wilmslow Road, Manchester, UK

[3]Christie Hospital NHS Trust, Wilmslow Road, Manchester, UK

[4]South Manchester University Hospitals Trust, Withington Hospital, Manchester, UK

Abstract

Voice quality is of fundamental importance to the patient following treatment of cancer of the larynx. Current techniques for voice analysis are slow, mainly subjective, and based on limited numbers of retrospective studies. This study is concerned with the development of an on-line system which encapsulates the expert knowledge of the Speech and Language Therapist in such a way as to provide an objective and consistent assessment of voice quality for staging and treatment monitoring of cancer of the larynx.

After discussions with the Speech and Language Therapist it was concluded that their expert knowledge was related to subtle variations in the frequency structure in a patient's stylised speech. In order to identify the frequency components that can be used to provide an objective classification and assessment of a patient's voice quality, appropriate parameters were extracted from a segment of speech recorded from 20 male patients with cancer of the larynx and 20 male volunteers who were considered as having normal voice quality. These parameters were then presented to a feed-forward Artificial Neural Network known as the Multi-Layer Perceptron. This Multi-Layer Perceptron was shown to be able to distinguish between normal, i.e. non-cancerous, subjects and patients having cancer of the larynx, achieving a classification accuracy of between 85% and 90%. These results provide the basis for an extension of this work into a practical system that may be utilised by the Speech and Language Therapist during clinical examinations to provide an objective measure of voice quality.

1. Introduction

1.1. Treatment of Cancer of the Larynx

There are two main approaches to treating larynx cancer. Surgical management of the neck is similar to that of other sites in the aero-digestive tract. In those patients with substantial and multi-site disease, radical neck dissection is usually employed in conjunction with a primary resection, unless the primary tumour has been treated with curative radiation. In those patients with minimal neck disease or with clinically negative necks, radiation alone can suffice, or any one of a variety of selected neck dissections can be employed as a means of removing gross disease from the neck in preparation for radiation. Chemoprevention is defined as the administration of natural or synthetic agents to reverse or suppress carcinogenesis before the development of an invasive cancer.

1.2. Rationale for treatment

An increasingly important factor in deciding which method of treatment should be chosen is the quality of voice retained post-therapy. While radiation therapy ensures a higher level of voice function than surgery, this observation must be weighed against the risk of recurrence of the cancer. The level of preserved voice quality must be measured to give a realistic indication to the patient of the achievable results post-treatment. A further concern is the inability of Speech and Language Therapists (SALT) to provide a consistent classification of voice quality and the separation of their assessment from that of the patient. However, it is clear that an absolute measure of voice quality cannot be formulated. Instead, a relative scale must be used to determine the enhancement or degradation in quality prior to and following treatment.

1.3. Data Capture

The usual tool for capturing speech sequences is an Electrolaryngograph PCLX system [1]. This system is used to capture electrical impedance signals using impedance pads placed either side of the neck synchronously with acoustic signals using a microphone.

The Electrolaryngograph provides four-channel 16-bit analogue-to-digital conversion and two-channel 16-bit digital-to-analogue conversion. A TI TMS320C25 50MHz DSP chip carries out digital signal processing functions. The two channels used in this work are the impedance and acoustic channels; this paper presents the results of analysis of the impedance channel. The speech data used in this study were collected from 20 male volunteers, who were considered to have normal voice quality and 20 male patients with cancer of the larynx at the Christie and Withington Hospitals in Manchester. In the remainder of the discussion these two groups will be referred to as *normal* and *abnormal* subjects respectively.

Data was collected following the exact procedure used by SALTs - capturing acoustic and impedance signals synchronously using the Electrolaryngograph. The recordings were made at 20kHz (allowing frequencies up to a Nyquist Critical Frequency of 10kHz to be represented) for around ~3.5 seconds while the subject was trying to say an 'ah' sound as steadily as possible. This sound was chosen as the SALTs find it the most informative and easily interpreted when displayed as a waveform on the screen.

1.4 Rationale for Project

In this work, a set of features have been obtained which provide a good level of classification accuracy between normal and abnormal subjects. This is an extension of earlier work [2] where more salient features have been extracted from the power spectrum of the impedance data. These features take into account the knowledge obtained from discussions with a SALT and from the physical interpretation of their description of voice quality. Recent research [3] suggests that Multilayer Perceptrons (MLPs) can be used to successfully classify acoustic signals. Also, non-Artificial Neural Network (ANN) methods have been used to identify and provide a measure of voice quality [4][5]. Given the different methods available in identifying these pathologies, a consistent framework needs to be developed that will provide the SALT with a useful system to provide an objective measure of voice quality.

2. Knowledge Extraction and Representation

In order to provide a consistent measure of voice quality, one must first elicit the knowledge used by the SALT in their own perceptual analysis of voice quality. The usual assessment of voice quality involves a SALT making a perceptual analysis of stylised speech in terms of pitch, loudness and

Phonation Type	Physical Description
Whisper	The inability to fully close the vocal folds resulting in higher frequency components
Creak	Tense vocal cords resulting in an irregular fundamental frequency with limited intensity, and higher frequency components
Vocal Fry	Pulsatile-like production of speech resulting in a low and irregular fundamental frequency
Harsh	Inability to open and close vocal folds in a precise manner resulting in spurious mid-range frequencies
Shimmer	Inability to sustain a constant amplitude level resulting in a cycle to cycle variation of amplitude
Jitter	Inability to sustain a constant frequency resulting in a cycle to cycle variation of fundamental frequency

Table 1. Physical description of phonation types

intonation from taped speech from the patient. The purpose of the assessment is to identify how well the patient's voice is returning to normal, and then modify the therapy program as necessary. Not only is this approach very subjective, but one speech therapist may provide a completely different diagnosis and staging of the patient's recovery from another. This inconsistency arises because of the difficulty in defining the terms used to describe voice quality and their physical interpretation. Typical terms used by a SALT to describe the different disorders brought on by the cancer and its treatment and their physical interpretation are listed in Table 1.

To some extent, all voices exhibit these characteristics. For example, normal voices have jitter of 0.5-1.0%, e.g. 1Hz, and shimmer of about 0.04-0.21db. These variations are not easily discernible below the levels of 2% jitter or 1 db shimmer [6]. It is the extent to which these characteristics are present that needs to be quantified. Using this measure, a description of voice quality against a statistically normal voice can be provided.

During examination the patient reproduces vowels and phonetically balanced sentences. The SALT is looking for regularity in voice quality. One measure of this 'regularity' can be obtained using an electrical impedance signal that is transmitted through the vocal tissue surrounding the larynx. A fast decrease in impedance at the onset of speech is regarded as a sign of a healthy vocal tract. A slower decrease in impedance, which results in a prolonged onset of speech, is regarded as a sign of poor speech quality. This can be viewed in an idealised laryngograph waveform (Lx) as a sharp decrease in impedance as the vocal folds close at the onset of speech. A diagram of an idealised Lx waveform is shown in Figure 1. Note the relationship between the four phases of the waveform and the vocal fold position.

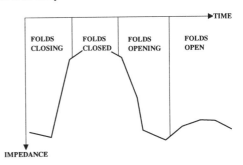

Figure 1. Idealised Lx waveform

Increased tension in the vocal cords results in a less periodic and higher frequency waveform. For example, in Creak where there is increased tension in the vocal tract, the acoustic waveform becomes more erratic with high local variance. Furthermore, the impedance waveform displays a small then large Lx waveform that is apparently as a result of 'bouncing' vocal folds.

The approach taken has been to elicit the expert knowledge used by the SALT during the assessment of a patient's voice. This has involved analysing a selection of the stylised speech samples and those aspects of voice quality considered to be significant by the SALT. It was observed that the effect of the radiotherapy was to distort the balance of the formant frequencies, to the extent that they are almost absent immediately after radiotherapy but can reappear after a year.

In addition the SALTs listen for jitter which is a shift in the fundamental frequency (see Table 1). This problem occurs frequently among cancer of the larynx patients, particularly in the male group, which constitute the bulk of the cases as they form the main group of smokers. While it was concluded that the prime knowledge used by SALTs related to subtle changes in the frequency structure of the patient's speech as it returned to normal after radiotherapy, it was difficult to be more precise about the specific changes that were taking place. It was, however, felt that an ANN might be built on this information and configured to learn and later recognise these changes in frequency structure as a means of providing the objective assessment of the quality of the speech.

From empirical analysis of the speech waveforms, it is apparent that the most discriminant information lies in the 0-5kHz range. This report concentrates on developing a classifier to distinguish between normal and patient data using this frequency range. The results presented in this paper detail the tests performed upon two data sets. The first data set contains a frequency range of 0Hz to 10kHz. The second data set contains a frequency range of 0Hz to 1kHz and 4kHz to 5kHz. These ranges were selected for analysis from our observations of the frequency structure of both normal and abnormal subject profiles.

3. Data Analysis

In general terms the data analysis involved a Power Spectral Analysis of 1000 sample sequences from the impedance data, and selections of these derived frequency components were fed to the MLP for the purpose of training and then classification.

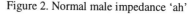
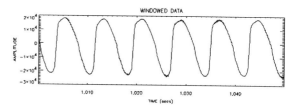

Figure 2. Normal male impedance 'ah'

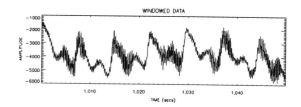

Figure 3. Abnormal male impedance 'ah'

Examples of a typical normal and abnormal Lx waveform are shown in Figures 2 and 3 respectively. In order to determine the most discriminant information present in the speech signal, the speech signals were processed in two different ways, and both of these derived data sets were fed to a variety of MLP structures, as described in the following sections.

3.1. Signal Processing and Feature Extraction

The speech signals were initially processed with no time-domain pre-processing. In this case a total of 56 overlapping windows of 1000 points were manually selected for input to the MLP. To cover the entire data capture period of ~2secs a total of 56 windows were chosen. An offset of ~1sec was used to allow for noise at the beginning of capture. The Fourier Transform of the window was computed and the full 10kHz range of positive frequencies were reduced to 20 bins by averaging and coded into a format suitable for feeding into the MLP.

The second data set was generated by first converting the data to stationarity by forward differencing in order to remove small but significant linear trends. Next, 56 overlapping windows of 1000 points were again selected for analysis by the MLP. The auto-covariance of each region was computed and multiplied with a half Hanning window. Finally, the Fourier transform was computed and frequencies in the range 0-1kHz and 4-5kHz were divided into bins by a process of averaging before being coded into a representation suitable for analysis by the MLP.

3.2. ANN topologies

There are many ANN topologies described in the literature such as feed-forward ANNs (including MLPs), feed-back ANNs, self organising ANNs and so on [7], [8], [9], [10]. However, in classification problems the most popular form of ANN in recent years has been the MLP trained with Back Propagation of Error algorithms. Much of the advances in the use of ANNs for classification has been performed since it was shown that a simple MLP can be used to directly estimate the Bayesian posterior probabilities of class membership [11]. There are many variations of the MLP and a commensurate number of training algorithms [9] that aim to improve upon the performance of earlier networks and training algorithms. However, in this research, we have chosen to use the popular two-layer MLP.

Two layer MLPs include an input layer, a single hidden layer, and a single output layer. It has been shown that two layer MLPs with non-linear activation functions are able to approximate a functional mapping with arbitrary accuracy [12]. The single input layer performs no processing, it simply distributes the inputs to the hidden layer; the single hidden layer and single output layer have been chosen to consist of logistic or softmax activation functions. In general, the activation function chosen for a given network should be determined by the problem to be represented, e.g. the required input to output mapping. The ability to view the results of an MLP classification as a function of probability also has an impact on the choice of activation function [see [10], §3.1.3 and §6.7.1]. In the first data set, two types of error function were tested, Sum Squared Error (SSE) and Multiple Entropy (ME). In the second data set, the Sum Squared Error function was used. The number of input nodes and hidden layer nodes varied on each test set and is described in the next section; a typical example is shown in Figure 4.

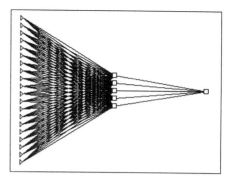

3.3. Data Representation

Figure 4. A 20-5-1 MLP

In total there were 26 normal subjects available for use in this study. However, the actual numbers used were limited to the same number as that available from the abnormal group, i.e. 20 subjects. Restricting the number of members of the normal group to be equal to those in the abnormal group allows the Bayesian posterior probabilities to be directly estimated by the MLP as shown by [11]. Unfortunately, this reduction in the amount of data available for use in training and validation of the MLP has an effect upon the number of free parameters recommended in the MLP if one is to achieve satisfactory learning with generalisation [7]. Tarassenko states that the number of training examples should be of the same order as the number of free parameters in the network. Those free parameters are the weights and biases that are adjusted during the learning process and which represent the MLPs knowledge upon completion of training.

The number of weights, W, for an I-J-K MLP is given as $W = (I+1)J + (J+1)K$, where I is the number of inputs, J is the number of hidden units, and K is the number of output units.

During this research various MLP structures were tested to elicit the most appropriate MLP structure for this classification problem. However, for the purpose of illustration, a 20-5-1 network would have 111 weights. Clearly, 40 male subjects are not enough test data to realise such a network. In total there were 23 test sets to allow for coverage of all reasonable combinations of nodes in the input and hidden layer of the MLP. Each test set consisted of 5 tests on the same structure with initially random weights having a Gaussian distribution and zero mean. Table 2 shows the MLP configuration, which was fixed for all tests.

Training Algorithm	BP
Learning Rate	0.05
Momentum	0.5
Data Scaling	Minimax
Data Scaling Min	0
Data Scaling Max	1
Initial Weight Distribution	Gaussian
Initial Weight Mean	0
Initial Weight SD	0.005
Normalisation	None

Table 2. ANN configuration

In order to increase the amount of data available to train and validate the MLP, it was decided to use more than one frame sequence from each patient as input to the MLP. In previous research [13] a single data sequence was constructed from each patient by selecting many windows and constructing an average time-domain representation. However, it is possible that the time-varying parameters inherent in speech production could be used as a discriminating factor in the MLP for classification of voice quality. Therefore, it was seen as appropriate to use more than one window from each subject for training and validation of the MLP.

The total numbers of patterns used to train, validate and test the MLPs are given in Table 3. The average test error and classification accuracy was determined from each test set and is presented in the next section.

Set	Subjects	Patterns
Training	14	784
Validation	14	784
Test	12	672

Table 3. ANN pattern set sizes

A low learning rate and higher momentum enables the MLP to reach satisfactory local minima although it may take a larger amount of iterations to achieve such minima. Furthermore, initialising the weights about a zero mean with a small standard deviation gives the activation value around the centre part of a non-linear sigmoidal activation function [7]. As with most problems solved using MLPs, the data must be scaled prior to training the MLP. This is due to the fact that the dynamic range of the input data may be very large with outliers having large consequences on the MLP performance. Further, using a logistic activation function with activation values in the range [0,1] requires that the data be scaled in order to lie within this range.

4. Results

The test results of the first (no time-domain processing) and second (time-domain processing) data sets extracted from the male impedance data and tested on various MLP configurations are shown in Table A1 in Appendix A. Figure 5a-d shows the error rate and classification accuracy for both data sets.

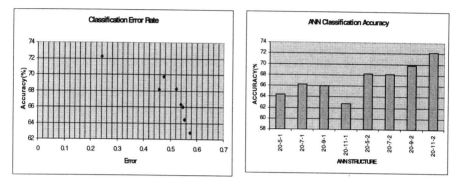

Figure 5a. Error rate for first data set

Figure 5b. Classification accuracy for first data set

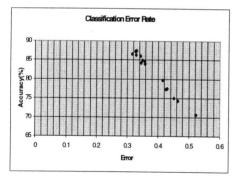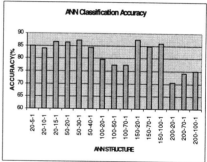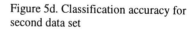

Figure 5c. Error rate for second data set

Figure 5d. Classification accuracy for second data set

From these results, one can see that the most accurate classification is achieved with a 150-20-1 configuration closely followed by the 50-30-1 configuration. These classification statistics are the average statistics from 5 tests performed on that network structure. The best classification performance overall was achieved with a 50-30-1 network with a maximum classification accuracy of 90.48%.

There is a large difference in the classification accuracy from the two data sets. The average classification accuracy of the first data set is 67.23% compared to 81.72%. From these statistics, it can be seen that pre-processing the signal in the time-domain to extract its harmonic and formant amplitudes and its periodicity gives a better set of discriminant features from which to classify the impedance signal. With the impedance data, an average classification accuracy of between 85% and 90% was achieved.

5. Conclusions and Further Work

This research has concluded that MLPs can be used with reasonable accuracy to distinguish the impedance signals derived from normal and abnormal subjects. This confirms the earlier observations of [2] where traditional MLPs were also used to classify impedance signals.

The ability of a patient to phonate a vowel at a constant level of pitch is one of the methods by which a SALT assesses the voice quality of a CAL patient. As suspected and proven in this research, it is the harmonic and formant amplitude that gives some the greatest measures of the quality of the signal.

Work is currently underway to achieve the same or better results with the acoustic data. An average classification accuracy of between 45% and 54% has been achieved. However, it is believed that the acoustic data contains far more information that will be valuable in quantifying the voice quality of patients across a range of disorders. Further work will concentrate on extracting a better set of features from a larger patient dataset that is currently being collected in order to develop a system capable of giving an objective measure across voice disorders arising from cancer of the larynx, such as those detailed in Table 1. Finally, it is hoped that this work will provide a platform for the development of other systems capable of utilisation across the range of disorders that a speech therapist encounters.

References

1. Fourcin AJ, Abberton E, Miller D, Howell D. Laryngograph: Speech pattern element tools for therapy, training and assessment. European Journal of Disorders of Comunication, 1995; 30; 2: 101-115.

2. Moore CJ, Slevin N, Ritchings RT & Chi KY. An approach to objective voice quality assessment for staging and treatment monitoring of cancer of the larynx. World Congress for Medical Physics and Biological Engineering, Nice, France, 1997.

3. Tadeusiewicz R, Wszolek W, Modrzejewski M. The evaluation of speech deformation treated for larynx cancer using neural network and pattern recognition methods. International conference on Engineering Applications of Neural Networks. EANN'98, Gibraltar, 1998.

4. Gavidia-Ceballos L, Hansen JHL. Direct speech feature estimation using an iterative EM algorithm for vocal fold pathology detection. IEEE Trans. on Biomedical Engineering. April 1996; 43; 4: 373-383.

5. Aref A, Dworkin J, Syamala D, Denton L, Fontanesi, J. Objective evaluation of the quality of voice following radiation therapy for T_1 glottic cancer. Radiotherapy and Oncology. 1997;45:149-153.

6. Akers G, Lennig M. Intonation in text-to-speech synthesis: Evaluation of algorithms. J. Acoustical Society of America. 1985;77:2157-2165.

7. Tarassenko L. A guide to neural computing applications. NCAF, Arnold, London, 1998.

8. Kohonen T. The Self-Organising Map. Proc. IEEE, 1990;78:1464-1480.

9. Haykin S. Neural Networks: A Comprehensive Foundation. Englewood Cliffs, NJ: Macmillan, 1994.

10. Bishop CM. Neural Networks for Pattern Recognition. Oxford University Press, Oxford, 1995.

11. Richard MD, Lippman RP. Neural network classifiers estimate Bayesian a-posteriori probabilities. Neural Computation, 1991;3:461-483.

12. DeVilliers J, Barnard E. Backpropagation neural nets with one and two hidden layers. IEEE Transactions on Neural Networks, 1992;4:136-141.

13. Moore CJ, Winstanley, S, Woods, et al. Computerising the evaluation of voice quality from impedance data for patients with cancer of the larynx. Unpublished, 1997.

Appendix A

Test Set	I-J-K	Activation Function	Error Function	Test Error	Normal Correct	Abnormal Correct	Classification Accuracy (%)
1	20-5-1	Logistic	SSE	0.5534			64.404
2	20-7-1	Logistic	SSE	0.5409			66.302
3	20-9-1	Logistic	SSE	0.5475	132	311	65.98
4	20-11-1	Logistic	SSE	0.5747	115	307	62.8
5	20-5-2	Softmax	ME	0.52242	194	265	68.24
6	20-7-2	Softmax	ME	0.4575	197	261	68.15
7	20-9-2	Softmax	ME	0.4754	214	255	69.76
8	20-11-2	Softmax	ME	0.24206	216	269	72.2
9	20-5-1	Logistic	SSE	0.3509	268	302	84.88
10	20-10-1	Logistic	SSE	0.3576	268	297	84.02
11	20-15-1	Logistic	SSE	0.3158	270	312	86.58
12	50-20-1	Logistic	SSE	0.3295	301	279	86.28
13	50-30-1	Logistic	SSE	0.3273	307	279	87.20
14	50-40-1	Logistic	SSE	0.3456	286	280	84.26
15	100-20-1	Logistic	SSE	0.4142	282	253	79.64
16	100-50-1	Logistic	SSE	0.4294	269	252	77.5
17	100-70-1	Logistic	SSE	0.4248	265	255	77.41
18	150-20-1	Logistic	SSE	0.3305	295	292	87.35
19	150-70-1	Logistic	SSE	0.3563	286	283	84.7
20	150-100-1	Logistic	SSE	0.3442	284	294	86.04
21	200-20-1	Logistic	SSE	0.5228	174	300	70.60
22	200-70-1	Logistic	SSE	0.4636	206	293	74.29
23	200-100-1	Logistic	SSE	0.4514	223	281	75

Table A1. Results of ANN classification tests

REVIEW PAPER

Case-Based Reasoning is a Methodology
not a Technology

Ian Watson
AI-CBR, University of Salford,
Salford, M5 4WT, UK
ian@ai-cbr.org
www.ai-cbr.org

Abstract: This paper asks whether case-based reasoning is an AI technology like rule-based reasoning, neural networks or genetic algorithms or whether it is better described as a methodology for problem solving, that may use any appropriate technology. By describing four applications of CBR, that variously use: nearest neighbour, induction, fuzzy logic and SQL, the author shows that CBR is a methodology and not a technology. The implications of this are discussed.

1. Introduction

Artificial Intelligence is often described in terms of the various technologies developed over the last three or four decades. Technologies such as logic programming, rule-based reasoning, neural networks, genetic algorithms, fuzzy logic, constraint-based programming and others. These technologies are characterised by specific programming languages or environments (e.g., Prolog or rule-based shells) or by specific algorithms and techniques (e.g., A*, the Rete algorithm or back propagation). Each also has, to a lesser or greater extent, laid down particular ways or methods of solving problems (e.g., depth first search, generate and test) that best use the characteristics of each technology.

Case-based reasoning (CBR) is a relative newcomer to AI and is commonly described as an AI technology like the ones listed above. This paper will show, by examining four very different CBR applications, that CBR describes a methodology for problem solving but does not prescribe any specific technology. The first section of the paper briefly describes CBR and identifies what characterises a methodology in this context. The next four sections each describe an application whose authors each felt could be described as case-based reasoners. The paper then concludes by discussing the implications of viewing CBR as a methodology.

2. Case-Based Reasoning

CBR arose out of research into cognitive science, most prominently that of Roger Schank and his students at Yale University [1, 2, 3 & 4]. It is relevant to the argument presented in this paper that CBR's origins were stimulated by a desire to understand how people remember information and are in turn reminded of information; and that subsequently it was recognised that people commonly solve problems by remembering how they solved similar problems in the past. The classic definition of CBR was coined by [5]:

"A case-based reasoner solves problems by using or adapting solutions to old problems."

Note that this definition tells us *"what"* a case-based reasoner does and not *"how"* it does what it does. Conceptually CBR is commonly described by the CBR-cycle.

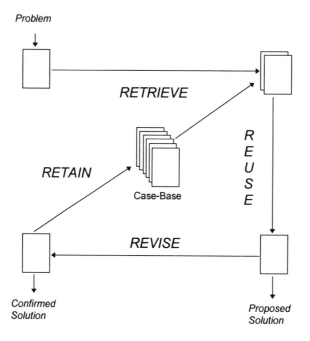

Figure 1 The CBR-cycle after Aamodt & Plaza [6]

This cycle comprises four activities (the four-REs):
1. *Retrieve* similar cases to the problem description
2. *Reuse* a solution suggested by a similar case
3. *Revise* or adapt that solution to better fit the new problem if necessary
4. *Retain* the new solution once it has been confirmed or validated.

Once again, what is being described here is a methodology for solving problems not a specific technology. Peter Checkland [7] describes a methodology as:

"an organised set of principles which guide action in trying to 'manage' (in the broad sense) real-world problem situations" [7, p.5]

The CBR-cycle fits very nicely into this definition of a methodology as a *"set of principles which guide action"*.

What then are the set of principles which guide CBR? The first of these is a desire by the problem solver to solve a problem by explicitly trying to reuse a solution from a similar past problem. Thus, a CBR must *retrieve* cases from a case-library and in someway assess the *similarity* of cases in the library to the current problem description. Second, a CBR system should attempt to *reuse* the solution suggested by a retrieved case, either with or without *revision*. Finally, a CBR system should seek to increase its knowledge by *retaining* new cases.

The subsequent sections will show how four different applications use this set of principles, defined as CBR, to solve real-world problems.

3. CBR Using Nearest Neighbour

Nearest neighbour techniques are perhaps the most widely used technology in CBR since it is provide by the majority of CBR tools [8]. Nearest neighbour algorithms all work in a similar fashion. The similarity of the problem (target) case to a case in the case-library for each case attribute is determined. This measure may be multiplied by a weighting factor. Then the sum of the similarity of all attributes is calculated to provide a measure of the similarity of that case in the library to the target case. This can be represented by the equation:

$$Similarity(T, S) = \sum_{i=1}^{n} f(T_i, S_i) \times w_i$$

where:
T is the target case
S is the source case
n is the number of attributes in each case
i is an individual attribute from 1 to n
f is a similarity function for attribute i in cases T and S and
w is the importance weighting of attribute i

This calculation is repeated for every case in the case-library to rank cases by similarity to the target. Algorithms similar to this are used by most CBR tools to perform nearest neighbour retrieval. Similarities are usually normalised to fall within a range of zero to one (where zero is totally dissimilar and one is an exact match) or as a percentage similarity where one hundred percent is an exact match. The use of nearest neighbour is well illustrated by the Wayland system [9].

3.1 Wayland - Setting up Aluminium Die-Casting Machines

Wayland is a CBR system that advises on the set up of aluminium pressure die-casting machines. Wayland was implemented using a very simple CBR tool called CASPIAN [10], which can be downloaded from the Internet (www.aber.ac.uk/~cjp/getting-caspian.html). Pressure die casting involves injecting molten metal at very high pressure into a mould (a die), where it cools to make a casting. Machine settings are critical for successful pressure die casting, and there is a compromise between factors such as the cost of producing the casting, maximising the die life, and the quality of the final product. The die parameters are strongly interrelated, making the problem non-decomposable. A change in one parameter can be compensated for by altering another.

CBR is an appropriate technology for this problem, because each foundry will tend to have a particular way of working. Engineers refer to records of previous dies with similar input requirements, and adjust the parameters for a similar die to reflect the different requirements of the new die being built. The records of previous dies are good examples of working compromises between the different operating requirements: such compromises might well have been found by costly adjustments performed in the foundry after the die was built.

Wayland automates the identification of past dies with similar characteristics, alters the die settings to take into account the differences between the past die and the new one being designed, and validates that the new solution is within design limits.

```
CASE INSTANCE die_no_5014 IS
weight_of_casting = 240.00;
weight_of_casting_and_overflows = 310.00;
weight_of_total_shot = 520.00;
no_of_slides = 0.00;
projected_area_of_casting = 19.50;
total_projected_area = 35.50;
average_no_of_impressions = 1.00;
machine_type = t400;
metal_type = lm24;
SOLUTION IS
imagefile = 'dn5014.gif';
gate_velocity = 6414.09;
cavity_fill_time = 13.77;
length_of_stroke = 3.10;
percentage_fill = 16.24;
gate_area = 135.00;
gate_width = 90.00;
gate_depth = 1.50;
plunger_velocity = 225.00;
pressure_on_metal = 8000.00;
tip_size = 70.00;
cycle_time = 35.00;
END;
```

Figure 2 A Case from Wayland

Wayland has a case base of some 200 previous die designs, extracted from a database of records of actual die performance maintained at the foundry. Only dies with satisfactory performance had their values entered into the case base, so the foundry personnel are confident that each case provides a good basis for calculating new solutions. Cases are fixed format records, with a field for each of the values as shown in Figure 2. Some of the fields may be blank, if complete records for a die have not been available.

Cases are retrieved using an algorithm similar to that described above. Each of the retrieved cases is assigned an overall *match value* by assigning a match score to each field and summing the total. Each field is given a weight which expresses its significance (e.g. the number of impressions is an important field to match: it specifies how many of the parts are made at once in the die). The case with the highest overall mark is the *best* match. After a case is retrieved it then has adaptation rules applied to it in order to produce the correct machine settings.

Once a case has been accepted, and the die casting has been found to be successful in practice, the case is entered into Wayland's case-base by an engineer, thus, completing the CBR-cycle.

4. CBR Using Induction

Induction techniques are commonly used in CBR since many of the more powerful commercially available CBR tools provide this facility (e.g., KATE from AcknoSoft, ReCall from ISoft, CBR-Works, from TecInno, and ReMind from Cognitive Systems [8]. Induction algorithms, such as ID3, build decision trees from case histories. The induction algorithms identify patterns amongst cases and partition the cases into clusters. Each cluster contains cases that are similar. A requirement of induction is that one target case feature is defined (i.e., the feature that the algorithm will induce). Essentially the induction algorithms are being used as classifiers to cluster similar cases together. It is assumed (usually correctly) that cases with similar problem descriptions will refer to similar problems and hence similar solutions.

4.1 Troubleshooting CFM 56-3 Engines on Boeing 737s

A good example of the use of inductive techniques for CBR was described by Richard Heider of CFM-international [11]. The project, called Cassiopee, developed a decision support system for the technical maintenance of the CFM 56-3 engines used on Boeing 737 jets. One of the business motivations of this project, in addition to improving problem diagnostics, was to create a corporate memory of troubleshooting knowledge (the *retain* part of the CBR-cycle).

30,000 cases were obtained from a database of engine failure descriptions. Each failure report contained both a structured section that described the *failure symptom* (e.g., high oil consumption, abnormal noise, thrust deficiency, etc.), and the faulty equipment (i.e., a list of engine parts that needed replacing or maintaining), and a free form text narrative describing the failure event. The textual narratives were analysed by maintenance specialists to identify a further 70 technical parameters that further defined the failure symptoms. Eventually 1500 cases were selected by a specialist as being representative of the range of engine failures. These became Cassiopee's case-base.

The induction algorithm of the tool KATE generated a fault tree from these cases extracting relevant decisions knowledge from the case histories. Retrieval of a similar case is obtained by walking the fault tree to find the cluster of cases that are most similar to the problem description. Once a fault tree is generated retrieval is extremely fast.

In use airline maintenance crews are prompted (via dialogs) to select a failure symptom and to provide additional information about the symptom. The system uses the induced fault tree to find the case or cluster of cases that are most similar to the problem description and provides a list of possible solutions. The cases that provide the solutions can be browsed by the users to help them confirm or reject the solutions.

5. CBR Using Fuzzy Logic

Fuzzy logics are a way of formalising the symbolic processing of fuzzy linguistic terms, such as *excellent, good, fair,* and *poor,* which are associated with differences in an attribute describing a feature [12]. Any number of linguistic terms can be used. Fuzzy logics intrinsically represent notions of similarity, since good is closer (more similar) to excellent than it is to poor. For CBR A fuzzy preference function can be used to calculate the similarity of a single attribute of a case with the corresponding attribute of the target.

For example, In Figure 3, a difference of 1 unit in the values of an attribute would be considered excellent, a difference of 2 would be good, 3 would be fair, and 4 would be poor. The result of using fuzzy preference functions is a vector, called the fuzzy preference vector. The vector contains a fuzzy preference value for each attribute. The values in this vector can be combined, through weighted aggregation, to produce a robust similarity value. The use of fuzzy preference functions allows for smooth changes in the result when an attribute is changed unlike the large changes that are possible when step functions are used. A fuzzy preference function is used to transform a quantifiable value for each attribute into a qualitative description of the attribute that can be compared with the qualitative description of other attributes. Thus, a fuzzy preference function allows a comparison of properties that are based on entirely different scales such as cost measured in cents per pound and spectral curve match measured in reflection units.

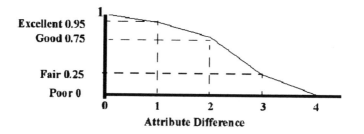

Fig. 3. A Fuzzy Preference Function, after Cheetham & Graf, [13]

5.1 Colour Matching Plastics at General Electric

A case-based reasoning system for determining what colorants to use for producing a specific colour of plastic was created at General Electric (GE) and has subsequently been patented by them. The selection of colorants needs to take many factors into consideration. A technique that involved fuzzy logic was used to compare the quality of the colour match for each factor. The system has been in use for two years at a growing number of GE Plastics sites and has shown significant cost savings [13].

When presented with a required colour for a new batch of plastic engineers at GE would select the closet match from samples on thousands of colour swatches in a reference collection. The colour formulae of dies from the closest matching swatch would be reused or adapted slightly to produce the required new colour. A swatch of the new colour would then be created and added to the reference collection. This is a pure case-based process being performed by people.

Based on discussions with experts and work to classify previous matches into various sets of linguistic terms GE were able to create fuzzy preference function for each of the following attributes of the colour match:
- colour similarity,
- total colorant load,
- cost of colorant formula,
- optical density of colour, and
- colour shift when moulded under normal and abusive conditions.

Each of the above properties including spectral colour match, loading level, cost, optical density, and colour shift due to processing conditions, is based on different scales of units. But, by mapping each of these properties to a global scale through the use of fuzzy preferences and linguistic terms such as excellent, good, fair, and poor, it was possible to compare one attribute with another. Then these values were input into a typical nearest neighbour algorithm to provide a summed, weighted and normalised score for each colour sample. Thus, fuzzy logic is being used to assess similarity in this system.

6. CBR Using Database Technology

At its most simple CBR could be implemented using database technology. Databases are efficient means of storing and retrieving large volumes of data. If problem descriptions could make well formed queries it would be straightforward to retrieve cases with matching descriptions. The problem with using database technology for CBR is that databases retrieve using exact matches to the queries. This is commonly augmented by using wild cards, such as "WEST*" matching on "WESTMINSTER" and "WESTON" or by specifying ranges such as "< 1965". The use of wildcards, Boolean terms and other operators within queries may make a query more general, and thus more likely to retrieve a suitable case, but it is not a measure of similarity.

220

However, by augmenting a database with explicit knowledge of the relationship between concepts in a problem domain it is possible to use SQL queries and measure similarity.

6.1   SQUAD - Sharing Experience at NEC

The SQUAD system was developed at NEC in Japan as a software quality control advisory system [14]. Real-world deployment imposed several key constraints on the system. Of these one in particular forced the developers to consider database technology: the system had to be part of the corporate information system and provide a fast response time to over 150,000 users. The use of a commercial RDBMS as a case-manager where each case is represented as a record of a relational database table offered several key advantages such as: data security, data independence, data standardisation and data integrity.

The developers of SQUAD were able to create a set of SQL expressions for similarity-based retrieval by referring to abstraction hierarchies as in Figure 4.

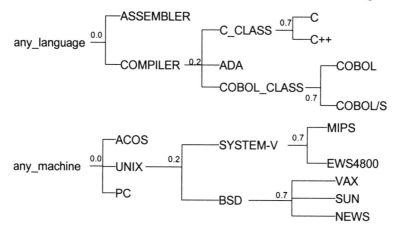

Figure 4. Examples of Abstraction Hierarchies, after Kitano & Shimazu, [14]

By referring to the abstraction hierarchies for concepts in the problem domain SQUAD can generate a set of similarity values associated with a set of SQL expressions as in Table 1. If a user with a problem identified ADA as the *language* and VAX as the *machine* the SQL specifications shown in Table 1 would be generated and sent to the RDBMS as queries. In this way SQUAD is able to assess the similarity of records (cases) returned by the RDBMS.

Over 3,000 cases were added to SQUAD each year whilst it was in use resulting in over 25,000 cases, which were accessed by employees all over the global organisation. The developers at NEC believe that this would not have been possible without the scalability, security and robustness provided by a commercial RDBMS system.

Rank	Similarity	SQL Specification (only WHERE clause is shown)
1	1.00	(language = ada) and (machine = vax);
2	0.89	(language = ada) and (machine in (sun, news, ...))
3	0.66	(language in (c, c++, cobol, cobol/s)) and (machine = vax);
4	0.54	(language = ada) and (machine in (mips, ews4800, ...))
4	0.54	(language in (c, c++, cobol, cobol/s)) and (machine in (sun, news,));

Table 1. SQL Specifications from SQUAD, after Kitano & Shimazu, [14]

7. Conclusions

Each of the systems described above uses different technologies but they all follow the same set of guiding principles:

- each explicitly attempts to solve problems by reusing solutions to old problems,
- the retrieval of past problems (cases) involves assessing the similarity of the problem to cases in a case-library, and
- once a new problem is solved it is added to the case library to retain the problem solving experience for future reuse.

The developers of the systems described above were therefore correct to describe their systems as case-based reasoners since they adhere to the CBR methodology.

"It has become clear that CBR is a generic methodology for building knowledge-based systems, rather than an isolated technique that is capable of solving only very specific tasks." [15 p.327]

If you now accept that CBR is a methodology for problem solving and not a technology you may now be able to see ways of applying it using techniques other than those described here. However, if you now think that CBR can use nearest neighbour, induction, fuzzy logic or database technology you have missed the point of this paper. A case-based reasoner can use *any* technology provided the system follows CBR's guiding principles. This is analogous to agent research since agent systems typically adhere to a set of principles or characteristics (e.g., agents typically exhibit: *autonomy, communication, collaboration* and *intelligence*) but can be implemented using any number of techniques [16].

This view of CBR as a methodology also has implications for *hybrid* systems. It is not uncommon in the CBR literature to see systems that combine nearest neighbour retrieval with rules for adaptation described as hybrid systems. Unfortunately this distinction is unsupportable if CBR is viewed as a methodology because CBR systems *must* use other technologies; since CBR has no technology to call its own per se (e.g. nearest neighbour derives from operational research, inductive indexing from machine learning). Thus, a hypothetical CBR system that used nearest neighbour to index and retrieve cases, neural networks and fuzzy logic to assess similarity, and rules and constraint satisfaction to adapt cases would not be a hybrid CBR system, although (perhaps confusingly) it would be a hybrid AI system. A true hybrid CBR system is one that combines two or more problem solving methodologies. For example a medical system that used CBR to diagnose a patient's illness and then used a rule-based system to design a unique treatment regime based upon a deep causal knowledge of treatments and their effects.

I believe that viewing CBR as a methodology and not a technology is important to its continued development. If CBR is viewed just as a technology it might seem that research into CBR is largely completed since, for example, nearest neighbour and inductive retrieval (the most commonly used techniques) are mature and reliable techniques. But if CBR is viewed as a methodology researchers have the challenge of applying any number of technologies. For example, it has been proposed that neural networks can be used to assess similarity since a neural network can tell us, with a degree of certainty, whether two patterns (such as finger prints) are similar [17]. Thus we can redraw the CBR-cycle and indicate where different technologies may be used.

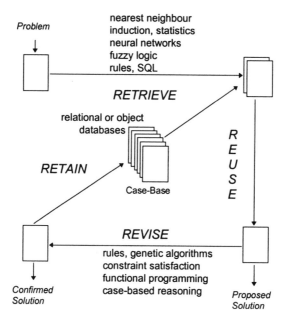

Figure 5. Technologies and the CBR-cycle

Figure 5 is not a complete diagram; you could I'm sure add other technologies to the cycle. Moreover, AI will surely develop new technologies in the future, some of which may prove very suitable for use in the CBR-cycle. Consequently, it is as a methodology that CBR's future is ensured.

References

[1]   Schank, R., & Abelson, R. (Eds.) (1977). Scripts, Plans, Goals and Understanding. Hillsdale, NJ: Erlbaum.

[2]   Schank, R. (Ed.) (1982). Dynamic Memory: A Theory of Learning in Computers and People. New York: Cambridge University Press.

[3]   Kolodner. J.L. (1983). Reconstructive memory, a computer model. Cognitive Science, 7(2), pp.281-328.

[4]   Hammond, K.J. (1988). Case-Based Planning: Viewing planning as a memory task. In, Proceedings of the DARPA Case-Based Reasoning Workshop, Kolodner, J.L. (Ed.), Morgan Kaufmann, Calif., US.

[5]   Riesbeck, C.K., and Schank, R. (1989). Inside Case-Based Reasoning. Northvale, NJ: Erlbaum.

[6]   Aamodt, A. & Plaza, E. (1994). Case-Based Reasoning: Foundational Issues, Methodological Variations, and System Approaches. AI Communications, 7(i), pp.39-59.

[7]   Checkland, P. & Scholes, J. (1990). Soft Systems Methodology in Action. Wiley.

[8]   Watson, I. (1977). Applying Case-Based Reasoning: techniques for enterprise systems. Morgan Kaufmann, Calif., US.

[9]   Price, C.J., & Pegler, I. (1995). Deciding Parameter Values with Case-Based Reasoning. In, Progress In Case-Based Reasoning, Watson, I. (Ed.). Lecture Notes in Artificial Intelligence 1020, Springer-Verlag.

[10]   Pegler, I., & Price, C.J. (1996) Caspian: A freeware case-based reasoning shell. In, Proceedings of the 2nd UK Workshop on Case-Based Reasoning. Watson, I. (Ed.), Salford University, Salford, UK.

[11]   Heider, R. (1996). Troubleshooting CFM 56-3 Engines for the Boeing 737 Using CBR & Data-Mining. In, Advances in Case-Based Reasoning, Smith, I. & Faltings, B. (Eds.), pp.513-18. Lecture Notes in AI 1168, Springer.

[12]   Mendel, J. (1995). Fuzzy Logic Systems for Engineering: A Tutorial, In, Proc. of the IEEE, 83(3).

[13]   Cheetham, W. & Graf, J. (1997). Case-Based Reasoning in Colour Matching. In Proc. ICCBR-97, Leake, D. & Plaza, E. (Eds.) LNAI, Springer.

[14]   Kitano, H., & Shimazu, H. (1996). The Experience Sharing Architecture: A Case Study in Corporate-Wide Case-Based Software Quality Control. In, Case-Based Reasoning: Experiences, Lessons, & Future Directions, Leake, D.B. (Ed.). AAAI Press / The MIT Press, Menlo Park, Calif., US.

[15]   Kamp, G. Lange, S. & Globig, C. (1998). Case-Based Reasoning Technology: Related Areas. In, Case-Based Reasoning Technology: From Foundations to Application. Lenz, M. et al (Eds.) LNAI # 1400 pp.325-351. Springer-Verlag, Berlin.

[16]   Russell, S., & Norvig, P. (1995). Artificial Intelligence: A Modern Approach. Morgan Kaufmann, San Francisco, US.

[17]   Thrift, P. (1989). A Neural Network Model for Case-Based Reasoning. In, Proceedings of the DARPA Case-Based Reasoning Workshop, Hammond, K.J. (Ed.), Morgan Kaufmann, Calif., US.

information on all aspects of CBR can be found at www.ai-cbr.org

AUTHOR INDEX

Aknine, S.	29
Barruffi, R.	96
Basden, A.	114
Boswell, R.	58
Chadwick, D.W.	114
Coenen, F.	44
Conroy, G.V.	198
Coulondre, S.	77
Craw, S.	58
Crémilleux, B.	159
Dahlstrand, F.	173
Evans, J.B.	114
Frietas, A.A.	147
Gao, W.	189
Goldberg, D.E.	3
Lamma, E.	96
Ling, C.X.	189
McGillion, M.A.	198
McSherry, D.	15
Mello, P.	96
Milano, M.	96
Montanari, R.	96
Moore, C.J.	198
Ragel, A.	159
Ritchings, R.T.	198
Slevin, N.	198
Thompson, S.	133
Visser, P	44
Watson, I.	213
Winstanley, S.	198
Woods, H.	198
Young, A.	114
Zhu, T.	189